D0900802

Mauzy's
Comprehensive Handbook of
Depression Glass Prices
10th Edition

Barbara & Jim Mauzy

4880 Lower Valley Road • Atglen, PA 19310

Designed by Douglas Congdon-Martin & Sue Taylor
Type set in Zurich BT

ISBN: 978-0-7643-4280-6
Printed in China

Published by Schiffer Publishing Ltd.
4880 Lower Valley Road
Atglen, PA 19310
Phone: (610) 593-1777; Fax: (610) 593-2002
E-mail: info@schifferbooks.com
For the largest selection of fine reference books on this and
related subjects, please visit our website at
www.schifferbooks.com
This book may be purchased from the publisher.
Please try your bookstore first.

We are always looking for people to write books on new
and related subjects. If you have an idea for a book, please
contact us at
proposals@schifferbooks.com

In Europe, Schiffer books are distributed by
Bushwood Books
6 Marksbury Ave.
Kew Gardens
Surrey TW9 4JF England
Phone: 44 (0) 20 8392-8585; Fax: 44 (0) 20 8392-9876
E-mail: info@bushwoodbooks.co.uk
Website: www.bushwoodbooks.co.uk

CONTENTS

The numbers C-1 to C-32 refer to the
color identification photos found
between pages 96 & 97

DEDICATION

This book is dedicated to all National Depression Glass Association members. We thank you for your ongoing support for and love of the glass presented in our books. We hope this tool assists your endeavors to add to your collections. If you aren't a member, please visit www.ndga.net and join.

ACKNOWLEDGMENTS

The maintenance of this book is a huge endeavor and many unsung heroes participate. For all of you who have shared glass and information pertaining to glass, we greatly appreciate your openness. We provide of list of hundreds of contributors in the front of *Mauzy's Depression Glass* (the big, hardback that accompanies this handbook); providing these names in this diminutive handbook is impossible. We do wish to single out our very, very special friend, David G. Baker, for his ongoing dedication to the buying, selling, and sharing of Depression Glass. Without David, our books wouldn't even have a cover. Without David, we would laugh less, too. Thanks, David, and thanks to all who have helped and who are using Mauzy books.

Barbara and Jim Mauzy

ABOUT THE VALUES

As Americans observe the fluctuation of Wall Street values and suffer through the shrinking of one's retirement, the question of values must be addressed. Depression Glass is a "want" and not a "need;" it is a luxury item and not a necessity. During the past few years we watched the values of several patterns suffer through the impact of reproductions and the general malaise of the economy.

You might be expecting woe and gloom to follow those opening statements, but such is not the case. Dealers have consistently reported to us that sales are stronger than they had been since the publication of the ninth edition of the *Mauzy Handbook*. We experienced the best Christmas season ever in 2011, with sales that continued at a brisk pace up to the time of this writing. The Antiques Extravaganza held in July 2012 in south central Pennsylvania saw sales way up from 2011 despite temperatures above 100!

Does the economic turmoil of Greece influence the values show within these pages? Happily, we can provide an unequivocal, "No!"

Here are a few thoughts regarding trends, keeping in mind that Depression Glass values are a function of supply and demand. If buyers are demanding specific items, these pieces should increase in value, so it is important to note these developments. First, collectors aren't simply building a set of glassware based on a pattern of choice. Many collectors have shifted from buying a single pattern to buying a color and mixing patterns. If you are a dealer, this is excellent news as it provides greater ease in making a sale. Next, the disinterest in Fire-King has faded into history and it has again become a line of glassware in great demand. Look for values in the eleventh edition to reflect this if the demand for Fire-King continues; we don't like to adjust values too quickly.

The values presented are suggested, not dictated. They are meant to reflect an accurate indication of the worth and availability of the patterns and pieces showcased in this book. There are no Glass Police, and certainly a seller has the freedom to require a customer to pay more than this suggested value, and the wisdom to sell for less than the suggested value.

Neither the authors nor the publisher are responsible for any outcomes resulting from consulting this reference.

OUR GUARANTEE

This book comes with a one year guarantee on the binding. If the binding does not maintain its integrity for one year Schiffer Publishing Ltd. will replace it with another copy of the same copyright at no charge to you.

Simply return the defective book with a letter that includes your address to the publisher's address shown in this handbook.

HOW TO REACH THE AUTHORS

We enjoy hearing from you because we know that collectors are the ultimate authority regarding the pattern(s) they collect. We do not open e-mails with attachments; they are deleted! If you wish to share images, please send them to:

Barbara & Jim Mauzy
PO Box 1417
Kitty Hawk NC 27949-1417

If you provide an e-mail address with your correspondence we can respond promptly. For a written response, or to have the images returned, please include a self-addressed stamped envelope.

Our e-mail address: TPTT@aol.com
Our eBay store name: Barbara and Jim Mauzy
Our eBay auctions listed as:
todays_pleasures_tomorrows_treasures

To purchase any of our books, including Barbara's new Schwoe series for kids ages 0-11, contact us by mail or by e-mail.

Barbara and Jim Mauzy

HOW TO USE THIS HANDBOOK

In the back of the book we have provided a thorough index. If you can not locate a pattern in the alphabetically arranged *Contents* check the *Index*. The "C" numbers in both the *Contents* and the *Index* refer to the Color Identification section following page 96. We have made every effort to provide pricing for every piece known in every important pattern, regardless of color. If we have missed an item or you would like to see a pattern included in the next edition, please contact us!

We want this book to be helpful to **you**! For this reason we have created other features such as a column labeled "Qty" found throughout the book. This is designed with the collector in mind to maintain an accurate, up-to-date record of items owned. Don't miss the ruler on the back cover! If you need to double check a measurement it is there for your use. By the way, we opted to round off measurements to the nearest quarter inch to simplify the inconsistencies in Depression Glass.

You will find an italicized *R* after each piece that has been reproduced as a signal to the buyer to use caution. Then, at the end of the pricing we have provided information to discriminate old Depression Glass from new glassware.

The numbers shown in the columns are the values in US dollars. These values are listed vertically by color and horizontally by item. Thus, "45" means $45.00.

ABOUT THE GLASS

A few remarks need to be made regarding Depression Glass and its very nature. As poorer quality glassware that was often given away with the purchase of a product or service, Depression Glass is full of flaws. Newbies to this wonderful DG World often struggle with some of the characteristics that many know are expected. We hope this short presentation will help.

A straw mark is a line on the surface of glassware that is a result of manufacture. A straw mark is not a crack and it will not get larger. A crack will have a dimensional look that will catch the light and often look silver or gray while a straw mark will show up only on the surface if the glassware is tilted just so in the right light. A straw mark should not negatively effect the value of an item.

It is normal to find bumps of extra glass, especially along mold lines. We recommend the "fingernail test." Run your fingernail along exposed edges. If your nail feels a protruding bump look carefully for extra glass. This is normal, perfectly fine, and does not diminish the value of the item in any way. If your fingernail seems to go down it is time to stop and examine the spot in question. It may still be an imperfection and not a chip.

You may find pieces that lean to one side, wobble on the counter top, and seem slightly misshapen. Two identical items may have slightly different dimensions. One pattern may have several shades of the same color. This is Depression Glass!

We do offer a warning. Foggy, cloudy, and lime-deposited glass can not be cleaned! Buyer beware. Likewise, buying outside on a dewy morning can cause one to inadvertently purchase "sick" glass. Dew can mask the real surface of the glassware leaving one with an unhappy surprise later in the day.

When in doubt rely on a reputable dealer and our handbook! Together you can buy with confidence!

ADAM *Reproduced*
(1932-1934 Jeannette Glass Company)

	Pink	Green	Qty
Ashtray, 4.5"	38	40	____
Bowl, 4.75" berry, 1.5" deep	28	30	____
Bowl, 5.75" cereal	65	68	____
Bowl, 7.75" berry	40	42	____
Bowl, 9" w/o lid	40	42	____
Bowl, 9" w/lid	90	115	____
Bowl, 10" oval vegetable, 2.5" deep	45	45	____
Butter dish base *R*	40	175	____
Butter dish lid *R*	90	275	____
Butter complete	130	450	____
Butter w/Adam bottom & Sierra/Adam lid	trtp*		____
Cake plate, 9.75"	38	45	____
Candlestick, ea.	60	75	____
Candy jar w/lid, 2.5"	160	175	____
Coaster	32	34	____
Creamer, 3"	32	34	____
Cup	32	34	____
Lamp	2500	2500	____
Lid for 9" bowl	50	75	____
Pitcher, round base	110		____
Pitcher, square base	70	80	____
Plate, 6" sherbet	10	12	____
Plate, 7.75" salad	22	24	____
Plate, 9" dinner	40	44	____
Plate, 9" grill	30	30	____
Platter, 11.75" x 7.75"	38	35	____
Relish, 8", 2-part	30	34	____
Salt & pepper	95	130	____
Saucer *R*	8	8	____
Sherbet, 3.5" diam.	32	37	____
Sugar base, 3.25"	32	32	____
Sugar lid	35	48	____
Tumbler, 4.5"	45	48	____
Tumbler, 5.5" tall, 3.5" diam	95	100	____
Vase, 7.5"	400	150	____

Reproduction information: New butter base: points aimed at corners rather than middle of side edges. New butter lid: leaf veins disjointed rather than touching center. New saucer: pattern is turned and incomplete.

Note: Delphite candlesticks: $150 each, 9" bowl: $300. Yellow cup: $100. Round 7.75" salad plate & saucer in pink or yellow: $120. Iridescent pink 4.75" berry bowl: $75. Crystal pitcher with round foot: $75. Crystal ashtray, $80. Other pieces of crystal 1/2 value of pink. Satinized pink lamp, $2500

*trtp = too rare to price

AMERICAN PIONEER

(1931-1934   Liberty Works)

	Pink	Green	Qty
Bowl, 4.25" mayonnaise	65	100	____
Bowl, 5" w/2 handles	30	30	____
Bowl, 8" w/foot		125	____
Bowl, 8.75" w/lid	125	145	____
Bowl, 9.25" w/2 handles	35	45	____
Bowl, 9" w/lid & foot	125	145	____
Bowl, 10.5" console	65	80	____
Candlestick, 6.5", ea.	50	60	____
Candy jar w/lid, 8" tall	110	130	____
Candy jar w/lid, 10" tall	130	160	____
Cheese & cracker 2-pc. set	65	80	____
Coaster, 3.5"	35	35	____
Creamer, 3"	25	25	____
Creamer, 3.75"	25	25	____
Cup	18	18	____
Dresser set, 4-piece set	600	600	____
Cologne bottle, 4.5", ea.	175	175	____
Powder jar	150	150	____
Tray w/indents, 7.5"	100	100	____
Goblet, 3.25" diam. wine	60	60	____
Goblet, 6" water	60	60	____
Ice pail, 6" deep, 5.5" diam.	65	80	____
Lamp, 5"		250	____
Lamp, 5.5" round	90		____
Lamp, 8.5" tall (all glass)	150	150	____
Lamp, 9.5" tall (glass base, metal shaft)		75	____
Pitcher/urn, 5"	100	125	____
Pitcher lid for 5" urn	140	140	____
Pitcher/urn, 7"	140	140	____
Pitcher lid for 7" urn	125	125	____
Plate, 5", liner for 5" pitcher	60		____
Plate, 6"	18	18	____
Plate, 6" w/2 handles	18	18	____
Plate, 7" liner for 7" pitcher	65		____
Plate, 8"	18	18	____
Plate, 8.5" liner for 7" pitcher		65	____
Plate, 11" tray w/2 handles	30	30	____
Saucer	10	10	____
Sherbet, 4.5" tall, 4" diam.	18	20	____
Sherbet, 4.75" tall w/stem	40	50	____
Sugar, 2.25"	35	35	____
Sugar, 3.5"	25	25	____
Tumbler, 2.25", 1 oz. whiskey	70	100	____
Tumbler, 5 oz. juice	55	65	____
Tumbler, 4", 8 oz.	55	55	____
Tumbler, 5", 12 oz.	55	55	____
Vase, 7.5" cupped		120	____

AMERICAN PIONEER *(cont.)*

	Pink	Green	Qty
Vase, 7.5" ruffled		120	____
Vase, 8.25" cupped		120	____

Note: Crystal items half of pink. Amber items 50% more than pink.

AMERICAN SWEETHEART

(1930-1936 Macbeth-Evans Glass Company)

	Pink	Monax	Red	Blue	Trimmed rim	Qty
Bowl, 3.75" flat berry	100					____
Bowl, cream soup, 4.25"	100	125				____
Bowl, 6" cereal	20	22			60	____
Bowl, 6.5" diam., 2" deep, small console bowl		trtp*				____
Bowl, 9" berry	60	70			250	____
Bowl, 9.5" flat soup	100	100			150	____
Bowl, 11" oval vegetable	85	95				____
Bowl, 18" console		600	1250	1400		____
Creamer	22	20	200	200	125	____
Cup	20	12	110	165	100	____
Lamp shade, 6" tall, 11" wide		750				____
Lamp shade, 8.5"		750				____
Pitcher, 7.5", 60 oz	1200					____
Pitcher, 8", 80 oz.	900					____
Plate, 6" bread & butter	10	10			40	____
Plate, 6.5"		10				____
Plate, 8" salad	18	15	110	140	50	____
Plate, 9" luncheon		15			55	____
Plate, 9.75" dinner	40	25			125	____
Plate, 10.25" dinner		28				____
Plate, 11" chop plate		28				____
Plate, 12" salver	40	35	220	265	155	____
Plate, 15.5" server		300	425	500		____
Platter, 13"	80	85			250	____
Salt & pepper	750	550				____
Saucer	8	6	35	45	25	____
Sherbet, 3.75" diam., 2"deep	25					____
Sherbet, 4.25" diam., 2.25" deep	20	20			100	____
Sugar base	22	10	220	250	125	____
Sugar lid		600				____
Tid-bit, 2-tier (8" & 11" or 12" plates)	60	54	360	400		____
Tid-bit, 3-tier (8", 12", & 15.5" plates)		310	825	800		____
Tumbler, 3.5" tall, 2.5" diam. juice	100					____
Tumbler, 4.25" tall, 2.75" diam	90					____
Tumbler, 4.75" tall, 2.75+" diam	125					____

Note: Crystal sherbet in chrome base: $5. Cremax: 6" cereal, $15; 9" berry, $45; cup, $500; lamp shade, $800; oatmeal colored 6" cereal bowl, $250.
*trtp = too rare to price

AUNT POLLY

(Late 1920s   U.S. Glass Company)

	Blue	Green	Qty
Bowl, 4.25" berry,			
1.5" deep	20	8	_____
Bowl, 4.5", 2.75" deep	65		_____
Bowl, 4.75", 2" deep		18	_____
Bowl, 5.5" w/1 handle	25	15	_____
Bowl, 8" oval pickle			
w/2 handles, 3" deep	40	15	_____
Bowl, 7.75" berry, 3" deep	55	23	_____
Bowl, 8.25" oval,			
1.5" deep	130	50	_____
Butter dish base	130	75	_____
Butter dish lid	80	200	_____
Butter complete	210	275	_____
Candy base w/2			
handles, 5.5", 2.75" tall	45	30	_____
Candy/sugar lid	200	75	_____
Creamer	40	35	_____
Pitcher, 8"	200		_____
Plate, 6" sherbet	12	8	_____
Plate, 8" luncheon	20		_____
Salt & pepper, 3"	300		_____
Sherbet. 3.25" tall	14	10	_____
Sugar base	35	30	_____
Sugar/candy lid	200	75	_____
Tumbler, 3.75" tall, 3" diam.	35		_____
Vase, 6.5" tall, 3.5" diam.	55	35	_____

Note: Iridescent items ½ of Green EXCEPT for these: butter complete, $250; & pitcher, $200.

AURORA

(1937-1938   Hazel Atlas Company)

	Cobalt & Pink	Qty
Bowl, 4.5" diam., 2.25" deep	70	___
Bowl, 5.25" cereal	15	___
Creamer	25	___
Cup	12	___
Plate, 6.5"	10	___
Saucer	5	___
Tumbler, 4.75"	25	___

Note: Green and Crystal items ½ those in Cobalt and Pink.

AVOCADO *Reproduced*
(1923-1933...see note at bottom
Indiana Glass Company)

	Green	Pink	Crystal	Qty
Bowl, 5.25" olive				
w/2 handles, 1.5" deep	40	25	10	____
Bowl, 6.25" relish w/3 feet,				
1.5" deep	40	25	12	____
Bowl, 7.25" preserve				
w/1 handle	45	30	12	____
Bowl, 7.25" salad,				
1.75" deep	65	45	15	____
Bowl, 9" x 4.5" oval				
w/2 handles	35	23	10	____
Bowl, 9.25" salad, 3" deep	160	110	20	____
Creamer, 3.75"	35	35	12	____
Cup, 2 styles	45	40		____
Pitcher, 9"-9.25" 64 oz. *R*	trtp*	1100	400	____
Plate, 6.25" cheese	30	20	8	____
Plate, 8.25" salad	30	20	8	____
Plate, 12.5" x 10.5" cake				
w/2 handles	70	50	12	____
Saucer, 6.5"	30	25		____
Sherbet/Sundae, 3.5" tall	65	65		____
Sugar, 3" at lowest pt.	35	35	12	____
Tumbler, w/foot 5.25" tall,				
almost 3.5" diam *R*	250	300		____

Reproduction information: The following are new colors so
everything in these colors is new: amethyst, blue, frosted pink,
red, yellow, darker green, pink with an orange tint, frosted green.
These pieces are new: 6" plate, 8" plate, 8" bowl w/2 handles,
and tumblers with flared rims.

Note: Milk glass items made in 1950s. Milk white
pitcher, $400; tumbler, $40; bowl, $30. Luncheon plate w/apple
design, $15.

*trtp = too rare to price

BANDED SPIRAL
(1929-1940s Hocking Glass Company)

	Green	Qty
Ashtray, tilt style, 2 pcs.	35	____
Base: 3" deep, 3.75" diam.		
Insert: 1.25" deep, 3.25" diam.		
Cup	12	____
Goblet, 6" tall, 3-3.25" diam.	30	____
Sherbet with stem	18	____
Tumbler, 5" tall, 2.75" diam.	25	____

Note: Candy jar in pink, base: 5" diameter opening, 2.5" deep; lid: 5" diameter, $75.

BEADED BLOCK

(1927-1930s...see note below
Imperial Glass Company)

	All Colors	Opal-es-cent	Crystal	Qty
Bowl, lily, 2.5" deep, 3" base, 4" opening	50	55	50	____
Bowl, lily, 3" tall, 3.5" base, 4.5" opening	50	55	50	____
Bowl, lily, 3" tall, 3.5" base, 5" opening	50	55	50	____
Bowl, 4.5" round lily	45	55	20	____
Bowl, 4.75-5" diam., 2" deep jelly w/2 handles (looks like a cream soup)	35	50	20	____
Bowl, 5.25" round lily, 2.5" deep			35	____
Bowl, 5.5" square	70	80	20	____
Bowl, 5.5" w/1 handle, olive	35	50	20	____
Bowl, 6" round, lily	50	60	20	____
Bowl, 6" square w/ ruffled rim			75	____
Bowl, 6.25" diam., 2.25" deep round with flared rim	50	60	20	____
Bowl, 6.5" round nappy	50	60	20	____
Bowl, 6.5" pickle w/2 handles	60	70	20	____
Bowl, 6.75" round	50	60	20	____
Bowl, 7.25" round & flared	60	70	20	____
Bowl, 7.5" round salad	60	70	20	____
Bowl, 7.75" round w/fluted rim	60	70	20	____
Bowl, 8.5" celery	85	95	25	____
Candy jar, pear-shaped	350	375	325	____
Comport, 4.5" tall, 5" diam.			50	____
Comport, 4.75" tall, 4.5" diam.	55		55	____
Creamer	35	50	20	____
Jelly, 4.5" stemmed	65	75	20	____
Jelly, 4.5" stemmed & flared	65	75	20	____
Pitcher, 5.25"	200	250	125	____
Plate, 7.75" square	70	80	20	____
Plate, 8" round	50			____
Plate, 8.75" round	75	75	30	____
Plate, 9" round	45			____
Sugar, 4.25"	35	50	20	____
Syrup, 4.25"			250	____
Vase, 6" bouquet	30			____

BEADED BLOCK *(cont.)*

(1927-1930s...see note below
Imperial Glass Company)

Note: White made in 1950s. Later issued pieces in other colors from 1970s & 1980s marked "IG" for Imperial Glass. Yellow pear-shaped candy jar, $400, green pear-shaped candy jar, $500. 6" vase (go along) pink and cobalt, $38. Cobalt items twice prices found in first column. Red 2x values of "All Colors."

BLOCK OPTIC
(1929-1933 Hocking Glass Company)

	Green	Pink	Topaz	Qty
Bowl, 4.25", 1.25" deep	14	14		____
Bowl, 4.5", 1.5" deep	30	30		____
Bowl, 5.25" cereal	18	35		____
Bowl, 7.25" salad, 2.5" deep	150	150		____
Bowl, 8.5" berry	40	40		____
Bowl, 11.75" console w/rolled edge, 2" deep	100	100		____
Butter dish base	60			____
Butter dish lid	25			____
Butter complete, 3" x 5" rectangle	85			____
Candlestick, ea.	45	40		____
Candy jar w/lid, 2.25" tall	65	65	65	____
Candy jar w/lid, 6.25" tall	70	140		____
Creamer, 5 varieties	14	14	16	____
Cup, 4 styles	8	8	8	____
Cup, black foot	30			____
Goblet, 3.5" wine	trtp*		trtp*	____
Goblet, 4" cocktail, 2.25" diam.	45	45		____
Goblet, 4.5" wine	45	45		____
Goblet, 5.75", 3" diam.	40	40		____
Goblet, 7.25", just over 3" diam.			45	____
Ice bucket w/metal handle	85	125		____
Ice/butter tub w/2 tab handles	90	120		____
Ice tub, 4.5" diam., 1.75" deep with tab handles	500			____
Lid, for tall sugar, 2" tall, 3" diameter		75		____
Mayonnaise comport, 4" across	80	80		____
Mug	90			____
Pitcher, 7.5", 54 oz.	90	185		____
Pitcher, 8", 80 oz.	110	115		____
Pitcher, 8.5", 54 oz.	65	75		____
Pitcher, 9"	100			____
Plate, 6" sherbet	7	7	7	____
Plate, 8" salad	10	10	12	____
Plate, 9" dinner	35	50	50	____
Plate, 9" grill	70	70	70	____
Plate, 10.25" sandwich	35	40		____
Plate, 12.75"	40		35	____
Reamer	45			____
Salt & pepper, short	130			____
Salt & pepper, tall w/foot	50	85	100	____

BLOCK OPTIC *(cont.)*

	Green	Pink	Topaz	Qty
Sandwich server w/center handle	75	75		____
Saucer, 5.75"	10	10		____
Saucer, 6.25"	10	10		____
Sherbet, cone-shaped	8			____
Sherbet, 3.25" round	12	10	10	____
Sherbet, squared low foot, 3.75" diam.			20	____
Sherbet, 4.75" stemmed sundae, 3.5" diam.	18	18	24	____
Sugar base, 3 styles	14	14	16	____
Sugar lid, 2" tall, 3" diameter		75		____
Tray, figure 8, 6.5" x 10", .75" deep for use under tumble-up night set	250			____
Tumbler, 1.75", 1 oz. whiskey, 1.25" diam.	45	45		____
Tumbler, 2.25", 2 oz. whiskey, 1.75" diam.	38	38		____
Tumbler, 2.5", 3 oz.	25	25		____
Tumbler, 3.25", 3 oz. w/foot	30	30		____
Tumbler, 3.5", 5 oz. 2.25" diam.	25	25		____
Tumbler, 3.75", 9.5 oz. flat	18	18	28	____
Tumbler, 4.75", 12 oz. flat	30	30		____
Tumbler, 4.75", w/foot		25		____
Tumbler, 5", 10 or 11 oz. flat, 2.75" diam.	25	20		____
Tumbler, 5.25", 15 oz. flat	45	40		____
Tumbler, 6", 10 oz. w/foot	35	35		____
Tumbler, 9 oz. w/foot	20	18	28	____
Tumble-up night set	380			____
Bottle, 5.75"	30			____
Tray, figure 8	250			____
Tumbler, 3"	100			____
Vase, 5.75"	350			____

Note: Amber: 11.75" rolled edge console bowl, $75; candle-sticks, $40 ea. Rectangular butter: green clambroth, $300; blue, $750; crystal, $100. Crystal: half of green. Green satinized sugar with lid - looks similar to sherbet, but base has rim - with or without handpainted flowers, $10.

*trtp = too rare to price

BOWKNOT
(1931   Belmont Tumbler Company)

	Green	Qty
Bowl, 4.25" berry, 1.75" deep	24	____
Bowl, 5.25" cereal, 2" deep	40	____
Cup	7	____
Plate, 6.75" salad	18	____
Sherbet	18	____
Tumbler, 4.75" flat	24	____
Tumbler, just under 4.75" w/foot	20	____

BUBBLE *Reproduced*
(1934-1965   Hocking Glass Company)

	Blue & Ruby Flash	Green	Red	White & Crystal	Qty
Bowl, 4" berry	34			4	____
Bowl, 4.5" dessert *R*	15	12	12	4	____
Bowl, 5.25" cereal	18	18		4	____
Bowl, 7.75" flat soup	20			10	____
Bowl, 8" soup		75			____
Bowl, 8.25" vegetable *R*	30	30	34	7	____
Bowl, 9" flanged	trtp*				____
Candlestick, ea.		120	40	15	____
Creamer	35	18		7	____
Cup	5	10	10	3	____
Lamp, 3 styles				40	____
Pitcher, 8.25"			60	175	____
Plate, 6.75" pie or salad	5	20		2	____
Plate, 7" x 4.5" leaf	100				____
Plate, 9.25" dinner	12	35	35	5	____
Plate, 9.25" grill	20				____
Plate, 9.5" dinner		40			____
Plate, 10" dinner		40			____
Platter, 12"	18			12	____
Saucer	2	6	5	1	____
Sugar	20	20		7	____
Tidbit, 2-tier			50	50	____
Tumbler, 3.25", 8 oz. old fashioned			16	3	____
Tumbler, 3.75" juice			12	3	____
Tumbler, 4.5" water			12	3	____
Tumbler, 5.75", 12 oz. iced tea			18	6	____
Tumbler, 6", 16 oz. lemonade				8	____

Note: Pink: 8.25" berry bowl, $34; cup, $100; saucer, $50. Jade-ite 8.25" berry bowl, $50; 5.25" diameter, 1.5" deep bowl, trtp*. Dark blue: cup & saucer, $125 for set; 6.75" bread & butter plate, $45. Iridescent: 4" berry bowl, $7; 8.25" berry bowl, $10; cup, $5; saucer, $2; 6.75" pie plate, $20; 9.25" dinner plate, $25; 7.75" soup bowl, $25. Yellow: 4.5" dessert bowl, $100. Light green: cup, saucer, 6.75" pie plate, 8" soup bowl, 7" diameter, 1.5" deep bowl, $85 each. Ruby flash same value as blue. Black candlestick, $150. Amber creamer, $80.

Reproduction information: In Ruby only 4.5" and 8" bowls with Anchor trademark on bottom are reissues.

*trtp = too rare to price

CAMEO *Reproduced*
(1930-1934   Hocking Glass Company)

	Green	Topaz	Pink	Crystal (Platinum trim)	Qty
Bottle, water/Whitehouse Vinegar (dark green)	25				____
Bowl, 4.25" sauce				8	____
Bowl, 5" diam. cream soup	185				____
Bowl, 5" cereal	35	35	200	8	____
Bowl, 5.5" diam., 1.5" deep w/3 feet	trtp*				____
Bowl, 7.25" salad	75				____
Bowl, 8.25" berry	45		200		____
Bowl, ruffled/crimped	trtp*				____
Bowl, 9" soup	100		150		____
Bowl, 10" oval vegetable	55	70			____
Bowl, 11" console w/3 feet	90	130	100		____
Butter dish base	100				____
Butter dish lid	150				____
Butter dish complete	250	trtp*			____
Cake plate, 10" w/3 feet	45	trtp*			____
Cake plate, 10.5" no feet (same as rimmed 10.5" dinner) *R*	125		250		____
Candlestick, ea.	80				____
Candy jar w/lid, 4" tall, base 2.5" tall, 4.25" opening, lid 5" diam. *R*	100	120	500		____
Candy jar w/lid, 6.5" tall	225				____
Cocktail shaker w/metal lid, 11.25"				1000	____
Comport, 5" mayonnaise	65		250		____
Cookie jar/lid *R*	85				____
Creamer, 3.25"	25	25			____
Creamer, 4.25"	35		150		____
Cup, 2 styles	15	8	100	8	____
Decanter w/stopper, 10.25"	300			240	____
Decanter w/stopper, 10.25" frosted	90				____
Domino tray, 7" across handles w/ 3" indent	200				____
Domino tray, 7" no indent			350	200	____
Goblet, 3.25" wine	1500		1000		____
Goblet, 4" wine, 2.5" diam	90		250		____
Goblet, 6" water	65		200		____
Ice bowl/Open butter, 3" tall x 5.5" wide	220		850	300	____
Ice tub, 6.5" diam.	250				____
Jam jar w/lid, 6" diam., base 2" deep, lid 2.5" tall	320			250	____
Lid for Juice Pitcher	700				____
Pitcher, 5.75" milk or syrup, 20 oz.	375	trtp*			____
Pitcher, 6" juice, 36 oz.	90				____
Pitcher, 8.5" water, 56 oz., 2 styles	90		trtp*	500	____
Plate, 6" sherbet	10	6	110	4	____

24

	Green	Topaz	Pink	Crystal	Qty
Plate, 7" salad				5	____
Plate, 8.25" luncheon	16	18	50	4	____
Plate, 8.25" with 3.5" indent	50				____
Plate, 8.5" square	90	300			____
Plate, 9" ruffled	1200				____
Plate, 9.5" dinner	30	15	135		____
Plate, 10" sandwich	35		75		____
Plate, 10.5" dinner, rimmed (same as 10.5" cake plate)	125		250		____
Plate, 10.5" grill no handles	20	15	55		____
Plate, 10.5" grill w/tab handles	75	20			____
Plate, 10.5" w/tab handles	20	22			____
Platter, 12" w/tab handles	30	45			____
Relish, 7.5", 3-part w/3 feet	40			160	____
Salt & pepper *R*	100		1000		____
Sandwich server w/center handle	trtp*				____
Saucer	250				____
Sherbet, 3.25", blown	25		80		____
Sherbet, 3.25" molded	18	40	85		____
Sherbet, 4.75" w/tall stem	35	55	110		____
Sugar, 3.25"	25	25			____
Sugar, 4.25"	35		155		____
Tray, Domino sugar, 7" w/indent	200				____
Tray, Domino sugar, no indent			350	200	____
Tumbler, 3 oz. juice w/foot, 3.25"	75		155		____
Tumbler, 3.5" juice, no foot			175		____
Tumbler, 3.75" juice, 5 oz., no foot	60		110		____
Tumbler, 4" water, 9 oz., w/foot	40		90	10	____
Tumbler, 4.75", 10 oz. no foot	40		110		____
Tumbler, 4.75", 9 oz., w/foot	40	20	130		____
Tumbler, 5", 11 oz., no foot	50	60	110		____
Tumbler, 5.25", w/foot	90		150		____
Tumbler, 5.25"			165		____
Tumbler, 5.75"	80		150		____
Tumbler, 6", w/foot	750		165		____
Vase, 5.75"	400				____
Vase, 8"	75				____

Reproduction information: All miniatures are new. Salt & pepper reproduced in blue, green, & pink; glass is too thick, green is too dark. No Cameo was originally made in cobalt blue. New cookie jar and low candy: color a bit too dark, motif not crisp. All cobalt blue, including miniatures, are new.
*trtp = too rare to price

CANADIAN SWIRL

(late 1930s-1940s   Dominion Glass Company Limited)

	Plain	Stippled	Qty
Bowl, 4.5" small berry	4	6	____
Bowl, 7.5" large berry	12	12	____
Bowl, 7.5" soup	20		____
Butter dish base	15	15	____
Butter dish lid	25	25	____
Butter dish complete	40	40	____
Creamer	6	6	____
Cup	5		____
Pitcher, 4.5", 20 oz.	15	15	____
Pitcher, 7.75", 60 oz.	20		____
Plate, 6" sherbet	5	5	____
Plate, 8" salad	8		____
Plate, 9.75" dinner	18		____
Salt & pepper	10		____
Saucer	2		____
Sherbet	5		____
Sugar base	6	6	____
Sugar lid	25		____
Tumbler, 3.75" flat, 9 oz.	8		____
Tumbler, 4" w/foot, 5 oz.	8		____
Tumbler, 5" w/foot, 9.5 oz.	20		____

Note: Fired-on colors: Dinners, cups, saucers are found in blue, green, red, & yellow. Creamer found in yellow, sugar found in red. Salt & pepper found in dark green, gray, and gold. Add 50% for fired-on colors. Cobalt (not fired-on) creamer & sugar, $35 ea.

CHERRY BLOSSOM *Reproduced*
(1930-1939 Jeannette Glass Company)

	Pink	Green	Delphite	Qty
Bowl, 4.75" berry, almost 1.5" deep *R*	30	30	24	____
Bowl, 5.75" cereal, almost 1.75" deep *R*	65	50		____
Bowl, 7.75" flat soup	105	105		____
Bowl, 8.5" berry, 2.5" deep *R*	60	60	65	____
Bowl, 9" oval vegetable, 6.75" deep	65	55	75	____
Bowl, 9" w/2 handles, 2.75" deep	55	70	40	____
Bowl, 10.5" fruit w/3 feet	100	100		____
Butter dish base *R*	30	40		____
Butter dish lid *R*	90	100		____
Butter complete *R*	120	140		____
Cake plate, 10.25" *R*	40	50		____
Casserole, base 9" diam., 2.5" deep, lid just over 7.5"	trtp*	trtp*		____
Coaster, 3.25"	24	20		____
Cookie Jar *R*	trtp*			____
Creamer *R*	30	30	35	____
Cup *R*	22	22	20	____
Mug, 7 oz., 2.75" diam., 3" deep	500	400		____
Pitcher, 6.25", scalloped base w/pattern all over *R*	85	85	100	____
Pitcher, 6.25", round base w/pattern all over	95	95		____
Pitcher, 6.75", flat pattern only at top		trtp*		____
Pitcher, 6.75", scalloped base w/pattern only at top	500			____
Pitcher, 8" footed w/pattern only at top	95	90		____
Pitcher, 8" flat w/pattern only at top	125	125		____
Plate, 6" sherbet *R*	14	16	18	____
Plate, 7" salad	30	30		____
Plate, 9" dinner *R*	34	34	30	____
Plate, 9.25" grill	35	30		____
Plate, 10.25" grill	trtp*	120		____
Platter, 9"	1000	1200		____
Platter, 11" x 7.5"	65	65	55	____
Platter, 13" & 13" divided *R*	150	150		____
Salt & pepper *R*	trtp*	trtp*		____
Saucer *R*	8	8	8	____
Sherbet, 2.75" tall *R*	24	28	24	____
Sugar base, 3"	30	30	35	____

CHERRY BLOSSOM *(cont.)*

	Pink	Green	Delphite	Qty
Sugar lid	30	35		____
Tray, 10.5″ sandwich w/2 handles *R*	45	45	35	____
Tumbler, 3.5″ no foot, pattern only at top	25	30		____
Tumbler, 3.75″ w/foot, pattern all over *R*	20	25	30	____
Tumbler, 4.25″ no foot, pattern only at top	30	30		____
Tumbler, 4.5″ w/round foot, pattern all over *R*	42	42	38	____
Tumbler, 4.5″ scalloped foot, pattern all over *R*	40	40	38	____
Tumbler, 5″ no foot, pattern only at top	125	100		____

Note: Yellow: 10.5″ 3-footed fruit bowl, $450; 8.5″ bowl, $450; 9″ dinner plate, $450. Translucent Green: grill plate, $400. Jadeite: saucer, $250; cup, 9.25″ grill plate, 4.5″ tall tumbler, $400; 5.75″ cereal bowl, 8.5″ diam., 2.5″ deep berry bowl, 8.75″ diam.,2.75″ deep bowl with two handles, 9″ x 6.75″ vegetable bowl, 10.5″ 3-ftd. fruit bowl, 7″ salad plate, 9″ Dinner plate, $600; 7.75″ diam., 1.5″ deep flat soup bowl, 10.25″ cake plate, 11″ x 7.75″ platter, $650; 10.25″ diam. 2-handled sandwich tray, $1000; butter dish; 6.25″ tall pitcher w/scalloped foot, $2000. Crystal: 3x price of pink.

Rarities in pink: bowl, about 2.25″ deep ruffled violet in pink; bowl, 4.75″ diameter, 1.5″ deep in pink with frosting; bowl, 8.55″ diameter, 2.75″ deep in pink with frosting; bowl, ruffled, made from pink 6″ sherbet plate; bowl, ruffled, made from pink 7″ salad plate; cookie jar in pink, base 6″ deep, 5″ opening, lid just over 5″ diameter; pitcher, pattern only at top in panels w/foot; plate, 8″ with 12 sides in pink; plate, 8.5″ with 12 sides in pink; plate, 9″ with rim and stippling in pink; plate, 10.25″ in pink; relish, 5-part in pink; tumbler, 4.25″ tall, 9 oz. with rolled-in rim.

Rarities in slag: bowl, 8.75″ diameter (11″ diameter handle to handle), 2.75-3″ deep bowl in orange slag with yellow-green trim; bowl, 10.5″ diameter, 3.25″ deep bowl with feet in orange slag with yellow-green trim; tray, 10.25″ diameter, (12.75″ diameter handle to handle) 2.75-3″ deep with two handles in orange slag with yellow-green trim.

Rarities in other colors: bowl, almost 9″ diameter (10.75″ diameter handle to handle) bowl in Amberina; comport, 2.75″ deep, 5.75″ diameter with a 2.5″ diameter starburst foot; plate, 9″ dinner in opalescent Delphite; pitcher, 6.5″ w/pattern only at top in green; tumbler, 4.5″ tall, 3″ diameter with foot in iridescence; tumbler, 4.5″ tall, 3″ diameter with foot in reddish hue. Opalescent clambroth 9″ dinner plate. 9″ dinner plate with rippled rim and green tint.

CHERRY BLOSSOM *(cont.)*

Reproduction information: New colors: blue (chalaine, transparent, cobalt, & delphite), iridescent, & red. Also reproduced in pink & green. 5.75" cereal bowl: *new* – 2" mold ring on bottom; *old* – 2 ½" mold ring on bottom. 8.5" round berry bowl: *new* - smooth edges to leaves, veins same size; *old* - irregular veins, realistically shaped leaf. Butter dish lid: *new* - 1 molded line in smooth area near base; *old* - 2 molded lines. Butter dish base: *new* - branches without texture and end about 1/4" from outer edge, leaves unrealistic; *old* - textured branch that ends very close to outer edge, realistic leaves. *New* cake plate: from underside of plate the design along the outside rim does not accurately line up with the rest of the design inside the rim. Cup: *new* - pattern is sparse on bottom; *old* - 4 cherries w/ pattern all over & many leaves on bottom. 6.75" pitcher: *new* - 7 cherries on smooth bottom; *old* - 9 cherries on textured bottom. 9" dinner plate, 6" sherbet plate, & saucer: *new* - crudely finished at outer edges so one can feel a ridge; *old* - smooth edges. 13" divided platter: *new* - too heavy & too thick, VERY DIFFICULT TO DISCERN; *old* - leaves still have more realistic design upon close examination. Salt & pepper: assume what you have found is new! 10.5" sandwich tray w/2 handles: *new* - if handles are at 9:00 & 3:00, center branch lines up horizontally; *old* - if handles are at 9:00 & 3:00, center branch with textures will be vertical. Tumblers with scalloped feet and pattern all over: *new* - 1 or 3 weak lines dividing pattern and smooth rim at top; *old* - 3 clearly distinct lines between pattern and rim at top and Cherry Blossom design entirely covers bottom of foot. Delphite scalloped-foot tumbler reproduced with a crude pattern, wrong color, and the line separating the pattern is incomplete. Creamer: reproduced in Delphite with a very crude design. Bowl, 4.75" Berry, pink & green are now being reproduced, but at this time we have no details. Sherbet: *old*–two complete cherries on foot, pattern continues on rim at top, glass is true pink; *new* – five complete cherries on foot, rim totally plain, glass has purple cast. Only one original cookie jar is known to exist; it is pink. Assume all cookie jars found to be new.

*trtp = too rare to price

Child's Junior Dinner Set
Reproduced

	Pink	Delphite	Qty
Creamer	40	50	____
Cup *R*	40	45	____
Plate, 6"	15	15	____
Saucer *R*	8	8	____
Sugar	40	50	____
14-piece set	332	372	____
Box (for pink)			

    in fairly reasonable condition: $35,
    mint condition: $50

Reproduction information: Butter dish: all are new regardless of color. Cup: lopsided handle, cherries may be upside down and off-color. Saucer: design not centered.

CHERRYBERRY

(1928-1931   U.S. Glass Company)

	Pink & Green	Crystal & Iridescent	Qty
Bowl, 4" berry	24	6	____
Bowl, 6.25"	120	50	____
Bowl, 6.5" salad	40	15	____
Bowl, 7.5" berry	50	15	____
Butter dish base	75	40	____
Butter dish lid	150	85	____
Butter complete	225	125	____
Comport, 3.5" tall, 5.5" dia.	45	18	____
Creamer, 3"	25	14	____
Creamer, 4"	40	16	____
Olive dish, 5" w/1 handle	30	14	____
Pickle dish, 8.25" oval	30	14	____
Pitcher, 7.75"	250	120	____
Plate, 6" sherbet	14	5	____
Plate, 7.5" salad	28	6	____
Sherbet	14	5	____
Sugar, small, 3"	25	14	____
Sugar base, large	35	14	____
Sugar lid (fits large)	65	36	____
Tumbler, 3.25"	50	20	____

CHINEX CLASSIC

(Late 1930s-1942   Macbeth-Evans Division Corning Glass Works)

	Castle decorations	Floral decoration	Plain	Qty
Bowl, 5.75", 1.5" deep dessert	12	8	4	____
Bowl, 6.75" salad	10	18	8	____
Bowl, 7" vegetable	30	20	8	____
Bowl, 7.75" coupe soup	30	20	8	____
Bowl, 9" vegetable	30	20	8	____
Bowl, 11"	35	25	15	____
Butter dish base	25	18	12	____
Butter dish lid	110	50	30	____
Butter complete (actually a covered utility dish)	135	68	42	____
Cigarette holder, 3" tall, 3" diam			20	____
Creamer	12	8	5	____
Cup	8	5	5	____
Lamp, 9" tall, 6" wide, urn shape	400			____
Planter, urn, 7" tall, 7" diam			85	____
Plate, 6.25" bread & butter	7	4	3	____
Plate, 9.25"-9.75" dinner	20	8	5	____
Plate, 11.5" salver	20	15	7	____
Saucer	5	3	3	____
Sherbet	18	8	6	____
Sugar	12	8	5	____

CHRISTMAS CANDY

(Late 1930s-early 1950s Indiana
Glass Company)

	Terrace green	Crystal	Qty
Bowl, 5.75" fruit		4	____
Bowl, 7.25" soup	65	8	____
Bowl, 9.5" vegetable	trtp*		____
Creamer, 3.5"	35	8	____
Cup	35	4	____
Mayonnaise 3-pc. set		30	____
Mayo. comport		20	____
Mayo. ladle		5	____
Mayo. under plate		5	____
Plate, 6" bread & butter	18	4	____
Plate, 8.25" luncheon	30	7	____
Plate, 9.5" dinner	50	10	____
Plate, 11.25" sandwich	75	15	____
Saucer	15	4	____
Sugar, 3.25"	35	8	____
Tidbit, 2 tier		18	____
Tumbler		trtp*	____

*trtp = too rare to price

CIRCLE

(1929-1930s   Hocking Glass Company)

	Green	Pink	Qty
Bowl, 4.5" diam., shallow	14		____
Bowl, 4.5" diam., 2" deep	38		____
Bowl, 5" diam. w/flared rim	24		____
Bowl, 5.25" diam.	14		____
Bowl, 7" diam. 2.75" deep	14		____
Bowl, 8" diam.	34		____
Bowl, 9.25" diam.	34		____
Creamer	15	15	____
Cup, 2 styles	10	10	____
Decanter, handled w/ stopper	90	90	____
Goblet, 4.5" wine	18	22	____
Goblet, 5.75", water	20	20	____
Pitcher, 60 oz.	65		____
Pitcher, 80 oz.	65		____
Plate, 6" sherbet	10	10	____
Plate, 8.25" luncheon	10	10	____
Plate, 9.5" dinner	42	42	____
Plate, 10" sandwich	20	20	____
Reamer (fits top of 80 oz. pitcher)	25	25	____
Saucer	8		____
Sherbet, 3" w/stem	8	8	____
Sherbet, 4.75" w/ stem	10	10	____
Sugar	15	15	____
Tumbler, 3.5" juice, flat	12		____
Tumbler, 4" water, flat	10		____
Tumbler, 5" iced tea, flat	18		____
Tumbler, 15 oz., flat	25		____

Note: Crystal items ½ of those in green. Crystal lid for 80 oz. pitcher, $50; vase, $35. Iridescent vase, $35.

CLOVERLEAF
(1930-1936   Hazel Atlas Glass Company)

	Green	Topaz	Black	Pink	Qty
Ashtray, 4"	100		150		____
Ashtray, 5.75"	125		85		____
Bowl, 4" dessert	50	35		25	____
Bowl, 5" cereal	80	75			____
Bowl, 7" salad	85	60			____
Bowl, 8"	115				____
Candy jar w/lid	125	125			____
Creamer	25	25	25		____
Cup	12	10	20	8	____
Plate, 6" sherbet	15	10	40		____
Plate, 8" luncheon	18	18	22	10	____
Plate, 10.25" grill	50	35			____
Salt & pepper	75	125	125		____
Saucer	6	6	8	4	____
Sherbet *(see note)*	12	12	20	7	____
Sugar	25	25	25		____
Tumbler, 3.75" flat	80				____
Tumbler, 4" flat	60			35	____
Tumbler, 5.75" w/foot	40	35			____

Note: Crystal cup, $5; saucer, $3. Sherbet found with and without design on foot.

COLONIAL, "KNIFE & FORK"

(1934-1938   Hocking Glass Company)

	Pink	Green	Crystal	Qty
Bowl, 3.75" berry	65			___
Bowl, 4.75" diam, 1.5" deep berry	20	20	10	___
Bowl, 4.75" diam, 2"deep cream soup	70	70	40	___
Bowl, 5.25" diam, 1.25" deep cereal	70	175	20	___
Bowl, 7.25" diam, 1.75" deep low soup	70	70	20	___
Bowl, 8.75" diam, 2.5" deep berry	35	35	20	___
Bowl, 10" x 8", 1.75" deep oval vegetable	40	40	20	___
Butter dish base, 7" diam, 1" deep	500	55	25	___
Butter dish lid, 5" diam	200	25	15	___
Butter complete	700	80	40	___
Celery/spoon holder, 5.5"	135	125	50	___
Cheese dish		260		___
Creamer, 5" (same as 5" milk pitcher)	80	45	16	___
Cup	18	12	5	___
Goblet, 3" tall, 2 oz., 2" diam.	30	25	8	___
Goblet, 3.75" tall, 1.5"+ diam cordial, 1 oz.		25	8	___
Goblet, almost 4" tall, 2" diam cocktail, 3 oz.		24	6	___
Goblet, 4.25"+ tall, 2.25" diam cocktail		24		___
Goblet, 4.5" tall wine, 2.5 oz.		24	6	___
Goblet, 5.25" tall, 2.5" diam claret, 4 oz.		24	6	___
Goblet, 5.75" tall, 3.25" diam water, 8.5 oz.		30	12	___
Mug, 4.5" tall, 3" diam	trtp*	1000		___
Pitcher, 5" milk/creamer	80	45	20	___
Pitcher, 7.25", 54 oz w/or w/out ice lip	85	75	30	___
Pitcher, 7.25", 68 oz w/or w/out ice lip	85	95	30	___
Plate, 6" sherbet/saucer	10	10	5	___
Plate, 8.25" luncheon	30	30	4	___
Plate, 9.75" dinner	65	70	25	___
Plate, 9.75" grill	30	25	10	___
Platter, 12" x 9"	50	45	15	___
Salt & pepper	180	180	60	___
Saucer/sherbet plate	12	10	4	___
Sherbet, 3"	25			___

COLONIAL, "KNIFE & FORK"
(cont.)

	Pink	Green	Crystal	Qty
Sherbet, 3.75" diam	14	15	5	____
Spoon holder/celery, 5.5"	135	135	60	____
Sugar base, 4"	28	18	10	____
Sugar lid	60	30	15	____
Tumbler, 2.25" tall, 1.75" diam whiskey or toothpick, 1.5 oz., flat	25	20	12	____
Tumbler, 3.25" tall, 2.25" diam juice, 5 oz., flat	25	25	10	____
Tumbler, 3.25", 2" diam, 3 oz. w/foot	22	27	10	____
Tumbler, 4", 2.5" diam 5 oz. w/foot	35	45	15	____
Tumbler, 4" tall, almost 3" diam water, 9 oz., flat	25	25	10	____
Tumbler, 5" tall, 2.75" diam, 11 oz., flat iced tea	36	45	15	____
Tumbler, 5" tall, 3" diam 12 oz. flat iced tea	65	65	20	____
Tumbler, 5.25" tall, 3.25" diam 10 oz. w/foot	50	50	20	____
Tumbler, 5.75" tall, 3"+ diam 15 oz. lemonade, flat	70	80	40	____

Note: Beaded top pitcher, $1300. Ruby tumblers, $150. White: cup, $5; saucer, $2. Flower pot, 2.25" tall, 2.25" diam. in variety of fired-on colors, $12. Cranberry goblet, $125.

*trtp = too rare to price

COLONIAL BLOCK

(1930s, White in 1950s   Hazel Atlas
Glass Company)

	Pink & Green	Qty
Bowl, 4" diam	12	____
Bowl, 5" diam	15	____
Bowl, 6" diam	18	____
Bowl, 7" diam, 2.5" deep	35	____
Bowl, 8" diam	35	____
Butter dish base	20	____
Butter dish lid	40	____
Butter complete	60	____
Butter tub	60	____
Butter tub lid	80	____
Candy jar w/lid, 8.75"	40	____
Creamer, 4"	15	____
Goblet, 5.75" tall, 3" diam	15	____
Pitcher	75	____
Powder jar w/lid	40	____
Sherbet	10	____
Sugar base	15	____
Sugar lid	20	____
Tumbler, 5.25" small stem and foot	30	____

Note: White creamer, sugar base, $7; sugar lid $8. Black powder jar w/lid, $40. Crystal items half of those in pink and green. Cobalt creamer: $250.

COLONIAL FLUTED
(1928-1933   Federal Glass Company)

	Green	Qty
Bowl, 4" berry	10	____
Bowl, 6" cereal	12	____
Bowl, 6.5" salad (deep)	20	____
Bowl, 7.5" berry	25	____
Creamer	14	____
Cup	5	____
Plate, 6" sherbet	8	____
Plate, 8" luncheon	10	____
Saucer	3	____
Sherbet	10	____
Sugar base	14	____
Sugar lid	30	____

Note: Crystal items worth ½ of those in green.

COLUMBIA *Reproduced*
(1938-1942   Federal Glass Company)

	Crystal	Pink	Qty
Bowl, 5" cereal	15		____
Bowl, 8" soup	20		____
Bowl, 8.5" salad	15		____
Bowl, 10.5" fruit w/ruffled rim	18		____
Butter dish base	5		____
Butter dish lid	12		____
Butter complete	17		____
Cup	5	20	____
Pitcher	100		____
Plate, 6" bread & butter	6	15	____
Plate, 9.5" luncheon	10	30	____
Plate, 11" chop	12		____
Saucer	1	8	____
Tumbler, 2.75" 4 oz. juice *R*	25		____
Tumbler, 4" 9 oz. water	30		____

Note: Ruby flashed butter, $25. Other flashed or satinized butters, $20.

Reproduction information: Juice glasses marked "France" on bottom are new.

COREX
(1948 Corning Glassworks of Canada)

	Ivory	Qty
Bowl, 5" berry	7	____
Bowl, large berry	15	____
Bowl, 7.75" soup	18	____
Creamer	8	____
Cup	4	____
Mug, 8 oz.	25	____
Plate, 6.75" sherbet	5	____
Plate, 7.5" salad	8	____
Plate, 9.25" dinner	12	____
Plate, 12" salver	18	____
Saucer	2	____
Sherbet, 4.5"	12	____
Sugar	7	____
Tumbler, 9 oz.	15	____

CORONATION *Reproduced*
(1936-1940 Hocking Glass Company)

	Pink	Ruby	Green	Qty
Bowl, 4.5" diam, 1.5" deep berry w/2 handles	12	10		____
Bowl, 4.25" diam with no handles	80		60	____
Bowl, 6.5" diam, 2.25" deep w/2 handles	18	18		____
Bowl, 8" diam, 2.75" deep berry w/2 handles	25	25		____
Bowl, 8" diam w/no handles	150		180	____
Cup	8	12		____
Pitcher, 7.75"	1000			____
Plate, 6" sherbet/saucer	6			____
Plate, 7.5" long, 4.5" wide, crescent-shaped			60	____
Plate, 8.5" luncheon	15	30	60	____
Saucer/6" sherbet plate	8			____
Sherbet, squatty, 4" diam, 2.75" tall	10		90	____
Sherbet, stemmed	300			____
Tumbler, 4.75" tall *R*	40		180	____

Note: Crystal with or without gold trim: saucer, $3, cup, $3.

Reproduction information: Newly made: 4" and 7" tall footed tumblers, 7" goblets, 10" dinner plates, and 6.5" diameter bowls.

CREMAX

(Late 1930s-early 1940s   Macbeth-Evans
Division Corning Glass Works)

	Cremax	All other colors w/or w/out decorations	Qty
Bowl, 6" dessert/cereal	5	8	____
Bowl, 7" bowl	8	14	____
Bowl, 7.75" coupe soup	8	14	____
Bowl, 9" vegetable	8	14	____
Creamer	6	10	____
Cup	5	6	____
Cup, demitasse, 2.25" deep	12	12	____
Egg cup, 2.25" tall	8		____
Plate, 6" bread & butter	5	7	____
Plate, 9.75" dinner	6	10	____
Plate, 12" salver	6	8	____
Saucer	3	4	____
Saucer, demitasse, 4.5" diam	3	4	____
Sugar	6	10	____

CROW'S FOOT

(1930s Paden City Glass Company)

	Red	Black, Blue & Amethyst	Other colors	Qty
Bowl, 4.25" diam, 2.25" deep	30			____
Bowl, cream soup, 4.5" diam 2.25" deep	25	30	12	____
Bowl, 4.75" square	30	35	12	____
Bowl, 5" diam, 1.5" deep	50			____
Bowl, 5.25" diam, 2.75" deep	50			____
Bowl, 5.75" diam, 4.5" tall w/foot	50			____
Bowl, 6" round	28	30	12	____
Bowl, 6.5" round	45	50	20	____
Bowl, 7" diam, 4.25" tall w/foot	50			____
Bowl, 7" diam, 3.75" tall w/foot, square shape	60			____
Bowl, 7" diam, 6" deep cupped rim w/3 feet	65			____
Bowl, 7" 2-spout sauce	40	35	18	____
Bowl, 7.25" w/foot & flat rim	50	50	20	____
Bowl, 7.5" x 5" oval, 4.5" tall w/foot	60			____
Bowl, 8.5" square w/ 2 handles	40	50	20	____
Bowl, 8.5" punch w/cover & chrome ring	750	450	400	____
Bowl, 8.75" square	40	50	20	____
Bowl, 9" w/ foot, flared	50	45	20	____
Bowl, 9.5" x 7", 2.25" deep oval vegetable	60	60	30	____
Bowl, 9.75" w/foot & flat rim	60	60	30	____
Bowl, 10" w/3 feet	70	70	30	____
Bowl, 10" square, w/crimped rim	125	95	65	____
Bowl, 10" square, 3.5" deep, w/2 handles, flared rim	60	70	30	____
Bowl, 10.25" x 8" oval, 1.25" deep shallow vegetable/platter	80	70	40	____
Bowl, 11" oval	30	40	15	____
Bowl, 11" round			30	____
Bowl, 11" square	60	70	30	____
Bowl, 11" square w/rolled edge	60	70	30	____
Bowl, 11.5" round w/3 feet	90	120	50	____
Bowl, 11.75" console w/rolled edge	85	100	45	____

CROW'S FOOT *(cont.)*

	Red	Black, Blue & Amethyst	Other colors	Qty
Bowl, 11.75" diam, 3" deep console w/flat rim	90	80	40	____
Bowl, 11.75" diam, 4" deep square shape w/flared rim	90	80	40	____
Bowl, 12" console w/foot	95	85	45	____
Bowl, 12" console w/3 feet	120	100	50	____
Bowl, 12" console w/flared rim	95	85	45	____
Bowl, Nasturtium w/3 feet	200	225	100	____
Bowl, whipped cream w/3 feet	50	60	20	____
Cake plate, 9.5" square	75	90	40	____
Cake plate, 12.5" w/foot	160	150	70	____
Candlestick, 2.5" tall, round base, ea.	40	45	20	____
Candlestick, 2.5" tall, square "mushroom", ea.	15	20	12	____
Candlestick, 5", 2-light w/fan, ea.	100	85	45	____
Candlestick, 5.25", stem, ea.	40	35	25	____
Candlestick, 5.75" tall, ea.	55			____
Candlestick, 6.5", 3-light w/fan, ea.	120	110	60	____
Candlestick, 7" ea.	70	65	30	____
Candy w/lid, 6.25" across	170	200	90	____
Candy w/lid, 6.5" across, 2 sections	65			____
Candy w/ lid, 6.5" 3-sections, 2 styles	65	80	30	____
Cheese stand, 5"	25	35	15	____
Comport, 2.25" tall, 2 styles	40	30	15	____
Comport, 3.75" tall, 2 styles	25	35	15	____
Comport, 4.25" tall	50	65	40	____
Comport, 6.5" tall, 2 styles	65	80	40	____
Comport, 6.75"	100	90	30	____
Comport, 7" tall, 7.25" diam	65	55	30	____
Creamer, flat or footed	15	18	8	____
Cup, flat or footed	10	15	5	____
Gravy boat, flat, 2 spouts	100	120	50	____
Gravy boat, pedestal, 1 spout	150	175	75	____
Mayonnaise, 3 feet	40	55	25	____
Plate, 5.75"	10	15	5	____
Plate, 6" square	18			____
Plate, 6.25"	18	12	8	____
Plate, 7.5"	20	15	8	____
Plate, 7.5", liner for gravy boat/sherbet plate	18	12	8	____

CROW'S FOOT *(cont.)*

	Red	Black, Blue & Amethyst	Other colors	Qty
Plate, 8"	12	16	4	____
Plate, 8.5" square	12	16	7	____
Plate, 9.25"	45	35	15	____
Plate, 9.25" small dinner	35	40	15	____
Plate, 9.5" 2 handles	60	70	35	____
Plate, 10.25" round w/2 handles	50	60	20	____
Plate, 10.25" square w/2 handles	50	60	30	____
Plate, 10.5" dinner	100	125	50	____
Plate, 11" cracker	40	50	20	____
Plate, 11.75" square w/2 handles	60			____
Plate, 12"	20	40	15	____
Platter, 11.5" x 8.5" oval	60	50	20	____
Relish, 11", 3 sections	100	120	50	____
Sandwich server, round w/center handle, 10.75" diam	60	70	30	____
Sandwich server, square w/center handle	40	50	15	____
Saucer, round	8	12	4	____
Saucer, square	10	15	6	____
Sugar, flat or footed	15	18	8	____
Tumbler, 2.5", punch/roly-poly	15	12	8	____
Tumbler, 4.25" tall, 2.75" diam	80	100	40	____
Vase, 4.5"	60	75	40	____
Vase, 7.5", cupped	200	150	50	____
Vase, 7.75", flared	200	120	50	____
Vase, 8.25", cupped	200			____
Vase, 10.25", curved in	110	130	50	____
Vase, 10.25", curved out	95	110	40	____
Vase, 11.75"	150	185	70	____

Note: Add 20% for sterling overlay. White bowl, 12" square, 2.25" deep, $40.

CROWN

(1940s   Pyrex, Macbeth-Evans Division of
Corning Glass Works)

	Turquoise	Qty
Bowl, 4.75" small berry	6	____
Bowl, 6" oatmeal	10	____
Bowl, 7.75" soup	22	____
Bowl, 9" large berry	30	____
Creamer	10	____
Cup	5	____
Mug	35	____
Plate, 6.75" sherbet	6	____
Plate, 9" dinner	15	____
Plate. 12" salver	27	____
Saucer	2	____
Sugar	10	____

CUBE
(1929-1933   Jeannette Glass Company)

	Pink	Green	Qty
Bowl, 4.5" dessert, pointy rim	12	10	_____
Bowl, 4.5" deep	12		_____
Bowl, 6.5" salad, pointy rim	22	22	_____
Bowl, 7.5" salad, pointy rim	18	22	_____
Butter dish base	40	40	_____
Butter dish lid	60	60	_____
Butter complete	100	100	_____
Candy jar w/lid, 6"	45	55	_____
Coaster, 3.25"	12	12	_____
Creamer, 2.5"	8		_____
Creamer, 3.25"	12	14	_____
Cup	12	14	_____
Pitcher, 9.75"	225	225	_____
Plate, 6" sherbet	10	8	_____
Plate, 8" luncheon	14	14	_____
Powder jar w/lid, 5", w/3 feet	40	45	_____
Relish, 7" w/3 feet (like Windsor)	trtp*		_____
Salt & pepper	60	60	_____
Saucer	6	6	_____
Sherbet	10	12	_____
Sugar, 2.5"	8		_____
Sugar base, 3"	12	14	_____
Sugar lid/candy lid	22	22	_____
Tumbler, 4"	80	80	

*trtp = too rare to price

Note: Ultramarine: 4.5" bowl, $50; 6.5" bowl, $85. Amber: small creamer & sugar, $10 ea. White: small creamer & sugar, $3 ea. Crystal: tray for larger creamer & sugar, $5; 6" sherbet plate, $5; 2.5" tall, 3.25" custard cup, $10; other items, $1. Creamer and sugar with ruby flash and clear handles, $12 each.

CUPID
(1930s Paden City Glass Company)

	Green & Pink	Qty
Bowl, 8.5" oval w/foot, 4.25" deep	300	____
Bowl, 8.5" fruit w/foot	300	____
Bowl, 9" w/center handle	300	____
Bowl, 10.25" fruit	225	____
Bowl, 11" w/rolled edge	225	____
Bowl, 13.25" console w/rolled edge	225	____
Bowl, 14" console	225	____
Cake plate, 11.25"	200	____
Cake stand, 2" tall, 11.25" diam.	225	____
Candlestick, 5" diam., 2" tall, ea.	110	____
Candy jar w/lid, 3-part flat, 6" diam., 1.5" deep	300	____
Candy jar w/lid, 7" tall, 6" diam.	400	____
Casserole w/lid, base: 12" x 8.75", 1.75" deep	450	____
Cheese & cracker	600	____
10.5" plate w/indent	300	____
3" tall comport	300	____
Comport, 3.5" tall, 3 styles	200	____
Comport, 5.5" tall, 8.25" diam.	200	____
Comport, 6.25" tall, 8" diam., 3 styles	200	____
Creamer, 3" w/foot	175	____
Creamer, 4.25" w/foot	150	____
Creamer, 5" w/foot	150	____
Cup	90	____
Ice bucket, 6.25", 5.25" diam.	320	____
Ice tub, 4.25", 5.5" diam.	320	____
Ice tub cover	380	____
Lamp w/silver overlay	500	____
Mayonnaise, 3-piece set	250	____
Mayo. comport, 6.5" diam., 4" tall	150	____
Mayo. ladle	50	____
Mayo. underplate, 7.75"	50	____
Plate, 8.25"	200	____
Plate, 10.5"	175	____
Platter, 10.75"	300	____
Samovar	1100	____
Saucer	40	____
Sugar, 3", w/foot	175	____

CUPID *(cont.)*

	Green & Pink	Qty
Sugar, 3.75", w/foot	175	____
Sugar, 4.25" w/foot	150	____
Sugar, 5" w/foot	150	____
Tray, 10.5" w/center handle	200	____
Tray, 11" x 5" oval w/foot	250	____
Vase, 8.25" elliptical	600	____
Vase, 8", fan-shaped	425	____
Vase, 8", round bottom, flared rim	400	____
Vase, 10"	325	____
Vase, 11.75"	500	____
Vase, 12"	850	____

Note: Black: covered casserole, $650. Peacock blue: comport, $250; mayonnaise, $375; 10.5" plate, $250; samovar, $2000. Aqua: 30% more than value shown for green & pink. Add 20% for sterling overlay.

DAISY

(1933 crystal, 1940 amber, others till 1980s
Indiana Glass Company)

	Amber & Fired-on red	Green	Crystal	Qty
Bowl, 4.5" diam, 2.25" deep cream soup	10	5	4	____
Bowl, 4.75" berry	8	7	4	____
Bowl, 6" cereal	30	12	7	____
Bowl, 7.25" berry	12	8	7	____
Bowl, 9.25" berry	30	15	12	____
Bowl, 10" oval vegetable, w/tab handles	15	12	8	____
Creamer, 4.25"	12	8	7	____
Cup	7	6	3	____
Plate, 6" sherbet	6	5	1	____
Plate, 7.25" salad	8	6	3	____
Plate, 8.5" luncheon	8	6	3	____
Plate, 9.25" dinner	10	10	5	____
Plate, 10.25" grill	9	8	4	____
Plate, 10.25" grill w/indent (fits cream soup)	18	18		____
Plate, 11.5" cake/sandwich	15	8	6	____
Platter, 10.75"	15	10	6	____
Relish, 7.5" 3-part w/3 feet	30		8	____
Saucer	5	3	1	____
Sherbet, 3"	8	6	4	____
Sugar, 4"	12	8	7	____
Tumbler, 9 oz., 4.75"	18	10	8	____
Tumbler, 12 oz., 6.5"	35	20	15	____

Note: White sugar, $10.

DELILAH BIRD

(1930s Paden City Glass
Manufacturing Company)

	Any color	Qty
Biscuit jar w/lid	600	____
Bowl, 4.75"	50	____
Bowl, 6.5", 2" deep	75	____
Bowl, 8.75"	125	____
Bowl, 8.75" w/handles	125	____
Bowl, 9" x 10" w/foot	100	____
Bowl, 9.25" w/center handle	150	____
Bowl, 11.75", console	150	____
Candlestick, ea., 5" tall	85	____
Candy box w/lid	200	____
Cheese & cracker	200	____
Comport, 3.25" tall	85	____
Comport, 4.25" tall	85	____
Creamer, 2.75"	95	____
Cup	85	____
Goblet, 5.75" tall	125	____
Plate, 5.75" sherbet	25	____
Plate, 8.5" luncheon	70	____
Plate, 10.5" w/handles	100	____
Plate, sandwich w/center handle	85	____
Saucer	25	____
Sherbet, 2 sizes	75	____
Sugar, 2.75"	95	____
Tumbler, 4"	100	____
Tumbler, 5.25"	100	____
Vase, 6.5"	400	____
Vase, 8.25" elliptical	300	____
Vase, 10"	225	____

DELLA ROBBIA

(1928-1940s   Westmoreland Glass Company)

	Crystal w/applied colors	Qty
Basket, 9", flared	100	___
Basket, 9", rolled	100	___
Basket, 12"	125	___
Bowl, 4" finger	34	___
Bowl, 4.5"	30	___
Bowl, 6"	25	___
Bowl, 6.75"x 8.5" w/1 handle	25	___
Bowl, 7", flared	30	___
Bowl, 7.5" x 9" w/1 handle	30	___
Bowl, 8"	35	___
Bowl, 8" w/handles	40	___
Bowl, 8.25" x 9" heart w/1 handle	100	___
Bowl, 9"	45	___
Bowl, 11.5", no. 1067	75	___
Bowl, 12" w/foot	120	___
Bowl, 13" w/rolled edge	80	___
Bowl, 14" oval	100	___
Bowl, 14" punch	250	___
Bowl, 15"	100	___
Candlestick, no. 1067, pyramid style, ea.	40	___
Candlestick, 4" 1-light, ea.	20	___
Candlestick, 4" 2-light, ea.	35	___
Candy, chocolate, round & flat	50	___
Candy jar w/lid, scalloped edge, 7" tall	90	___
Comport, 6.5" mint, 3.5" tall	50	___
Comport, 5.75" tall, flat	50	___
Comport, 6" tall, cupped	50	___
Comport, 6" tall, crimped	60	___
Comport, 8" sweetmeat	25	___
Comport, 12"	80	___
Comport, 13"	80	___
Creamer	18	___
Cup	15	___
Cup, punch	12	___
Pitcher, 8"	300	___
Plate, 6" liner for 4" finger bowl	12	___
Plate, 6.25" bread & butter	12	___
Plate, 7.25" salad	20	___
Plate, 9" luncheon	22	___
Plate, 10.5" dinner	125	___

DELLA ROBBIA *(cont.)*

	Crystal w/applied colors	Qty
Plate, 14" torte	50	____
Plate, 14" salver/cake w/foot	85	____
Plate, 18"	100	____
Plate, 18" liner for punch bowl w/upturned rim	150	____
Platter, 14"	100	____
Punch bowl	250	____
Punch bowl 15-piece set	600	____
Salt & pepper	60	____
Saucer	8	____
Stem, 4.25", 3 oz. wine	25	____
Stem, 3.25 oz. cocktail	25	____
Stem, 5 oz. sherbet, 4.75"	20	____
Stem, 4.75", 5 oz. champagne	25	____
Stem, 6 oz. champagne	25	____
Stem, 8 oz. water, 6"	25	____
Sugar	18	____
Tumbler, 5 oz. ginger ale, flat	25	____
Tumbler, 8 oz. w/foot	25	____
Tumbler, 8 oz. water, flat	25	____
Tumbler, 11 oz. iced tea w/foot	30	____
Tumbler, 12 oz. iced tea, flat	30	____
Tumbler, 12 oz. iced tea, w/foot	35	____
Tumbler, 12 oz. iced tea, 5.25" without usual "bell" or flare at rim	35	____

Note: Green candlesticks, 3.25" tall, $100 ea; bowl, 12" diam. 3.5" deep, $75.

DIAMOND CUT
Formerly known as
Anniversary
(1947-1949 Pink...see note at bottom Jeannette Glass Company)

	Pink	Crystal	Amber-escence	Qty.
Bowl, 4.75" berry	12	4	4	____
Bowl, 7.25" soup	22	8	8	____
Bowl, 9" fruit	34	12	20	____
Butter dish base	40	20		____
Butter dish lid	35	10		____
Butter complete	75	30		____
Candy, 5.75" w/3 feet, open	15		8	____
Candy jar w/lid	60	25		____
Cake plate, 12.5" round	35	8		____
Cake plate, 12.5" square		30		____
Cake plate cover, round (metal lid)	12			____
Cake plate cover, square (metal lid)	20			____
Candle holder, 4.75" ea.		14	15	____
Comport w/3 feet, 5.75"	24	5	8	____
Comport, ruffled w/3 feet, 5.75"		7		____
Creamer, 3.5"	14	5	8	____
Cup	10	5	4	____
Goblet, 2.5 oz. wine	20	12		____
Plate, 6.25" sherbet	10	2	4	____
Plate, 9" dinner	35	5	7	____
Plate, 10" snack w/cup ring		7	15	____
Plate, 10"			40	____
Plate, 12.5" sandwich	30	6	10	____
Relish, 8"	24	5	10	____
Relish, 4-part w/metal base		15		____
Saucer	6	2	2	____
Sherbet	14	3		____
Sugar base, 3.25"	14	5	8	____
Sugar lid	100	25	15	____
Tid-bit, 2-tier (made from 4.75" berry on top of 9" fruit bowl)		20		____
Tray w/ tab handles for creamer & sugar, 5" x 9"	25			____
Vase, 6.5"	80	15		____
Vase, wall pin-up, 6.5"	100	40		____

Note: Crystal and Iridescent pieces made in 1960s & 1970s. Shell pink: cake plate & pin-up vase, $200 ea. Shell pink cake plate, $75.

DIAMOND QUILTED

(Late 1920s-early 1930s
Imperial Glass Company)

	Pink, Green, & Amber	Blue & Black	Qty
Bowl, cream soup	20	20	____
Bowl, 5" cereal	10	18	____
Bowl, 5.5" w/1 handle, 2.25" deep	10	18	____
Bowl, 6.25" footed w/cover (resembles a stemmed candy)	50	50	____
Bowl, 6.75", ruffled		50	____
Bowl, 7"	20	20	____
Bowl, 7" diam, 2.25" deep w/ crimped rim	15	30	____
Bowl, 7" footed, rolled edge (resembles a comport)	50	50	____
Bowl, 7.5" footed, straight rim (resembles a comport)	50	50	____
Bowl, 8.75" diam, footed w/rolled edge	350		____
Bowl, 9" diam, footed w/flat rim	350		____
Bowl, 9" diam, footed w/straight rim	350		____
Bowl, 10.5" console w/rolled edge	30	60	____
Candlestick, high and low, each	20	30	____
Candlestick, w/ruffled feet, each	115		____
Candy jar w/lid, low w/3 feet	125		____
Compote, 3.5", 6.5" dia.	50	50	____
Compote, 6" tall, 7.25" across	50		____
Compote w/lid, 11.25"	120		____
Creamer	12	18	____
Cup, 2 styles	12	18	____
Goblet, 1 oz. cordial	18		____
Goblet, 2 oz. wine	18		____
Goblet, 3 oz. wine	18		____
Goblet, 9 oz. champagne, 6.25"	15		____
Ice bucket	60	90	____
Mayonnaise, 3-pc. set	45	65	____
Mayo. comport	15	25	____
Mayo. ladle	20	30	____
Mayo. under plate	10	10	____

DIAMOND QUILTED *(cont.)*

	Pink, Green, & Amber	Blue & Black	Qty
Pitcher	70		____
Plate, 6.5" sherbet w/indent	8	8	____
Plate, 7" salad	10	10	____
Plate, 8" luncheon	12	14	____
Plate, 14" sandwich	20		____
Punch bowl	400		____
Punch bowl foot (base)	250		____
Salver, 8.25" (resembles a pedestal cake plate)	200	75	____
Salver, 10" (resembles a pedestal cake plate)	200	75	____
Sandwich server w/center handle	30	50	____
Saucer	6	5	____
Sherbet, 3.5"	10	15	____
Sugar	12	18	____
Tumbler, 1.5 oz. whiskey	25		____
Tumbler, 6 oz. w/foot	25		____
Tumbler, 9 oz. water, flat	30		____
Tumbler, 9 oz. water w/foot	30		____
Tumbler, 12 oz. iced tea, flat	36		____
Tumbler, 12 oz. iced tea w/foot	36		____
Vase	65	85	____

Note: Red items twice those in pink. 7.5" diam., 2.75" deep, 3-footed bowl, $200; basket with metal bail in a variety of sizes, $25-65. Larger baskets command higher prices. Black amethyst: 5.5" bowl w/1 handle, $30.

DIANA *Reproduced*
(1937-1941 Federal Glass Company)

	Pink	Amber	Crystal	Qty
Ashtray, 3.75"	18		4	____
Bowl, 5" cereal, 2" deep	15	12	4	____
Bowl, cream soup, 5.5", 2.25" deep	50	35	4	____
Bowl, 9" salad, 3.75" deep	30	20	8	____
Bowl, 11" console, 3.75" deep	40	30	8	____
Bowl, 12.5" console w/scalloped rim	100		15	____
Candy jar w/lid; base 2.25" deep, 6" diam.; lid 6" diam.	50	50	12	____
Coaster, 3.75", with straight risers and .75" edge	30	30	8	____
Coaster, 3.75", with swirled risers and .75" edge	30	30	8	____
Creamer	12	12	4	____
Cup	20	10	2	____
Cup, demitasse, 2" tall, 2.5" diam.	40		7	____
Plate, 6" bread & butter	10	8	1	____
Plate, 9.5" dinner	30	22	4	____
Plate, 11.5" sandwich	25	20	8	____
Platter, 12" x 9"	40	30	8	____
Rack (metal) to hold 6 demitasse sets	25			
Salt & pepper	90	110	35	____
Saucer	8	5	1	____
Saucer, demitasse, 4.25"	10		3	____
Sherbet, 4" diam., 3" deep	12	12	2	____
Sugar	12	12	4	____
Tumbler, 4" tall, 3" diam.	60	50	12	____

Note: Green: ash tray, $10; sherbet, $12. Red demitasse cup, $12; saucer, $8. Frosted with red trim: 5.5" cream soup bowl, $15; salt & pepper shakers, $60. Crystal tumbler w/stripes, $20. Add $10 for ormolu.

Reproduction Information: 13.25" scalloped-edge bowl is new.

DOGWOOD

(1930-1934 Macbeth-Evans Glass Company)

	Pink	Green	Monax & Cremax	Qty
Bowl, 5.5" cereal	35	45	10	____
Bowl, rolled edge cereal	85	85		____
Bowl, 8.5" diam, 3" deep berry	65	130	40	____
Bowl, 9.75" diam., 3.5" deep	600	130		____
Bowl, 10.25" fruit	600	300	150	____
Cake plate, 11"	1250			____
Cake plate, 13"	150	150	200	____
Chandelier, 9" tall, 12" wide using 4 cereal bowls			300	____
Coaster, No Mess w/spoon rest	trtp*			____
Coaster, 3.25"	trtp*			____
Creamer, 2.5" thin, no foot	30	50		____
Creamer, 3.25" thick, ftd	22			____
Cup, thin	22	45		____
Cup, thick	15		40	____
Lamp shade (10.25" bowl w/hole)	125	125	50	____
Pitcher, 8", almost straight sided	290	590		____
Pitcher, 8", "fat" w/ice lip (similar to American Sweetheart pitcher)	675			____
Plate, 6" bread & butter	10	10	24	____
Plate, 8" luncheon	12	12		____
Plate, 9" dinner	35			____
Plate, 10.5" grill w/ pattern only in center	100			____
Plate, 10.5" grill w/ pattern only on rim	20	20		____
Plate, 10.5" grill with pattern all over plate	30			____
Plate, 12" salver	40		18	____
Platter, 12"	800			____
Saucer, thick	6	6	15	____
Saucer, thin	8	8	18	____
Sherbet, 2 styles	35	150		____
Stem, 5"+ tall, 3.75" diam.	trtp*			____
Sugar, 2.5" thin, no foot	30	45		____
Sugar, 2.75" thin, no foot	30	45		____
Sugar, 3.25" thick, footed	20			____
Tidbit, 8" & 12" plates	75			____
Tumbler, 3.25" tall, 2.25" diam. juice	trtp*			____
Tumbler, 3.5"	400			____
Tumbler, 4"	50	120		____
Tumbler, 4.75"	60	125		____

DOGWOOD *(cont.)*

Tumbler, 4.75" tall, 2.5" diam., molded w/decorated band near top	30		___
Tumbler, 5"	100	145	___
Vase, 7.5" tall, 6.5" diam		trtp*	___

Note: Yellow cereal and luncheon plate, $75 each. Crystal with or without gold trim: 8" luncheon plate, cup and saucer, 5.5" cereal bowl, $10 each; tumbler, 3.25" tall, 2.25" diam. juice, trtp*. Iridescent creamer & sugar, $700 each. Red 8.5" berry bowl, trtp*.

*trtp = too rare to price

DORIC

(1935-1938   Jeannette Glass Company)

	Pink	Green	Del-phite	Qty
Bowl, 4.5" diam., 1.5" deep, berry	12	12	50	____
Bowl, 5" cream soup	500	500		____
Bowl, 5" diam., 2" deep, cereal	80	100		____
Bowl, 8" diam., 3" deep, berry	35	35	150	____
Bowl, 8.75" diam., 2.75" deep, w/2 handles	25	25		____
Bowl, 9.5" x 7.25" x 2" deep oval vegetable	38	44		____
Butter dish base	25	35		____
Butter dish lid	55	65		____
Butter complete	80	100		____
Cake plate, 10.25"	40	30		____
Candy dish, 3 parts	12	12	14	____
Candy dish, 3 parts in Hammered aluminum tray	75	75	75	____
Candy jar w/lid, 8"	50	50		____
Coaster, 3"	20	20		____
Creamer	18	18		____
Cup	14	14		____
Pitcher, 5.5", flat	60	75	1400	____
Pitcher, 7.5", footed	700	1200		____
Plate, 6" sherbet	10	10		____
Plate, 7" salad	28	28		____
Plate, 9" dinner	30	30		____
Plate, 9.25" grill	25	28		____
Platter, 12" x 8.75"	30	30		____
Relish tray, 4" x 4"	20	20		____
Relish tray, 4" x 8"	30	40		____
Relish tray, 2-tier, 4" x 4" over 4" x 8"	85	85		____
Relish tray, 8" x 8"	50	50		____
Salt & pepper	45	40		____
Saucer	8	8		____
Sherbet	14	18	5	____
Sugar base	18	18		____
Sugar lid	22	32		____
Tray, 10.25" w/handles	20	20		____
Tumbler, 4.25" tall, 3" diam.	70	90		____
Tumbler, 4.5", flat	70	100		____
Tumbler, 5" tall, 3" diam.	80	150		____

Note: Yellow 7.5" pitcher, too rare to price. 3-part candy dish, iridescent from 1970s, Ultramarine, $30. Serrated 9" dinner, $200. Light blue 9" dinner plate, $200. Yellow fired-on candy dish, $12.

DORIC AND PANSY
(1937-1938 Jeannette Glass Company)

	Ultramarine	Pink	Qty
Bowl, 4.5" berry	25	15	____
Bowl, 8" berry	100	40	____
Bowl, 9" w/handles	70	30	____
Butter dish base	75		____
Butter dish lid	375		____
Butter complete	450		____
Creamer	130		____
Cup	25	15	____
Plate, 6" sherbet	22	12	____
Plate, 7" salad	55		____
Plate, 9" dinner	45		____
Salt & pepper	300		____
Saucer	10	7	____
Sugar	130		____
Tray, 10" sandwich w/2 open handles	35		____
Tumbler, 4", 10 oz.	110		____
Tumbler, 4.5", 9 oz.	trtp*		____

*trtp = too rare to price

Note: Crystal items 1/2 of ultramarine. Satinized lampshade, 8.25" diameter, 3" deep, $250.

"Pretty Polly Party Dishes"
Child's Set

	Ultra-marine	Pink	Qty
Creamer	50	40	____
Cup	35	30	____
Plate, 5.75"	15	10	____
Saucer	10	8	____
Sugar	50	40	____
14-piece set	340	272	____

EMERALD CREST
called "GREEN CREST" in 1949
(1949-1955 Fenton Art Glass Company)

	White w/green rim	Qty
Basket, 5"	90	____
Basket, 6"	90	____
Basket, 7" w/smooth sides	120	____
Basket, 7" w/beaded sides	175	____
Bottle w/ stopper, 5.5"	150	____
Bowl, 4" low dessert	25	____
Bowl, 5" finger	25	____
Bowl, 5" crimped bonbon	30	____
Bowl, 5.5" soup	50	____
Bowl, 7" w/crimped rim	40	____
Bowl, 8.5" w/flared rim	50	____
Bowl, 9.5"	60	____
Bowl, 10.5" low salad	80	____
Cake plate, 13" w/foot	125	____
Candle holder, ea.	90	____
Comport, 3.75" w/5.5" diam.	45	____
Comport, 3.75" w/7" diam.	45	____
Comport, 6"	45	____
Creamer, 3.25" w/green twisted handle	50	____
Cup	50	____
Flower pot w/attached saucer, 4.5" tall	70	____
Mayonnaise, 3 pieces w/green ladle	100	____
Mayonnaise bowl	35	____
Ladle, crystal	10	____
Ladle, green	40	____
Under plate	25	____
Pitcher, 6" "beaded melon" w/twisted handle	75	____
Plate, 6.5" sherbet	20	____
Plate, 7"	45	____
Plate, 8"	55	____
Plate, 10.25" dinner	65	____
Plate, 11.5"	55	____
Plate, 12"	75	____
Plate, 13" cake w/foot	95	____
Plate, 16" torte	75	____
Relish, handled leaf	80	____
Saucer	18	____
Sherbet	30	____
Sugar, 3" w/twisted handles	50	____

EMERALD CREST *(cont.)*

	White w/green rim	Qty
Tidbit, 8.75" plate over 12" plate	60	____
Tidbit, 3-tier w/bowls	125	____
Tidbit, 3-tier w/plates	85	____
Top hat	45	____
Vase, 4" w/crimped rim	45	____
Vase, 4.5" fan	25	____
Vase, 5.5" w/1 turned-up side	50	____
Vase, 6" w/crimped rim	45	____
Vase, 6" w/1 turned up rim	65	____
Vase, 6.5" fan	40	____
Vase, 8" w/crimped rim	60	____
Vase, bud w/ beaded sides	50	____

ENGLISH HOBNAIL *Reproduced*
(1928-1950, Crystal & Amber until 1983 Westmoreland Glass Company)

	Pink & green	Turquoise/ Ice blue	Amber & Crystal	Qty
Ashtray, 3"	20		5	____
Ashtray, 4.5" round or square		25	5	____
Basket, 5" w/handle			30	____
Basket, 6" w/ handle			40	____
Bon bon, 6.5" w/1handle	25	40	15	____
Bottle, toilet, 6.25" tall, 1.75" opening	40			____
Bottle, toilet, 6.25" tall, 1.75" opening with labels	120			____
Bottle, 5 oz. toilet, 7" tall	35	60	25	____
Bottle, wide mouth	50			____
Bowl, 3" cranberry	20			____
Bowl, 4" rose (curves inward)	50		15	____
Bowl, 4.5" finger	18		10	____
Bowl, 4.5" round nappy	15	30	10	____
Bowl, 4.5" square finger w/foot	18	35	10	____
Bowl, 5" round nappy	18	40	10	____
Bowl, cream soup			15	____
Bowl, 5.5" bell nappy			12	____
Bowl, 6" crimped dish, flat	20		14	____
Bowl, 6" rose (curves inward)			20	____
Bowl, 6" mayonnaise, flat w/flared rim	20		10	____
Bowl, 6" round nappy	17		10	____
Bowl, 6" square nappy	17		10	____
Bowl, 6.5" grapefruit w/ inner rim	25		12	____
Bowl, 6.5" round nappy	22		14	____
Bowl, 6.5" square nappy			14	____
Bowl, 7" w/6 points (pinched and crimped)			25	____
Bowl, 7" oblong spoon			20	____
Bowl, 7" preserve			15	____
Bowl, 7" round nappy	25		15	____
Bowl, 7.5" bell nappy			18	____
Bowl, 8" cupped nappy (curves inward)	30		25	____
Bowl, 8" w/foot	50		30	____
Bowl, 8" 2-handled hexagonal w/foot	75	125	50	____
Bowl, 8" pickle, flat *R*	30		15	____
Bowl, 8" round nappy	35		25	____

	Pink & green	Turquoise/ Ice blue	Amber & Crystal	Qty
Bowl, 8"w/6 points (pinched and crimped)			25	____
Bowl, 9" bell nappy			30	____
Bowl, 9" celery, flat	35		18	____
Bowl, 9.5" round, crimped			30	____
Bowl, 10" flared, flat	55		35	____
Bowl, 10" crimped oval			35	____
Bowl, 11" bell			35	____
Bowl, 11" rolled edge	50	100	30	____
Bowl, 12" celery, flat w/outward roll	35		20	____
Bowl, 12" flanged console	60		30	____
Bowl, 12" w/flare			35	____
Bowl, 12" crimped oval			40	____
Butter dish, rectangular			85	____
Candelabra, each			20	____
Candlestick, each, 3.5"	15	20	10	____
Candlestick, each, 5.5"			10	____
Candlestick, each, 9"	25		10	____
Candy dish w/lid, 6" w/3 feet	60		30	____
Candy jar w/lid, ½ lb., diamond-shaped, 7.25"-8" tall, 5.25" diam.	65	120	35	____
Candy jar w/lid, master, 9" tall	250		150	____
Chandelier, 17" shade w/prisms			500	____
Cheese and cover, 6"			40	____
Cheese and cover, 8.75"			60	____
Cigarette box w/cover, 4.5" x 2.5"	40	60	25	____
Cigarette Jar w/cover (round)	40	70	25	____
Coaster 3"			8	____
Compote, 5", round & square foot	30		15	____
Compote, 5.5" sweetmeat (ball at base of stem)			40	____
Compote, 5.5" bell, round & square foot			20	____
Compote, 6" honey, flat w/ round foot	35		18	____
Compote, 6" honey, flat w/square foot			18	____
Compote, 8" sweetmeat	70		40	____
Creamer, w/foot, 4", hexagonal *R*	25	50	10	____
Creamer, flat hex, 2.25" tall			10	____
Creamer, square w/foot	50		10	____

	Pink & green	Turqu- oise/ Ice blue	Amber & Crystal	Qty
Cup	20	30	10	____
Cup, demitasse	60		30	____
Cup, punch			8	____
Decanter w/stopper, 20 oz.			70	____
Egg cup			18	____
Hat dish, high			20	____
Hat dish, low			18	____
Ice tub, 4"	50	80	25	____
Ice tub, 5.5"	75	100	50	____
Icer, square base			50	____
Ladle for punch bowl			30	____
Lamp, candlestick (several styles)			40	____
Lamp, 6" tall, 3" diam. foot (oil)	80	80	80	____
Lamp, 6.25" (electric)	75		40	____
Lamp, 7" tall (oil)	100			____
Lamp, 7.75" tall (oil)	100			____
Lamp, 9.25" (electric)	150	150	50	____
Lamp, 9.25" (oil)	110	175	110	____
Lamp, 10.75" tall (oil)	100			____
Lamp, 11" tall (oil)	100			____
Lamp, 11.25" tall, 4" diam. base, straight shaft			100	____
Lamp, 11.25" tall, 5" diam. base, tapered shaft			100	____
Lampshade, 12.5" diam.		125		____
Lampshade, 13"	200		200	____
Marmalade w/cover	50	75	30	____
Mustard w/cover, square			28	____
Nut, individual, w/foot	15		8	____
Oil cruet w/stopper, 2 oz. (1 handle)			20	____
Oil cruet w/ stopper, 6 oz. (1 handle)			30	____
Oil-vinegar combination bottle, 6 oz. (no handles)			40	____
Parfait, round foot, 5.5" tall, 2.25" diam			15	____
Pitcher, 23 oz., round	150		60	____
Pitcher, 32 oz., straight sides	200		70	____
Pitcher, 38 oz., round	250		80	____
Pitcher, 60 oz., round	320		90	____
Pitcher, 64 oz., straight sides	350		100	____
Plate, 5.5"	10	10	5	____
Plate, liner for cream soup			8	____
Plate, 6" square liner for				

ENGLISH HOBNAIL *(cont.)*

	Pink & green	Turquoise/ Ice blue	Amber & Crystal	Qty
finger bowls	10		5	____
Plate, 6", square			5	____
Plate, 6.5"	10		7	____
Plate, 6.5" round liner for finger bowls	10		7	____
Plate, 6.5" w/ depressed center			7	____
Plate, 8"	14		8	____
Plate, 8.5"	14	30	15	____
Plate, 8.5", plain edge			10	____
Plate, 8.5" w/ 3 feet			10	____
Plate, 8.75"			10	____
Plate, 10"	60	70	15	____
Plate, 10" square			15	____
Plate, 10.5" grill			15	____
Plate, 12" square			25	____
Plate, 14" torte	65		30	____
Plate, 12" square			35	____
Plate, 20.5" torte			65	____
Puff box w/lid, 6" round	50	80	30	____
Punch bowl			225	____
Punch bowl stand, 4.75" tall			75	____
Relish, 8" w/3 sections			18	____
Salt & pepper, flat	150	225		____
Salt & pepper, round foot, 4.5"	85		30	____
Salt & pepper, square foot			30	____
Saucer	5	8	3	____
Saucer, square			3	____
Saucer, demitasse, 4.25"	15		10	____
Saucer, demitasse, square			10	____
Sherbet, low w/ 1 glass ball on stem			8	____
Sherbet, short stem, round foot, 3.5" tall, 3.75" diam.		15	8	____
Sherbet, short stem, square foot	12		8	____
Sherbet, tall stem, round foot	18		10	____
Sherbet, tall stem, square foot	18	40	10	____
Sherbet, tall, 2 balls of glass on stem, round foot			10	____
Stem, 1 oz. cordial, glass ball on stem, round foot, 3" tall, 1.75" diam			15	____
Stem, 1 oz. cordial, round foot, 3.25" tall, 1.75" diam			15	____

ENGLISH HOBNAIL *(cont.)*

	Pink & green	Turquoise/ Ice blue	Amber & Crystal	Qty
Stem, 1 oz. cordial, square foot			15	___
Stem, 2 oz. wine, square foot	30	60	10	___
Stem, 2 oz. wine, round foot			10	___
Stem, 2.25 oz. wine, glass ball on stem, round foot 3.5" tall, 1.75" diam			10	___
Stem, 3 oz. cocktail, round foot, 4.5" tall, 2" diam	20	40	10	___
Stem, 3 oz. cocktail, square foot, 4.5" tall, 2.25" diam			10	___
Stem, 3.5 oz. cocktail, glass ball on stem			8	___
Stem, 5 oz. claret, round foot			15	___
Stem, 5 oz. oyster cocktail, square foot	20		10	___
Stem, 4.5" tall, 2.25" diam			10	___
Stem, 6" tall, 3.25" diam goblet, square foot			40	___
Stem, 8 oz. water, square foot	30	50	10	___
Stem, champagne, 2 glass balls on stem, round foot			10	___
Sugar, w/foot, 4", hexagonal *R*	25	50	10	___
Sugar, flat hex, 2.25" tall			10	___
Sugar, square foot	50		10	___
Tid-bit, 2 tier	50	80	30	___
Tumbler, 1.5 oz. whiskey			15	___
Tumbler, 3 oz. whiskey, 2.25" tall, 2.25" diam			13	___
Tumbler, 5 oz. ginger ale, flat, 3.25" tall, 3" diam			10	___
Tumbler, 5 oz. old fashioned			10	___
Tumbler, 5 oz. ginger ale, round foot			10	___
Tumbler, 5 oz. ginger ale, square foot			10	___
Tumbler, 3.75" tall, 2.75" diam., w/foot			30	___
Tumbler, 4.75" tall, 2.5" diam. w/foot			30	___
Tumbler, 7 oz. juice, round foot			10	___
Tumbler, 7 oz. juice, square foot, 4" tall, 2.75" diam			10	___

ENGLISH HOBNAIL *(cont.)*

	Pink & green	Turquoise/ Ice blue	Amber & Crystal	Qty
Tumbler, 8 oz. water, glass ball on short stem, round foot, 5" tall, 3" diam			10	____
Tumbler, 8 oz. water, flat, 4"	35		10	____
Tumbler, 9 oz. water, glass ball on short stem, round foot			10	____
Tumbler, 9 oz. water, round foot			10	____
Tumbler, 9 oz. water, sq foot, 5.5" tall, 2.75" diam			10	____
Tumbler, 10 oz. iced tea, flat	30		15	____
Tumbler, 11 oz. iced tea, glass ball on short stem, round foot			10	____
Tumbler, 11 oz. iced tea, square foot			14	____
Tumbler, 12 oz. iced tea, flat	33		12	____
Tumbler, 12.5 oz. iced tea, round foot, 6.25" tall, 3" diam			10	____
Urn, 11" (w/lid 15")	400		50	____
Vase, 6.5" ivy bowl, squarefoot, crimped rim			35	____
Vase, 6.5" flower holder, square foot			25	____
Vase, 7.25" tall, 5.5+" diam.	100			____
Vase, 7.5" flip, 6" diam	100		30	____
Vase, 7.5", flip jar w/ cover	120		70	____
Vase, 8" w/square foot			35	____
Vase, 8.5", flared top	225	275	40	____
Vase, 9.5" tall, 5.25" diam.	100			____
Vase, 9.75" tall, 4" daim.	100			____
Vase, 10", Straw jar	190		75	____

Note: Cobalt and Black items 30% higher than Turquoise prices. Milk glass cigarette lighter, $25. Jade-ite sherbet, tumbler, and goblet, $250 ea. 8" trophy bowl with 6" diameter from the 1970s, $175. Crystal items with a blue base: candy jar, $300; candlesticks, $175 each; covered bowl, $300.

Reproduction Information: New hexagonal creamers and sugars have Westmoreland circular marks on bottom; old are unmarked. 8" flat pickle bowl new marked with Westmoreland mark; old unmarked. Individual nut with foot new made in other colors and may have "S" on bottom.

ENGLISH HOBNAIL *(cont.)*

Note: Rare Items In:	Cobalt blue	Olive green	Qty
Bottle, perfume, 6.75" tall	100		____
Bottle, wide mouth, 6.25" tall, 1.75" opening	200		____
Bowl, 3-3.5" diameter, 1.25"-1.5" deep, nut	75		____
Bowl, 8" diameter, 5.75" tall, trophy w/2 handles	200	85	____
Box, cigarette or pin, 4.5" x 3.25" x 1.25" deep w/lid	160		____
Candlestick, ea., 3.75" tall	50		____
Candlestick, ea., 8.25" tall	75		____
Cigarette or pin box, 4.5" x 3.25" x 1.25" deep w/lid	160		____
Comport, ruffled, 5" tall, 5.5" diameter		45	____
Electric lamp, 11.5" tall	150		____
Goblet, 6" tall, 3.25" diam. square feet	40		____
Goblet, 6" tall, 3.25" diam. round feet		12	____
Individual nut, 2" tall, 3" x 1.75" diam.,	45	25	____
Perfume bottle, 6.75" tall	100		____
Pin or cigarette box, 4.5" x 3.25" x 1.25" deep w/lid	160		____
Plate, 6.25"	35		____
Plate, 7.75" rolled to be 6" across fold	75		____
Lamp, electric, 11.5" tall	150		____
Lamp, oil, 6" tall	200		____
Lamp, oil, 11" tall	200		____
Oil lamp, 6" tall	200		____
Oil lamp, 11" tall	200		____
Sherbet, 2.5" tall, 4" diam.	30		____
Sherbet, stemmed, 4.5" tall, 3.75" diam., square feet	40		____
Sherbet, low stem, 3.5" tall, 3.5" diam, round feet		12	____
Stem, 3.25" tall, 1.5" diam, cordial, sq. ft.	40		____
Stem, 4.5" tall, 2" diam, wine, sqare feet	40		____

FIRE-KING ALICE

(1945-1949   Anchor Hocking Glass Corporation)

	Jade-ite	Blue trim	Vitrock	Qty
Cup	17	15	10	____
Plate, 9.5" dinner	40	35	18	____
Saucer	8	4	4	____

FIRE-KING BREAKFAST SET
Reproduced

(1954-1956   Anchor Hocking Glass Corporation)

	Jade-ite	Qty
Bowl, 5" cereal, 2.5" deep *R*	85	____
Cup, 9 oz. St. Denis cup w/round handle *R*	12	____
Egg cup, 4" tall	35	____
Pitcher, milk, 4.5" tall, 20 oz.	75	____
Plate, 9.25" dinner *R*	35	____
Saucer, 6" St. Denis *R*	8	____

Note: 5" cereal bowl with red ivy trim: Azurite, $60; Jade-ite, $150. 5" cereal with green ivy trim, $80. Peach Lustre milk pitcher, $100.

Reproduction Information: Cup, too heavy, unmarked, 2.75" tall. Saucer, too heavy, unmarked, 5.25" diameter; base is almost a .25" pedestal. Dinner plate, too heavy, unmarked, has a double rim on the underside, 10"; original plate is 9.25". **Note:** this glass is made in China. The color is a bit light and on the yellow side. The glass has minute ripples or lines that resemble sedimentary rock.

FIRE-KING CHARM
Reproduced
(1950-1956 Anchor Hocking Glass Corporation)

	Jade-ite, White, & Ivory	Azur-ite	Forest Green	Royal Ruby	Qty
Bowl, 4.75" dessert	20	18	20	8	____
Bowl, 6" soup	60	30	20		____
Bowl, 7.25" salad	60	50	35	30	____
Creamer	20	20	8		____
Cup	14	12	10	8	____
Plate, 6.5" salad	30	12	12		____
Plate, 8.25" luncheon	20	12	10	12	____
Plate, 9.25" dinner	50	30	35		____
Platter, 11" x 8"	65	50	35		____
Saucer	10	5	4	3	____
Sugar	20	20	8		____
Tidbit, 4.75" dessert bowl over 8.25" luncheon plate			37		____

Note: Pink saucer, $25. Azurite chili bowl marked "Fire-King Ovenware 4," $40. Azurite flower pot, $150; blossom bowl, $25.

Reproduction information: Ruby covered pedestal cake plates are new.

FIRE-KING FISH SCALE
(1939-1943 & 1963-1965 Anchor Hocking Glass Corporation)

	Vitrock	Vitrock w/red rim or deco-rations	Qty
Bowl, berry	8	20	
Bowl, cereal, 5.5" diam	10	35	____
Bowl, soup	15	45	____
Bowl, vegetable, 8.5" diam, 3" deep	20	65	
Cup	5	12	____
Plate, salad	5	20	____
Plate, dinner	5	20	____
Saucer	5	10	____

Note: Blue and pink rim or decorations worth 2x values of red. Copper Luster demitasse cup, $10; saucer, $5.

FIRE-KING JANE RAY

(1946-1965   Anchor Hocking Glass Corporation)

	Jade-ite	Qty
Bowl, 4.75" dessert	15	____
Bowl, 5.75" oatmeal	30	____
Bowl, 7.5" soup	25	____
Bowl, 8.25" vegetable	35	____
Bowl, 9" soup plate	trtp*	____
Creamer	25	____
Cup	12	____
Cup, demitasse	75	____
Plate, 6"	65	____
Plate, 7.75" salad	15	____
Plate, 9" dinner	15	____
Platter, 12"	35	____
Saucer	5	____
Saucer, demitasse	25	____
Sugar base	20	____
Sugar lid	35	____

*trtp = too rare to price

Note: Ivory & Vitrock items twice prices of Jade-ite.

FIRE-KING LAUREL *Reproduced*
(1951-1965   Anchor Hocking Glass Corporation)

	Gray	Peach Lustre	Ivory, White, & Ivory white	Qty
Bowl, 5" diam., 1.25" deep, dessert	12	4	12	____
Bowl, 7.5" diam., 1.25" deep, soup plate	24	10	25	____
Bowl, 8.25" diam., 2.25" deep, vegetable	35	10	40	____
Creamer	14	4	10	____
Cup *R*	10	4	8	____
Plate, 7.75" salad	17	8	15	____
Plate, 9" dinner	15	8	15	____
Plate, 11" serving	30	15	40	____
Saucer, 5.75"	5	1	5	____
Sugar	14	4	10	____
Tumbler, 3.25" tall, 2" diam., juice	15			____
Tumbler, 4.25" tall, 2.25" diam., water	15			____

Note: Jade-ite cup, too rare to price.

Reproduction Information: Jade-ite is made new in a totally wrong color with a bottom stamped "402," a diamond, and a "4." 5.75" Jade-ite plate is new. These are not saucers.

FIRE-KING MISCELLANEOUS JADE-ITE

(Anchor Hocking Glass Corporation)

	Jade-ite	Qty
Baby feeding plate, 7.5" diam 3-part	*trtp	____
Bowl, 4.5" diam	50	____
Bowl, 5" diam., 2.5" deep, bulb w/3 feet	45	____
Bowl, 6" diam, 2.75" deep w/vertical swirls	40	____
Bowl, batter .75" rim	35	____
Bowl, batter 1" rim	60	____
Bowl, Beaded Rim 4.75"	25	____
Bowl, Beaded Rim 6"	20	____
Bowl, Beaded Rim 7"	30	____
Bowl, Beaded Rim 8.5"	trtp*	____
Bowl, Chili, 5" diam., 2.25" deep	22	____
Bowl, Colonial Rim 6"	100	____
Bowl, Colonial Rim 7.25"	75	____
Bowl, Colonial Rim 8.75"	85	____
Bowl, Splash proof 6.75"	500	____
Bowl, Splash proof 7.5"	75	____
Bowl, Splash proof 8.5"	100	____
Bowl, Splash proof 9.5"	90	____
Bowl, Straight-sided 5"	35	____
Bowl, Swedish Modern, 1 pt., 6.5"	75	____
Bowl, Swedish Modern, 1 qt., 8"	175	____
Bowl, Swedish Modern, 2 qt., 9.5"	125	____
Bowl, Swedish Modern, 3 qt., 11"	125	____
Bowl, Swirl 5"	175	____
Bowl, Swirl 6"	30	____
Bowl, Swirl 7"	25	____
Bowl, Swirl 8"	20	____
Bowl, Swirl 9"	20	____
Bowl, 7.5" diam., 2.25" deep, swirled w/ruffled edge	45	____
Bowl, 4.75" vertical ribs	125	____
Bowl, 5.5" vertical ribs	75	____
Bowl, 7.5" vertical ribs	75	____
Butter dish base	125	____
Butter dish lid (clear)	40	____
Butter complete	165	____
Candy dish w/cover, rnd.	110	____
Custard	60	____

	Jade-ite	Qty
Flower pot, smooth or scalloped rim	30	____
Leaf & blossom set	35	____
leaf plate	15	____
blossom bowl	20	____
Maple leaf	30	____
Mug, thin 3.25" diam. "D" handle	25	____
Pie plate, Philbe juice saver	300	____
Pie plate, smooth	400	____
Pitcher, Bead & Bar	200	____
Pitcher, ball jug	500	____
Range Set (grease & 2 shakers)	175	____
Grease Jar w/tulip lid	75	____
Shaker w/tulip lids ea.	50	____
Refrigerator dish w/clear lid 4" x 4"	40	____
Refrigerator dish w/clear lid 4" x 8"	60	____
Refrigerator dish w/lid, Philbe 4.5" x 5"	60	____
Refrigerator dish w/lid, Philbe 5.25" x 9.5"	70	____
Sea shell	35	____
Skillet, 1 spout	80	____
Skillet, 2 spout	110	____
Spoon rest (Maple Leaf)	30	____
Vase, Deco 5.25"	25	____

*trtp = too rare to price

FIRE-KING RESTAURANTWARE
(1948-1967   Anchor Hocking Glass Corporation)

	Jade-ite	White	Qty
Bowl, 4.75" fruit (G294)	15	15	_____
Bowl, 5", handled	trtp*		_____
Bowl, cereal w/flanged rim, 8 oz. (G305)	30	30	_____
Bowl, 10 oz. (G309) w/beaded rim	30	30	_____
Bowl, deep, 15 oz. (G300) w/beaded rim	30	40	_____
Bowl, 9.25" flat soup (G298)	120	140	_____
Cup, 6 oz. straight (G215) (resembles a mug)	20	35	_____
Cup, 7 oz. extra heavy (G299) (resembles a coffee cup)	15	18	_____
Cup, demitasse	55		_____
Cup, handled soup	trtp*		_____
Gravy/sauce boat	trtp*	35	_____
Mug, coffee, 7 oz. (G212)	40	90	_____
Mug, slim hot chocolate, 6 oz.	65	400	_____
Pitcher, ball jug (G787)	900		_____
Plate, 5.5" bread & butter (G315)	25		_____
Plate, 6.75" pie (G297)	18	18	_____
Plate, 8" luncheon (G316)	70	45	_____
Plate, 8.75" oval partitioned/ indent platter (G211)	90		_____
Plate, 8.75" oval, no indent (G310)	120		_____
Plate, 9" dinner (G306)	25	35	_____
Plate, 9.5" 3-compartment/ grill w/or w/out a tab for stacking (G292)	30	30	_____
Plate, 9.5" 5-compartment (G311)	55		_____
Plate, 10.25" (G317)	trtp*		_____
Platter, 9" w/partition	100		_____
Platter, 9.5" oval (G307)	50	50	_____
Platter, 9.75" oval "football"	75		_____
Platter, 11.5" oval (G308)	40	40	_____
Saucer, 6" (G295)	10	15	_____
Saucer, demitasse	30		_____
Saucer for soup mug	trtp*		_____

Note: Azurite G294 Fruit bowl, $40. Roseite G299 Cup, $50. Crystal cup, trtp*.
*trtp = too rare to price

FIRE-KING SAPPHIRE BLUE

(1941-1956 Anchor Hocking Glass Corporation)

	Sapphire Blue	Qty
Baker, 1 pt., 4.5" x 5"	10	____
Baker, 1 pt., 5.5" round	10	____
Baker, 1 qt., 7.25" round	10	____
Baker, 1.5" qt., 8.25" round	12	____
Baker, 2 qt., 8.75" round	14	____
Bowl, 4.25" individual pie	25	____
Bowl, 4.25" diam. 1.5" deep, child's	trtp*	____
Bowl, 5.25" cereal	24	____
Bowl, 5.75", 2.75" deep	trtp*	____
Bowl, 16 oz., w/measures	30	____
Cake pan, 8.75"	40	____
Casserole, 4.75" individual w/lid	15	____
Casserole, 1 pt., 5.5" knob-handled lid	20	____
Casserole, 1 qt., 7.25" knob-handled lid	25	____
Casserole, 1 qt., pie plate lid	20	____
Casserole, 1.5 qt., 8.25" knob-handled lid	30	____
Casserole, 1.5 qt., pie plate lid	25	____
Casserole, 2 qt., 8.75" knob-handled lid	30	____
Casserole, 2 qt., pie plate lid	25	____
Cup, 1 spout 8 oz. liquid measure	35	____
Cup, no spout 8 oz. dry measure	trtp*	
Cup, 3 spouts, 8 oz. liquid measure	45	____
Custard cup, 2.75" deep	10	____
Custard cup, 3 shallower styles	8	____
Jelly jar, 3.25" diam. 2" deep	20	____
Loaf pan	10	____
Mug, thin	50	____
Mug, thick	35	____
Nipple cover, "Binky's Nipcap," 2.5" tall	250	____
Nursing bottle, 4 oz.	25	____
Nursing bottle, 8 oz.	40	____
Nursing bottle, 8 oz., Fyrock	35	____

	Sapphire Blue	Qty
Nursing bottle, 8 oz., "Tuffy"	35	____
Percolator top, 2.25"	8	____
Pie plate, 8.25"	10	____
Pie plate, 9"	10	____
Pie plate, 9.5"	10	____
Pie plate, 10.25", juice saver	150	____
Popcorn popper**	40	____
Refrigerator dish w/lid, 4.5" x 5"	30	____
Refrigerator dish w/lid, 5.25" x 9.25"	25	____
Roaster, 8.75"	85	____
Roaster, 10.25"	65	____
Skillet, 7" w/4.5" handle	trtp*	____
Silex 2-cup dripolator	60	____
Silex 6-cup dripolator	275	____
Trivet w/2 tab handles	22	____
Utility bowl, 1 qt., 6.75"	35	____
Utility bowl, 1.5 qt., 8.25"	30	____
Utility bowl, 2 qt., 10.25"	30	____
Utility pan, 8.25" x 12.5"	160	____
Utility pan. 10.5" x 6" x 2" deep	60	____

Note: insert for popcorn popper to hold oil and corn, $25.

Note: Ivory 1-quart casserole with Philbe design, $150; lid (pie plate style), $50.

*trtp = too rare to price

FIRE-KING 1700 LINE
Reproduced
(1946-1958   Anchor Hocking Glass Corporation)

	Jade-ite	Ivory	Milk white	Qty
Bowl, 5.75" cereal	20	25	8	____
Bowl, 7.5" flat soup *R*	20	35	12	____
Bowl, 8.5" vegetable		35		____
Cup, 8 oz. Coffee		10	6	
Cup, 9 oz. St. Denis w/round handle *R*	12	16	8	____
Cup, 9 oz. Ransom w/pointy handle	20	25	6	____
Plate, 7.75" salad			8	____
Plate, 9.25" dinner *R*	30	7	5	____
Platter, 9" x 12" oval		30	15	____
Saucer, 7.5" *R*	8	8	4	____

Reproduction Information: Cup, too heavy, unmarked, 2.75" tall. Saucer, too heavy, unmarked, 5.25" diameter; base is almost a .25" pedestal. Dinner plate, too heavy, unmarked, has a double rim on the underside, 10"; original plate is 9.25". Flat soup, too heavy, unmarked, 8.25" diameter. **Note:** this glass is made in China. The color is a bit light and on the yellow side. The glass has minute ripples or lines that resemble sedimentary rock.

FIRE-KING SHEAVES OF WHEAT
(1957-1959   Anchor Hocking Glass Corporation)

	Jade-ite	Crystal	Qty
Bowl, 4.5" dessert	100	6	_____
Cup	60	4	_____
Plate, 9" dinner	125	15	_____
Saucer	25	2	_____
Tumbler, juice		15	_____
Tumbler, water		18	_____

Note: Turquoise dinner plate, trtp*.

*trtp = too rare to price

FIRE-KING SHELL
(1965-1976   Anchor Hocking Glass Corporation)

	Jade-ite	"Mother of Pearl"	Other colors	Qty
Bowl, 4.75" diam, 1.25" deep dessert	10		4	____
Bowl, 6.25"diam, 1.75" deep cereal	20	12	10	____
Bowl, 7.75" diam, 1.5" deep soup	45	20	10	____
Bowl, 8.5" oval vegetable	trtp*			____
Bowl, 8.5" diam, 2.5' deep round vegetable	25	20	10	____
Creamer	25		3	____
Cup	8	7	3	____
Cup, demitasse		12	10	____
Plate, 7.25" salad	15	8	4	____
Plate, 10" dinner	20	12	4	____
Platter, 9" oval		18		____
Platter, 9.5" x 13" oval	75		10	____
Platter, 11.5" x 15.5" oval			20	____
Saucer	5	4	1	____
Saucer, demitasse		12	10	____
Sugar base	20	8	4	____
Sugar lid	80	12	8	____
Tidbit, 3-tier, saucer, 7.25" salad plate, 10" dinner	70			____

*trtp = too rare to price

FIRE-KING SWIRL

(1949-1962 Anchor Hocking Glass Corporation)

	Ivory w/red rim (Sunrise) & Azurite	Jade-ite	Pink	White (untrimmed looks almost Ivory)	Qty
Bowl, 4.75" dessert	12		15	7	____
Bowl, 5.75" cereal	25			15	____
Bowl. 7.75" soup	25		35	12	____
Bowl, 8.25" vegetable	30		35	15	____
Creamer	12		25	8	____
Cup	8	75	16	7	____
Plate, 7.25" salad	12		18	8	____
Plate, 9.25" dinner	12	110	18	8	____
Plate, 11"			25		____
Platter	25	trtp*		15	____
Saucer	4	25	8	3	____
Sugar base	12		20	8	____
Sugar lid	24		30	15	____

Note: Fired-on pink 9" mixing bowl, $65
*trtp = too rare to price

	Rose-ite	Qty
Bowl, 5" dessert, 1.5" deep	75	____
Bowl, 7.75" soup	100	____
Bowl, 8.5" oval vegetable	350	____
Cup	75	____
Creamer, footed	150	____
Plate, 7.25" salad	100	____
Plate, 9.25" dinner	125	____
Platter	250	____
Saucer	25	____
Sherbet, footed, 3.75" diam., 2.25" deep	100	____
Sugar, footed, 3.25" diam., 3.25" deep	150	____

Note: White trimmed in 22K gold worth half of untrimmed white. Azurite flower pot, $150; blossom bowl, $25. Ivory with red trim, 9" Swirl mixing bowl, $125.

FIRE-KING TURQUOISE BLUE

(1956-1958 Anchor Hocking Glass Corporation)

	Turquoise blue	Qty
Ashtray, 3.5"	30	____
Ashtray, 4.5"	30	____
Ashtray, 5.75"	40	____
Batter bowl, w/spout & 1 handle	400	____
Bowl, 4.5" diam, 1.5" deep dessert	30	____
Bowl, 4.75" diam, 2" deep	80	____
Bowl, 5" diam, 2" deep cereal	30	____
Bowl, 5" diam, 2.25" deep chili	30	
Bowl, 6.5" diam, 1.5" deep soup	50	
Bowl, 8" diam, 2.5" deep vegetable	40	
Bowl, Swedish Modern, 1 pt., 6.5"	65	____
Bowl, Swedish Modern, 1 qt., 8"	70	____
Bowl, Swedish Modern, 2 qt., 9.5"	70	____
Bowl, Swedish Modern, 3 qt., 11"	90	____
Bowl, Splash Proof, 1 qt., 6.75"	50	____
Bowl, Splash Proof, 2 qt., 7.5"	45	____
Bowl, Splash Proof, 3 qt., 8.5"	40	____
Creamer	20	____
Cup	18	____
Ice bucket, 2 quart Splash Proof bowl w/aluminum base & lid	100	____
Mug	40	____
Plate, 6.25" bread & butter	25	____
Plate, 7.25" salad	30	____
Plate, 9" dinner	20	____
Plate, 9" w/indent for cup	8	____
Plate, 10" serving	50	____
Plate, hard boiled egg w/ gold rim	20	____
Relish, 3-part w/gold rim	15	____
Saucer	10	____
Sugar	20	____

FLORAGOLD

(1950s   Jeannette Glass Company)

	Iridescent	Qty
Ashtray/coaster, 4"	7	____
Bowl, 4.5" square berry	8	____
Bowl, 5.5" salad	65	____
Bowl, 5.5" ruffled fruit	8	____
Bowl, 8.5" square	25	____
Bowl, 9.5" deep salad	50	____
Bowl, 9.5" ruffled	8	____
Bowl, 12" ruffled fruit	8	____
Bowl, 12" ruffled fruit, w/metal foot	20	____
Butter dish base (1/4 lb.)	35	____
Butter dish lid (1/4 lb.)	15	____
Butter complete (1/4 lb.)	50	____
Butter dish base (6.25" square base)	20	____
Butter dish lid (round to fit 6.25" base)	40	____
Butter dish complete (square base, round lid)	60	____
Butter dish, 5.5" complete (square base, rd. lid)	trtp*	____
Candlestick, ea.	35	____
Candy dish, 1 handle	12	____
Candy/Cheese dish w/lid, 6.75"	60	____
Candy, 5.25" oval scalloped w/4 feet	10	____
Comport, 5.25" smooth rim	trtp*	____
Comport, 5.25" ruffled rim	trtp*	____
Creamer	12	____
Cup	8	____
Goblet, 4" tall	trtp*	____
Pitcher, 8.25"	45	____
Plate, 5.25" sherbet/saucer	12	____
Plate, 8.25" square dinner	50	____
Platter, 11.25"	35	____
Salt & pepper	70	____
Sherbet	16	____
Sugar base	10	____
Sugar lid	14	____
Tid-bit, 2-tier, 5.5" bowl, over 9.5" bowl	40	____
Tid-bit, 3-tier, 5.5" bowl, 9.5" bowl, 12" bowl	50	____
Tid-bit, 2-tier, 9.5" ruffled bowl above 12" ruffled bowl	40	____

	Iridescent	Qty
Tray, 11.75" w/Iris edge	250	____
Tray, 13.5"	25	____
Tray, 13.5" w/center indent	75	____
Tumbler, 10 or 11 oz., 5" tall, both footed	20	____
Tumbler, 15 oz., footed, 5.75" tall	125	____
Vase/celery, 6" tall, 3.5" diam	500	____

Note: Shell Pink: comport, 6.25" tall, 9" diam, $50; 5.25" scalloped candy, $50; bowl with one handle, $400. Crystal: ashtray/coaster with indent for only one cigarette, $15; vase, $140; 5.25" scalloped candy w/gold trim, $20; 5.75" tall 3" diam. footed tumbler, $20; comport, 9" diam., 7" tall with motif on bottom of bowl, trtp*.

*trtp = too rare to price

FLORAL *Reproduced*

(1930-1935, Delphite in 1937   Jeannette Glass Company)

	Pink	Green	Delphite	Qty
Bowl, 4" berry, ruffled rim	175	175		____
Bowl, 4" diam, 1.75" deep berry	20	20		____
Bowl, 5.5" cream soup	850	850		____
Bowl, 7.5" salad, smooth rim	40	40	90	____
Bowl, 7.5" salad, ruffled rim	400	400		____
Bowl, 8" vegetable	35	45	85	____
Bowl, 9" x 6.75" oval vegetable	30	30		____
Butter dish base	40	35		____
Butter dish lid	85	75		____
Butter complete	125	110		____
Candlestick, 4" tall each	50	50		____
Candy jar w/lid	50	50		____
Coaster, 3.25"	18	14		____
Comport, 9" diam., 3.75" tall w/4" diam. foot	1000	1200		____
Cover for 8" vegetable bowl	30	30		____
Creamer	18	18	100	____
Cup	15	15		____
Dresser set		1800		____
powder jar, 4" diam., 1.75" deep, w/lid, ea. (set has 2 powder jars)		400		____
rouge box, 3" diam., 1.5" deep w/lid (1 per set)		600		____
tray, 9.25" x 6" w/1" rim		400		____
Frog, for vase		825		____
Ice tub, 3.5" tall, oval	1000	1000		____
Lamp	325	325		____
Pitcher, 5.5" flat		575		____
Pitcher, 8" with foot	55	50		____
Pitcher, 10.25" with foot (lemonade pitcher)	375	375		____
Plate, 6" sherbet	12	12		____
Plate, 8" salad	20	20		____
Plate, 9" dinner	25	25	300	____
Plate, 9" grill		350		____
Platter, 10.75"	25	25	250	____
Platter, 11", facetted rim	150	trtp*	trtp*	____
Refrigerator dish w/lid (inside of lid embossed w/Floral motif)		65	65	____
Relish, 2-part, 2 handles	25	25	200	____

	Pink	Green	Delphite	Qty
Salt & pepper, 4" footed *R*	65	60		____
Salt & pepper, 6" flat	65			____
Saucer	12	12		____
Sherbet	20	22	100	____
Sugar base	18	18	100	____
Sugar lid (same lid on candy jar)	30	30		____
Tray, 6.5" square w/tab handles, 7.5" handle-to-handle	50	60		____
Tray, 9.25" oval for dresser set		400		____
Tumbler, 3.5" w/foot		225		____
Tumbler, 4" tall, 3" diam., w/foot, juice	20	25		____
Tumbler, 4.5" flat		200		____
Tumbler, 4.75" water w/foot	28	30	250	____
Tumbler, 5.25" lemonade w/foot	64	65		____
Vase, rose bowl w/3 feet		850		____
with frog		1650		____
Vase, flared w/3 feet		700		____
Vase, 6.75" w/8 sides		600		____

Reproduction information: Shakers: red, cobalt, & dark green were never originally produced. Pink shakers: the color is wrong & the threads to screw on the lid should have two parallel threads; new shakers have one continuous thread winding around the top. New shakers missing Floral pattern on feet or pressed on top of feet; old - pattern on underside of feet.

Note: Jade-ite: Canisters (cereal, coffee, sugar, tea), 5.25" tall, square with Floral motif inside lid, $250 each. Jade-ite refrigerator dish, 5" square with Floral design inside lid, $75. Transparent green refrigerator dish, $65. Cremax 7.5" bowl, creamer, & sugar, $200 each. Crystal: 3-footed flared vase, $500; with frog, $950; 6.75" 8-sided vase, $450; 23" tall vase, trtp*. Black 4.75" tumbler with foot, trtp*.

*trtp = too rare to price

FLORAL AND DIAMOND BAND

(1927-1931   U.S. Glass Company)

	Pink & green	Qty
Bowl, 4.25" berry	12	____
Bowl, 5.75" w/handles	15	____
Bowl, 8" berry	18	____
Butter dish base (no design of any kind)	75	____
Butter dish lid	75	____
Butter complete	150	____
Compote, 5.5"	25	____
Creamer, small, 2.5"	15	____
Creamer, 4.75"	20	____
Pitcher, 8"	120	____
Plate, 8" luncheon	55	____
Sherbet	10	____
Sugar, small, 2.5"	15	____
Sugar base, 5.25"	20	____
Sugar lid	70	____
Tumbler, 4" water	30	____
Tumbler, 5" iced tea	65	____

Note: Iridescent butter & pitcher, $300 each. Crystal items ½ of pink & green.

FLORENTINE NO. 1 *Reproduced*
(1932-1934 Hazel-Atlas Glass Company)

	Green	Yellow	Pink	Cobalt	Qty
Ashtray, 3.75"	65	65			____
Ashtray, 5.5"	25	30	30		____
Bowl, 4.75" diam., 1.5" deep, berry	40	40	40	35	____
Bowl, 5.25" ruffled nut/ cream soup	25		25	65	____
Bowl, 6" cereal	60	60	70		____
Bowl, 8.5" berry	60	60	60		____
Bowl, 9.5" oval vegetable	70	80	85		____
Butter dish base	40	60	60		____
Butter dish lid	100	120	120		____
Butter complete	140	180	180		____
Coaster, 3.25" diam	20	20	25		____
Comport, 3.25" ruffled rim	50		30	75	____
Cover for 9.5" oval vegetable	40	45	45		____
Creamer, 3"	16	20	20		____
Creamer w/ruffled rim	50		40	75	____
Cup	12	12	12	100	____
Pitcher, 6.5" w/foot	85	85	85	trtp*	____
Pitcher, 7.5" flat with or without ice lip	85	200	150		____
Plate, 6" sherbet	14	14	14		____
Plate, 8.5" salad	22	22	22		____
Plate, 10" dinner	37	48	45		____
Plate, 10" grill	25	25	30		____
Platter, 11.5" x 8"	45	50	50		____
Salt & pepper *R*	50	60	70		____
Saucer	12	12	12	25	____
Sherbet	15	15	15		____
Sugar base	16	20	20		____
Sugar lid, glass	25	35	35		____
Sugar lid, metal	15				____
Sugar w/ruffled rim	50		40	75	____
Tumbler, 3.25" juice w/foot	22				____
Tumbler, 3.75" juice w/foot	40				____
Tumbler, 4" juice w/foot	25	30	30		____
Tumbler, 4" w/ribs	30		30		____
Tumbler, 4.75" water w/foot	40	48	48		____
Tumbler, 5.25", 9 oz. lemonade	275		150		____
Tumbler, 5.25", 12 oz. iced tea w/foot	45	65	55		____

Reproduction information: Shakers: Cobalt & red never originally produced. Pink: new poppy resembles a cauliflower, missing 7 distinct circles around blossom.

*trtp = too rare to price

Note: Crystal: comport, $10; cup, $5; sherbet, $5; 8.5" salad plate, $7; saucer, $3. Ruffled nut, $13; 5.5" vase, $200; creamer, $8, sugar, $8. Fired-on: 8" plate, $45; cup, $25; saucer, $20; salt & pepper shakers, $120. Crystal may be trimmed in gold.

FLORENTINE NO. 2 *Reproduced*
(1932-1935   Hazel-Atlas Glass Company)

	Green	Yellow	Pink	Qty
Ashtray, 3.75"	65	65		____
Ashtray, 5.5"	25	30	30	____
Bowl, 4.5" diam., 1.75" deep, berry	20	25	20	____
Bowl, cream soup, 4.75" diam., 2.25" deep	18	25	18	____
Bowl, 5.25", ruffled nut/cream soup	25		25	____
Bowl, 5.5"	60	65		____
Bowl, 6" diam., 2" deep, cereal	40	50		____
Bowl, 7.5"		100		____
Bowl, 8" diam., 2.5" deep, salad	30	40	40	____
Bowl, 9" oval vegetable	40	50		____
Bowl, 9" round	35			____
Butter dish base, 6.5" diam., 1" deep	40	60		____
Butter dish lid, 5"diam.	100	120		____
Butter complete	140	180		____
Candlestick, ea., 2.5" tall, 4.25" diam.	30	40		____
Candy jar w/lid, base 4.75" diam., 3.5" deep; lid 5" diam.	150	200	165	____
Coaster, 3.25" diam.	20	20	25	____
Comport, 3.25" w/ruffled rim	50	100	30	____
Cover for 9" oval vegetable	40	45		____
Creamer	10	10	12	____
Cup	12	10	12	____
Custard/jello, 3.75" diam., 2" deep	75	100		____
Gravy boat, 2.5" deep at handle		80		____
Pitcher, 6.25" w/foot		200		____
Pitcher, 7", 28 oz. w/foot *R*	50	50		____
Pitcher, 7", 48 oz. w/foot	85	225	150	____
Pitcher, 7", w/panels	750			____
Pitcher, 8.25" no foot	120	500	250	____
Plate, 5.75" sherbet	10	10		____
Plate, 6.25" w/indent	25	40		____
Plate, 8.25" salad	10	10	10	____
Plate, 10" dinner	20	20		____
Plate, 10.25" grill	15	15		____
Plate, 10.25" grill w/cream soup ring	45			____
Platter, 11" x 8.25"	25	25	30	____
Platter, 11.75" x 9" to elevate gravy boat		60		____
Relish, 9.75" x 6.75" x 1.25"		40		____

FLORENTINE NO. 2 *(cont.)*

	Green	Yellow	Pink	Qty
Relish, 10" x 6.25" x 1.25", 3-part	40		40	___
Relish, 10" x 6.25", 3-part divided in a Y	40	40	40	___
Salt & pepper	50	60		___
Saucer, 5.5" w/curve	8	8		___
Saucer, 6.25" flat	8	8		___
Sherbet, 3.75" diam., 2.75" tall	12	12		___
Sugar base	12	12		___
Sugar lid	25	25		___
Tray, 8.75", round with indents for salt, pepper, cream, sugar		100		___
Tumbler, 3.25" flat juice	22	28	22	___
Tumbler, 3.25" tall, 3" diam., footed juice	20	25	28	___
Tumbler, 3.5" tall, just under 2.25" diam., flat (blown) juice	30			___
Tumbler, 3.5" tall, 2.75" diam., juice w/foot	20	25	28	___
Tumbler, 4" tall, 2.75" diam., footed juice *R*	20	22		___
Tumbler, 4" tall, 3.25" diam., flat water	125			___
Tumbler, 4.25" tall, 3.25" diam., flat water	40	45		___
Tumbler, 4.75" tall, water w/foot	20	25	28	___
Tumbler, 5.25" tall, 3.25" diam., flat iced tea	45	65	55	___
Tumbler, 5.25" tall, 3.25" diam, paneled flat iced tea	55	75	65	___
Vase/parfait 6" tall, 3" diam., w/foot	50	75		___

Note: Crystal items ½ of Yellow EXCEPT for the crystal covered candy, $150; 5.5" vase, $200. Cobalt comport & tumbler, $75 each. Ice blue: pitcher, $750; 4.25" tall tumbler, $150; faceted sherbet, $120; tumbler, $450. Amber: tumbler & cup, $75 each; saucer, $20; sherbet, $50.

Reproduction information: Tumblers and pitchers are being made in colors not originally produced. Measurements for these items are a "tad" smaller than the old ones. Old tumblers measure 4" tall with a base of almost 4". New tumblers are about 1/8 inch smaller in both of these measurements and are missing pattern in center on underside of foot. New pitchers are 1/4" shorter with handles 1/8" wider than the 3/4" width of the old pitchers' handles. New pitchers and tumblers are heavier and may have bubbles in glass.

FLOWER GARDEN
WITH BUTTERFLIES
(Late 1920s   U.S. Glass Company)

	Black	Blue & Canary yellow	Pink, Blue-green, & Green	Amber & Crystal	Qty
Ashtray, 6" diam		200	200	175	____
Bon bon w/cover, 6.5" across	300				____
Bottle, cologne w/stopper, 8"		250	350		____
Bowl, 7.25" w/lid	400				____
Bowl, 8.5" console w/base	200				____
Bowl, 9" rolled edge w/base	250				____
Bowl, 11" orange w/foot	300				____
Bowl, 12" console w/rolled edge	250				____
Candle, 6.5"	350				____
Candlestick, 4" each	50	75	75	45	____
Candlestick, 6" each	250				____
Candlestick, 8" each	200	85	85	45	____
Candlestick, w/candle, 12" (candle is 6.5" tall and .75" square)	500				____
Candlestick, 10.25" tall, 4" base	350				____
Candy w/lid, 6.5" tall, 7.5" diam., no foot			175	150	____
Candy w/lid, 6.5" tall, base 4.75" diam., 3" tall, w/foot; lid 4.75" diam.			200		____
Candy w/lid, 7.5" tall, 6.5" diam.		150	200	100	____
Candy w/lid, 7.5" tall, base 4.75" diam., 4.5" tall, w/foot; lid 4.75" diam.			200		____
Candy w/lid, heart-shaped		trtp*	trtp*		____
Cheese & cracker, 10.25" base, 2.75" tall comport	400		400		____
Cigarette box w/lid, 4.25" long	200				____
Comport w/lid, 2.75" tall for 10" indented plate	250				____
Comport, 2.75" tall		50	50		____
Comport, 4.25" tall, 4.75" wide			50	100	____
Comport, 4.25" tall, 10" wide; tureen	300				____
Comport, 4.5" tall, 6.25" diam.			200		____
Comport, 4.75" tall, 6.25" diam.				200	____

	Black	Blue & Canary yellow	Pink, Blue-green, & Green	Amber & Crystal	Qty
Comport, 4.75" tall, 10.25" wide		80	100	65	____
Comport w/foot, 5.5" tall, 10" wide	250				____
Comport, 5.75" tall, 11" wide			120	75	
Comport w/foot, 7" tall	200				____
Comport, 7.25" tall, 8.25" wide		100		85	
Creamer		100	100		____
Cup		70	80		____
Mayonnaise, 3-piece set		150	175	100	____
Mayo. comport		75	85	50	____
Mayo. ladle		20	25	20	____
Mayo. under plate		55	65	30	____
Plate, 7.25"		35	50	25	____
Plate, 8.25", 2 styles		40	50		____
Plate, 10"		65	75		____
Plate, 10"-10.25" w/indent for comport w/3" foot	150	65	70	45	____
Powder jar, 3.5", no foot		120			
Powder jar, 6.25" w/foot		150	225	100	____
Powder jar, 7.5" w/foot		150	120	100	____
Sandwich server w/center handle	150	70	100	55	____
Saucer		35	40		____
Sugar		100	100		____
Tray, 5.5" x 10" oval		65		65	____
Tray, 7.75" x 11.75" rectangular		75	75	65	
Tumbler, 7.5 oz.				200	____
Vase, 6" Dahlia	150	120	175	80	____
Vase, 8" Dahlia	200				____
Vase, 9", wall	350				____
Vase, 10" w/2 handles	250				____
Vase, 10.5" Dahlia	300	150	250		____

*trtp = too rare to price

Note: 6" candlesticks in black amethyst, $500 each.

FOREST GREEN

(1950-1967   Anchor Hocking Glass Company)

		Qty
Ashtrays		
3" round	8	_____
3.5" square	8	_____
4.5" square	8	_____
5.75" square	10	_____
Hexagonal, 5.75"	12	_____
Pedestal, 3.5" & 4.5"	20	_____
Queen Mary, 3.5"	10	_____
Swedish Modern, 5" x 5.75"	20	_____
Bottle w/lid (ribbed)	50	_____
Bowls		
Batter, 7.5" w/tab handle & spout	30	_____
Bon-bon, triangular 6.25", 1.5" deep	10	_____
Bubble		
Dessert, 4.5"	12	_____
Cereal, 5.25"	18	_____
Vegetable, 8.25"	30	_____
Burple/Inspiration (vertical rows of balls & lines)		
Dessert, 4.5" diam., 2" deep	6	_____
Berry, 8.5" diam., 3" deep	18	_____
Charm (square)		
Dessert, 4.75"	20	_____
Soup. 6"	20	_____
Salad, 7.5"	35	_____
Mixing (add $5 for decorations)		
4.75" round w/ beaded rim	10	_____
5.5" Splash-Proof	12	_____
6" round w/ beaded rim	12	_____
7.25" round w/ beaded rim	18	_____
7.5" batter w/ tab handle & spout	30	_____
8" round w/ beaded rim	75	_____
Sandwich		
4.25" w/smooth rim	5	_____
6.75" w/scalloped rim	50	_____
7.5" salad w/scalloped rim	80	_____
8.25" w/scalloped rim	85	_____
Scalloped, ruffled & flared, 6.5"	10	_____
Scalloped, ruffled, flared, swirled, 7.5"	10	_____
Shell, 7"	10	_____
Swedish Modern		
Candy, 2.25" tall, 6.5" diam.	25	_____
Candy, 3.5" tall, 6.5" diam.	25	_____
Whirly Twirly (series of horizontal bulges), 3.75"	14	_____
Other Bowls		
4.75"	8	_____
5.25" popcorn	18	_____
6.25" w/3 feet, textured	10	_____
8.25" oval vegetable	35	_____
10" punch	30	_____

FOREST GREEN *(cont.)*

		Qty
Compote, 6" diam., 5.5" tall	30	___
Cookie Jar, Sandwich, never had a lid	20	___
Creamers		
Bubble	18	___
Flat, Charm (squarish)	8	___
Sandwich	45	___
Cups		
Bubble	10	___
Charm (square)	10	___
Punch	3	___
Sandwich, coffee	20	___
Custard, Sandwich, crimped rim	25	___
Custard, Sandwich, smooth rim	4	___
Custard Liner, Sandwich	4	___
Lamps, various styles	45	___
Leaf & Blossom Sets	30	___
Bowl, 4.5"	12	___
Plate. 8.25"	18	___
Maple Leaf (spoon rest)	10	___
Moskeeto-lites, ea.	25	___
Pitchers		
Milano (all-over bumpy texture)	40	___
Plain or decorated w/ice lip 36 oz., 10"	30	___
Plain 7" juice	25	___
Plain w/ice lip 86 oz.	35	___
Decorated 86 oz. w/ice lip, various styles	35	___
Roly Poly (flat bottom, smooth sides curve inward at base), 8"	35	___
Sandwich, 7" juice	200	___
Sandwich, 8.5" half gallon	500	___
Whirly Twirly (series of horizontal bulges), 8" at handle	85	___
Plates		
Custard Liner/Underplate, Sandwich	4	___
Sherbet, (round) 6.5"	8	___
Salad, Charm (square), 6.5"	12	___
Salad, Bubble, 6.75"	20	___
Luncheon, Charm (square), 8.25"	10	___
Dinner, Sandwich, 9"	140	___
Dinner, Bubble, 9.25"	40	___
Dinner, Charm (square), 9.25"	35	___
Platter, Charm, 11" x 8" (rectangular)	25	___
Punch bowl, 10"	30	___
Punch bowl base	50	___
Refrigerator Dishes (round ribbed "bowls" w/lids)		
5" base	30	___
5" lid (green)	35	___
6.25" base	30	___
6.25" lid (crystal)	15	___
7" base	30	___

FOREST GREEN *(cont.)*

		Qty
7" lid (green)	40	____
Relish Tray, 8.25" x 4"	18	____
Saucer		
Bubble	6	____
Charm (square)	4	____
Sandwich	18	____
Sherbets		
Baltic (rounded foot/base), 2.25" tall, 2.5" diam.,	7	____
Inspiration (twisted vertical rows of balls & plain glass), 3.75"	14	____
Spoon rest (Maple Leaf)	10	____
Sugars		
Bubble	20	____
Flat, Charm (squarish)	8	____
Sandwich	45	____
Tray, relish, 8.25" x 4"	18	____
Tumblers		
Baltic (rounded foot/base)		
Juice, 3.5"	8	____
Goblet, 4.5"	8	____
Belmont (slight bulge in center), 5"	8	____
Blown (Flared with 3 center rings)		
Juice, 3.75"	7	____
Tall, 4.5"	7	____
Iced Tea, 5.25"	8	____
Clear "bubble" foot		
Early American (rows of "balls" w/largest ones at outer edge)		
Cocktail, 3.5"	16	____
Sherbet, 4.25"	12	____
Juice, 4.5"	14	____
Goblet, 5.25"	14	____
Goblet, 6"	20	____
Inspiration (twisted vertical rows of balls & plain glass)		
Sherbet, 3.75" tall, 3" diam.	14	____
Sherbet, 4" tall, 3.75" diam.	14	____
Cocktail, 3.75"	14	____
Juice, 4.5"	16	____
Water, 5" tall, 2.75" diam.	14	____
Goblet, 5.75"	16	____
Iced Tea, 6.75"	22	____
Georgian (honeycomb-like bottoms), 4.25"	8	____
Milano (all-over bumpy texture)		
5.5" (12 oz.)	10	____
5.75" tall, 15 oz.	12	____
Roly Poly (flat bottom, smooth sides curve inward at base)		
Juice, 3.25"	5	____
Water, 4.25"	6	____

COLOR IDENTIFICATION PHOTOS

The following color plates give photo references for each pattern in this book. The number following the name indicates the page on which the pattern is found.

Adam, 10

American Pioneer, 11

American Sweetheart, 13

Aunt Polly, 14

Aurora, 15

Avocado, 16

Banded Spiral, 17

Above left, Beaded Block, 18

Above right, Block Optic, 20

Bowknot, 22

Bubble, 23

Cameo, 24

Canadian Swirl, 26

Cherry Blossom, 27

Cherryberry, 30

Chinex Classic, 31

Christmas Candy, 32

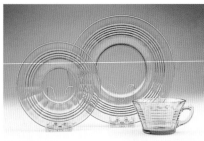

Circle, 33

Cloverleaf, 34

Colonial, "Knife and Fork," 35

Colonial Block, 37

C-4

Colonial Fluted, 38

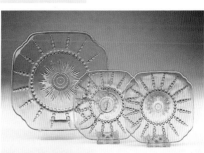

Columbia, 38

Corex, 39

Coronation, 40

Cremax, 41

Crow's Foot, 42

Crown, 45

Cube, 46

Cupid, 47

Daisy, 49

Delilah Bird, 50

C-6

Della Robbia, 51

Diamond Cut, 53

Right: Diamond
Quilted, 54

Below left: Diana, 56

Below right:
Dogwood, 57

Doric, 59

Doric and Pansy, 60

Emerald Crest, 61

English Hobnail, 63

Fire-King: Alice, 70

Fire-King:
Breakfast Set, 70

Fire-King: Charm, 71

Left: Fire-King: Fish Scale, 71

Below left: Fire-King: Jane Ray, 72

Below right: Fire-King: Laurel, 73

Fire-King: Restaurantware, 76

Fire-King: Sapphire Blue, 77

Fire-King: 1700 Line, 79

Fire-King: Sheaves
of Wheat, 80

Fire-King: Shell, 81

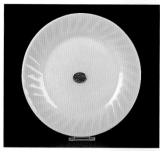

Fire-King: Swirl, 82

Fire-King: Turquoise
Blue, 83

Floragold, 84

Floral, 86

Floral and Diamond
Band, 88

Florentine No. 1, 89

Florentine No. 2, 90

Above left, Flower Garden with Butter-flies, 92

Above right, Forest Green, 94

Left, Fortune, 99

Frances, 100

Fruits, 101

Georgian Lovebirds, 102

Harp, 103

Heritage, 104

Hex Optic,
105

Hiawatha, 106

Hobnail, 107

Holiday, 108

Homespun, 109

Horseshoe, 110

Indiana Custard, 111

Inspiration, 112

Iris, 113

Jubilee, 115

Katy, 116

La Furiste, 117

Lace Edge (Old Colony), 119

Lake Como, 121

Laurel, 122

Lily Pons, 123

Lincoln Inn, 124

Lorain, 126

Madrid, 127

Manhattan, 129

Mayfair "Federal,"
131

Mayfair "Open
Rose," 132

Miss America, 135

Moderntone, 137

Moondrops, 139

Moonstone, 143

Moroccan
Amethyst, 144

Mt. Pleasant, 146

National, 148

New Century, 149

Newport, 150

Normandie, 151

Old Café, 152

Old English, 153

Orchid, 154

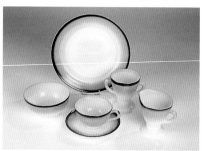

Ovide, 155

Oyster and Pearl, 156

Park Avenue, 157

Parrot (Sylvan), 158

Patrician, 159

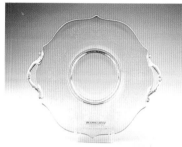

Patrick, 160

Peacock and Rose,
161

Pebble Optic, 163

Petalware, 164

Philbe, 165

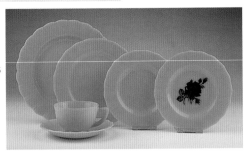

Piecrust, 166

Pillar Optic, 167

Pineapple and
Floral, 168

Pretzel, 169

Primo, 170

Princess, 171

Pyramid,
173

Queen Mary, 174

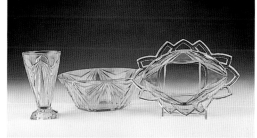

Radiance, 176

Rena, 178

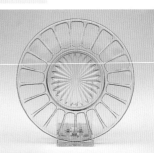

Ribbon, 179

Ring, 180

Rock Crystal
Flower, 182

Romanesque, 185

Rose Cameo, 186

Rosemary, 186

Roulette, 187

Round Robin, 187

Roxana, 188

Royal Lace, 189

Royal Ruby, 191

"S" Pattern, 195

Saguenay, 196

Sandwich (Anchor Hocking), 197

Sandwich
(Indiana), 199

Sharon, 201

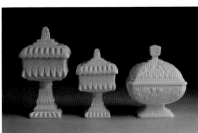

Shell Pink, 203

Sierra, 205

Spiral (Federal), 206

Spiral (Hazel-Atlas)
207

Above left, Spiral
(Hocking), 208

Above right, Spiral
Optic (Fostoria), 210

Right, Spiral Optic
(Hazel-Atlas), 212

Spiral Optic
(Hocking), 212

Spiral Optic
(Indiana), 212

Spiral Optic
(Jeannette), 213

Spiral Optic
(Tiffin), 213

Right: Starlight, 214

Below left: Stars &
Stripes, 214

Below right:
Strawberry, 215

Sunburst, 216

Sunflower, 216

Swirl, 217

Tearoom, 218

"Tendril," 220

Thistle, 220

Thumbprint, 221

Tulip, 222

Twisted Optic, 223

U.S. Swirl, 226

Vernon, 226

Victory, 227

Vitrock, 228

Waterford, 229

White Ship, 230

Windsor, 231

FOREST GREEN *(cont.)*

		Qty
Iced Tea, 5"	8	___
Sandwich		
Juice, 3"	8	___
Water, 4"	12	___
Straight sided		
4.75"	5	___
6"	5	___
6.25"	5	___
6.5" (Large Iced Tea) plain or decorated	5	___
7" (Giant Iced Tea w/foot)	8	___
Whirly Twirly (series of horizontal bulges w/foot)		
3.5"	10	___
4.25"	10	___
5"	10	___
6.5"	10	___
Windsor (small cube-like design at bottom), 4"	7	___
Others		
Bulbous base w/foot, 4"	6	___
Bulbous base w/foot, 5"	6	___
Bulbous base w/foot, 5.75"	6	___
Juice, 3.75" (similar to Whirly Twirly, less bumps)	6	___
Decorated, various styles 4.75"	5	___
Chinese Garden 4.75"	10	___
Davy Crockett 4.75"	20	___
Flying Geese/Cattails, 5.25" tall, 2.75" diam	10	___
Gay Nineties, 6.5"	5	___
Gazelle, 6.5" tall	10	___
Grape Vines, 3 colors, 4.5" tall	10	___
Lily of the Valley, 5.25" tall	10	___
Norfolk-Portsmouth Bridge Tunnel, 1952	7	___
Polka Dots, 4.75" tall, 2.75" diam	10	___
Polka Dots, 6.5" tall, 2.75" diam	12	___
Ruth Lyon 50/50 Club	7	___
Seagull Monument Utah, 5" tall	7	___
Seven-Up, 4.75" tall, 2.5" diam	10	___
Square Dance Set, 6.5" & 5.25"	5	___
Utah State Capital, 5" tall	7	___
Other decorated 3.75" glasses	5	___
Other decorated 6.5" glasses	5	___
Vases		
Ivy, 3.5" tall, 2.5" opening	5	___
Bud, 3.75" various styles	5	___
Narrow, 4" tall, 2"-2.25" opening	10	___
Bud, plain, 4" tall, 2.5" opening	5	___
Bud, decorated, 4.75"	10	___
Bud, crimped, 6.5"	8	___
Plain, ball at bottom, 3 ridges in middle, 6.25"	5	___
Plain, foot, wide middle, pinched		

FOREST GREEN *(cont.)*

		Qty
near top, 6.25"	5	____
Plain, foot, wide middle, pinched near top, 6.25," decorated,	10	____
Wide mouth, 7"	12	____
Crimped w/horizontal bulges, 6.5" tall, 3.25" opening	10	____
Crimped, 8"	8	____
Bud, (one bulge in middle) 9"	10	____
Paneled "Rocket," 9"	25	____
Plain, ruffled opening, 9"	20	____
Square textured bottom, flared top, 9"	20	____

Note: Unused tumblers found in paper carriers, add $20 for carrier in good condition. Crystal Inspiration plates: 6", trtp*; 8", $20.

*trtp=too rare to price

FORTUNE
(1936-1937   Hocking Glass Company)

	Pink	Qty
Bowl, 4" diam., 1.5" deep, berry	12	____
Bowl, 4.5" diam., 1.25" deep, w/one tab handle	12	____
Bowl, 4.5" diam., 1.75" deep, dessert	12	____
Bowl, 5.25" diam., 1.75" deep, w/flared top	20	____
Bowl, 8" diam., 2.75" deep salad	28	____
Candy dish w/lid, base 5.5" diam., 7" handle-to-handle, 2" deep; lid 5.75" diam.	45	____
Candy dish w/ Ruby lid	50	____
Cup	10	____
Plate, 6.75" sherbet	10	____
Plate, 8" luncheon	25	____
Saucer	5	____
Tumbler, 3.5" tall, 2.5"-2.75" diam., juice	15	____
Tumbler, 4"-4.25" tall, 3"-3.25" diam. water	18	____

Note: Crystal items ½ of pink, except for 8" diam., 2.75" deep bowl, $40.

FRANCES
(Late 1920s-early 1930s   Central Glass Works)

	Amber, Pink & green	Ice Blue, & Black	Crystal	Qty
Ashtray, 5" w/cover	140	175	85	____
Bowl, 2" diam, 2" tall w/2 handles, nut			35	____
Bowl, 5" diam, 2" deep, 3" opening, w/flower frog,	75			____
Bowl, nappy w/1 handle, 6" diam	225			____
Bowl, curved inward, 6" diam	20	50	20	____
Bowl, small berry	65	85	35	____
Bowl, 8" large berry	95	125	45	____
Bowl, 9.5"	95	125	45	____
Bowl, 10" w/3 ft, banana	60	80	35	____
Bowl, 10" round	60	80	35	____
Bowl, 10" 3-sided	60	80	35	____
Bowl, 11" diam., 2" deep rolled edge console w/3 ft	60	80	35	____
Bowl, trophy w/2 handles	95	125	40	____
Butter dish w/lid		200		____
Candlestick, ea., 3.25"-4" tall	45	65	25	____
Candy dish w/lid	75	95	45	____
Comport, 5" tall	50	65	35	____
Creamer, 6" tall	35	50	20	____
Cruet, 6.25" tall			40	____
Pitcher w/foot	225			____
Plate, 6.25"	35	35	25	____
Plate, 10.25" sandwich w/center handle	55	75	30	____
Plate, 12" w/3 ft., 2.5" tall, cake	65	85	30	____
Powder jar w/compartmentalized lid	125			____
Sugar	35	50	20	____
Tumbler	100	125	50	____
Vase, 7.75" tall w/foot		85	55	____
Vase, 8"-10.5" tall at highest point	75	95	45	____

Note: Trophy bowl with teal stippling, 175. 4" candlestick, pink top, iridescent base, trtp*. Orchid: 3 times the value of ice blue and black.

*trtp=too rare to price

FRUITS

(1931-1953   Hazel-Atlas Glass
Company & others)

	Green	Pink	Qty
Bowl, 5" cereal	50	30	____
Bowl, 8" berry	90	60	____
Cup	10	12	____
Pitcher	150		____
Plate, 8" luncheon	12	14	____
Saucer	6	8	____
Sherbet	10	10	____
Tumbler, 3.5" juice	60	50	____
Tumbler, 4" multiple fruits	20	20	____
Tumbler, 4.25" grapes	20		____
Tumbler, 4.25" single fruit shown	15	14	____
Tumbler, 5"	150		____

Note: Crystal & iridescent ½ of green items.

GEORGIAN LOVEBIRDS
(1931-1935   Federal Glass Company)

	Green	Qty
Bowl, 4.5" berry	15	____
Bowl, 5.75" cereal	30	____
Bowl, 6.5", deep	110	____
Bowl, 7.5" berry	80	____
Bowl, 9" oval vegetable	80	____
Butter dish base	35	____
Butter dish lid	65	____
Butter complete	100	____
Cold Cut Server (18.5" wooden lazy Susan w/7 indentations for 5" hot plate dishes)	trtp*	____
Creamer, 3"	14	____
Creamer, 4"	18	____
Cup	12	____
Hot plate dish, 5"	125	____
Plate, 6" sherbet	15	____
Plate, 8" luncheon	18	____
Plate, 9.25" dinner	45	____
Plate, 9.25" dinner, center design only	30	____
Platter, 11.25" w/tab handles	70	____
Saucer	8	____
Sherbet	15	____
Sugar base, 3"	14	____
Sugar lid for 3" base	50	____
Sugar base, 4"	18	____
Sugar lid for 4" base	300	____
Tumbler, 4"	85	____
Tumbler, 5.25"	150	____

Note: Crystal hot plate, $35. Amber sherbet, $40.

*trtp = too rare to price

HARP

	Crystal	Qty
Ashtray/coaster	8	____
Coaster	8	____
Cup	30	____
Cake stand, 9"	25	____
Plate, 7", 2 styles	20	____
Saucer	12	____
Tray w/2 open handles, 10" x 15.5"	40	____
Vase, 7.5"	35	____
Vase with 1" ball at base	trtp*	____

*trtp = too rare to price

Note: Colored glass cake stands, $100 each; transparent pink stands, $200; fired-on colors, $150. Ice blue stand found with more than one surface motif. Look for Harp design on pedestal. Clear cake stand found with and without rim or scalloped lip. Shell Pink cake plate $50, tray $100.

HERITAGE *Reproduced*
(1940-1955   Federal Glass Company)

	Crystal	Pink	Blue & Green	Qty
Bowl, 5" berry *R*	6	40	50	____
Bowl, 8.5" diam, 2.5" deep, berry *R*	35	110	175	____
Bowl, 10.5" diam, 3" deep fruit	10			____
Chip & Dip, 5" berry bowl & 10.5" fruit bowl	16			____
Creamer, 3"	25			____
Cup	6			____
Plate, 8" luncheon	8			____
Plate, 9.25" dinner	10			____
Plate, 12" sandwich	12			____
Plate, 12" lazy Susan	20			____
Saucer	4			____
Sugar, 3"	25			____

Reproduction information: All berry bowls marked "MC" or "N" connected to a horizontal bar are new. All amber pieces are new. Green pieces that are too dark are new.

HEX OPTIC

(1928-1932   Jeannette Glass Company)

	Pink & green	Qty
Bowl, 4.5" diam, 1.5"+ deep, berry, r.e.*	12	____
Bowl, 7" flat rim	75	____
Bowl, 7.5" berry	15	____
Bowl, 7.25" mixing, r.e.*	30	____
Bowl, 8" flat rim	75	____
Bowl, 8.25" diam, 4" deep mixing, r.e.*	30	____
Bowl, 9" flat rim	75	____
Bowl, 9" mixing, r.e.*	35	____
Bowl, 10" flat rim	75	____
Bowl, 10" mixing, r.e.*	32	____
Bucket reamer	65	____
Butter dish base (rect.)	50	____
Butter dish lid (rect.)	50	____
Butter complete	100	____
Creamer, 2 handle designs	12	____
Cup, 2 handle designs	12	____
Goblet, 5.75" tall, 3" diam	18	____
Ice bucket w/ metal handle	80	____
Measuring cup w/sunflower bottom	80	____
Pitcher, 5", no foot, w/ sunflower base	40	____
Pitcher, 8.25" flat, cylindrical	240	____
Pitcher, 8.75" flat	65	____
Pitcher, 9" w/foot, cone-shaped, water	65	____
Pitcher, 10.25" w/foot, cone-shaped, slightly elevated above foot	85	____
Plate, 6" sherbet	10	____
Plate, 8" luncheon	12	____
Platter, 11" round	30	____
Refrigerator dish, 4" x 4"	30	____
Refrigerator dishes, 3 rd. bases stacked w/1 lid	120	____
Salt & pepper	50	____
Saucer	8	____
Sherbet	12	____
Sugar, 2 handle designs	12	____
Tumbler, 2" whiskey	12	____
Tumbler, 3" flat	8	____
Tumbler, 4.75" w/foot	10	____
Tumbler, 5" flat, 2.75" diam.	8	____
Tumbler, 5.75" w/foot, cone-shaped, water	12	____

HEX OPTIC *(cont.)*

	Pink & green	Qty
Utility set		
base, bail handle & spout	80	___
reamer top	50	___

Note: Iridescent items worth ½ of those in pink & green. Tumblers may be found in thick & thin styles. Ultramarine 4.75" flat tumbler, $20.

*r.e.=ruffled edge

HIAWATHA

(Late 1930s-1940s   Dominion Glass Company Limited)

	Crystal	Qty
Bowl, berry	5	___
Butter dish base	8	___
Butter dish lid	8	___
Butter complete	16	___
Creamer	6	___
Plate, 6" sherbet	5	___
Sherbet	5	___
Sugar	6	___

Note: Red fired-on sherbet $8.

HOBNAIL

(1934-1936 Hocking Glass Company)

	Pink & crystal	Qty
Bowl, 5.5" cereal	10	____
Bowl, 7" salad	10	____
Creamer	10	____
Cup	8	____
Decanter w/stopper, 11.5"	45	____
Goblet, 3.5"	10	____
Goblet, 10 oz. water, 5.5"	10	____
Goblet, 13 oz. iced tea	10	____
Pitcher, 18 oz. milk	35	____
Pitcher, 67 oz.	45	____
Plate, 6" sherbet	8	____
Plate, 8.5" luncheon	14	____
Saucer, same as 6" sherbet plate	8	____
Sherbet	10	____
Sugar	10	____
Tumbler, 1.5 oz. flat whiskey, 2.5"	10	____
Tumbler, 3 oz. ftd. juice, 3.5"	10	____
Tumbler, 5 oz. flat juice, 3.5"	10	____
Tumbler, 5 oz. ftd. cordial	10	____
Tumbler, 9 or 10 oz. flat water, 4.75"	10	____
Tumbler, 15 oz. flat iced tea, 6.25"	12	____

Note: Items with red trim worth 50% more. "Buffalo Flour" plate, $30. Items with black trim, add 20%.

HOLIDAY
(1947-1949   Jeannette Glass Company)

	Pink	Qty
Bowl, 5.25" fruit dish	18	____
Bowl, 7.75" soup	65	____
Bowl, 8.5" berry	45	____
Bowl, 9.5" oval vegetable	30	____
Bowl, console, 10.75" diam., 3.75" deep	160	____
Butter dish base	25	____
Butter dish lid	70	____
Butter complete	90	____
Candlestick, ea.	75	____
Creamer	12	____
Cup, 2 styles	10	____
Pitcher, 4.75" milk	95	____
Pitcher, 6.75"	60	____
Plate, 6" sherbet	12	____
Plate, 9" dinner	25	____
Plate, 10.25" cake w/3 feet	125	____
Plate, 13.75" chop	125	____
Platter, 11.25"	35	____
Saucer	8	____
Sherbet	10	____
Sugar base	12	____
Sugar lid	40	____
Tray, 10.5" sandwich	25	____
Tumbler, 4" flat, 2 styles	25	____
Tumbler, 4" footed	50	____
Tumbler, 6" footed	175	____

Note: Iridescent pieces ½ the value of pink, except for 10.5" tray with open handles, "Windsor style," $75. Shell Pink 2x value of transparent pink. Crystal sugar, $25. Milk white, 10.75" console bowl, $100.

HOMESPUN

(1938-1940 Jeannette Glass Company)

	Pink	Qty
Ashtray/coaster, +/-4" sq.	20	____
Bowl, 4.5" berry		
w/tab handles	20	____
Bowl, 5" cereal		
w/tab handles	35	____
Bowl, 8.25" berry	40	____
Butter dish base	40	____
Butter dish lid	80	____
Butter complete	120	____
Coaster/ashtray, +/-4" sq.	20	____
Creamer	20	____
Cup	20	____
Plate, 6" sherbet	10	____
Plate, 9.25" dinner	20	____
Platter/tray, 13" x 8.25"		
w/tab handles	28	____
Saucer	10	____
Sherbet	25	____
Sugar	20	____
Tumbler, 3.75",		
5 oz. ftd. juice	12	____
Tumbler, 3.75", 7 oz.	30	____
Tumbler, 4", 8 oz.		
flat water w/flare	30	____
Tumbler, 4.25", 9 oz. flat	30	____
Tumbler, 4.75", 9 oz. flat	30	____
Tumbler, 5.25", 12.5 oz.		
flat iced tea	45	____
Tumbler, 5.75", 13.5 oz.		
flat iced tea	45	____
Tumbler, 6", 15 oz.		
w/foot	50	____
Tumbler, 6.5", 15 oz.		
w/foot	50	____

Note: Crystal items worth ½ value of pink.

Homespun Child's Tea Set

	Pink	Crystal	Qty
Cup	40	20	____
Plate, 4.5"	20	10	____
Saucer	25	10	____
Tea pot	60		____
Tea pot cover	150		____
Complete set			
Pink 14 items	550		____
Crystal 12 items		160	____

HORSESHOE

(1930-1933   Indiana Glass Company)

	Green	Yellow	Qty
Bowl, 4.5" berry	45	35	____
Bowl, 6" cereal	50	40	____
Bowl, 7.5" salad	45	35	____
Bowl, 8.5" vegetable	55	45	____
Bowl, 9.5"	65	55	____
Bowl, 10.5" oval vegetable	50	40	____
Butter dish base	trtp*		____
Butter dish lid	trtp*		____
Butter complete	trtp*		____
Candy dish, lid has designs & 3-part base is plain (may be in metal holder), 6.5" diam.	300		____
Creamer	25	25	____
Cup	12	15	____
Pitcher	425	525	____
Plate, 6" sherbet	12	12	____
Plate, 8.25" salad	18	18	____
Plate, 9.5" luncheon	18	18	____
Plate, 10.5" grill	125	175	____
Plate, 11.5" sandwich	28	38	____
Platter, 10.75"	30	40	____
Relish, 3-part	40	55	____
Saucer	10	10	____
Sherbet	18	20	____
Sugar	25	25	____
Tumbler, 4.25" tall, 2.75" diam flat	200		____
Tumbler, 4.75" tall, 3" diam flat	200		____
Tumbler, 9 oz. w/foot, 4.75" tall, 3" diam	30	40	____
Tumbler, 12 oz. w/foot, 3" diam	200	200	____

Note: Pink candy dish, $200

*trtp = too rare to price

INDIANA CUSTARD
(1933-1935   Indiana Glass Company)

	Ivory	Qty
Bowl, 5.5" berry	20	____
Bowl, 6.25" cereal	30	____
Bowl, 7.5" soup	40	____
Bowl, 9" berry	50	____
Bowl, 9.5" oval vegetable	40	____
Butter dish base	20	____
Butter dish lid	40	____
Butter complete	60	____
Creamer, 3.5"	20	____
Cup	40	____
Plate, 6" sherbet	12	____
Plate, 8" salad	25	____
Plate, 8.75" luncheon	25	____
Plate, 9.75" dinner	45	____
Platter, 12" x 9"	60	____
Saucer	10	____
Sherbet, 3" tall	125	____
Sugar base, 3.5"	20	____
Sugar lid	30	____

INSPIRATION
(1950s, Anchor Hocking Glass Company)

	Royal Ruby & Forest Green	Qty
Bowl, 4.5" diam., 2" deep	6	____
Bowl, 8.5" diam., 3" deep	18	____
Plate, 6" (only crystal)	trtp	____
Plate, 8" (only crystal)	25	____
Sherbet, 3.75" tall, 3" diam.	14	____
Sherbet, 4" tall, 3.75" diam.	14	____
Tumbler, 3.75" tall, 3" diam., cocktail	14	____
Tumbler, 4.5" tall; juice	16	____
Tumbler, 5" tall, 2.75" diam., water	16	____
Tumbler, 5.75" tall, goblet	16	____
Tumbler, 6.75" tall, 3.5" diam., iced tea	22	____

*trtp = too rare to price

IRIS *Reproduced*

(1943, iridescent in 1950 & 1969, white in 1970
Jeannette Glass Company)

	Crystal, Ruby Flash, & Satinized White	Iridescent	Qty
Bowl, 4.5" berry			
w/beaded rim *R*	50	25	____
Bowl, 5" sauce			
w/ruffled edge	15	30	____
Bowl, 5" cereal w/ruffle	trtp*		____
Bowl, 5" cereal			
w/straight side	145		____
Bowl, 7.5" coupe soup	185	75	____
Bowl, 8" berry			
w/ beaded rim	100	40	____
Bowl, 9.5" salad			
w/ ruffled edge	15	10	____
Bowl, 9.5" nut w/ metal			
foot and center	125		____
Bowl, 11" fruit w/ flat rim	70		____
Bowl, 11" fruit w/rolled rim	trtp*		____
Bowl, 12" fruit			
w/ruffled edge	15	10	____
Bowl, 12" flower			
w/ruffled edge	125		____
Bowl, 12" nut w/ metal			
foot and center	125	150	____
Bowl, 12" fruit w/ metal			
foot and center	125		____
Butter dish base	15	15	____
Butter dish lid	35	35	____
Butter complete	50	50	____
Cake Plate lid, 11.25"			
diam., 6.25" tall	trtp*		____
Candlesticks, ea.	25	25	____
Candy jar w/lid *R*	200		____
Chandelier	trtp*		____
Coaster *R*	140		____
Creamer	15	15	____
Cup, coffee	20	18	____
Cup, demitasse	50	200	____
Goblet, 4" wine		35	____
Goblet, 4.25" wine, 3 oz.			
2" diameter	18		____
Goblet, 4.25" cocktail, 4 oz.			
2.5" diameter	25		____
Goblet, 5.5", 8 oz. water			
3" diameter	25	225	____
Goblet, 5.75", 4 oz. wine			
2.25" diameter	25	225	____
Lamp shade, 11.5"	75		____

IRIS (cont.)

	Crystal, Ruby Flash, & Satinized White	Iridescent	Qty
Lamp, table w/Lucite-trimmed shade	250		____
Pitcher, 9.5"	40	50	____
Pitcher, 9.5" w/iris on foot	trtp*		____
Plate, 6"	15	15	____
Plate, 8" luncheon	130		____
Plate, 9" dinner *R*	60	45	____
Plate, 11.75" sandwich	45	35	____
Saucer, coffee	12	12	____
Saucer, demitasse	150	250	____
Sherbet, 2.5" w/foot	30	18	____
Sherbet, 4" w/stem, 3.5" diam	25	250	____
Sugar base	15	15	____
Sugar lid	20	25	____
Tumbler, 4" flat *R*	150		____
Tumbler, 6" w/foot	20	20	____
Tumbler, 6.5" w/foot *R*	40		____
Tumbler, 6.5" w/iris on foot	150		____
Vase, 9" *R*	30	20	____

Note: Items in green or pink, $125 each. Lamp shade frosted in pink, blue, or white, $65. Demitasse cups & saucers in other colors too rare to price. White vase, $10. Satinized yellow and blue items, $200 each.

Reproduction Information: Crystal 9" dinner plate: new- herringbone texture ends with an exacting zigzag .25" (1/4") from inner rim, old- herringbone texture ends in a "blur." The Iris design on new dinners looks "puffy" and the outer rim tilts down and may end with an fine but extra ridge of glass before dipping down to the eating surface. Crystal tumblers: new- herringbone texture is not crisp & rays on underside of the feet are pointy, old- herringbone background is crisp and even with smooth rays on the underside of the feet. Crystal 4.5" beaded rim bowl: new- irises have texture unlike the smooth, transparent old flowers. Candy jar: new- foot is missing rays found on foot of old jar. Coaster: new and old are same diameter, but side-by-side reproductions are a tad taller. Base of new, 3/8" thick; base of old, 1/8" thick. 10" dinner plates, all are new. Vases were reissued in the 1970s and 1980s. Tumblers, 4" flat *new* have crude bouquet of flowers on bottom and heavy 3/8" base of glass. Irises have no stems.

*trtp = too rare to price

JUBILEE
(1930 Lancaster Glass Company)

	Yellow	Pink	Qty
Bowl, 8" w/3 feet	250	350	____
Bowl, 9" fruit w/handles	150		____
Bowl, 11.5" fruit (flat)	175	225	____
Bowl, 11.5" w/3 feet	300	300	____
Bowl, 11.5" w/3 feet (curves inward)	250		____
Bowl, 13" w/3 feet	250	300	____
Candlestick, 2" tall, ea.	125	125	____
Candy jar w/lid (only 11 petals on this piece)	400	500	____
Cheese & cracker set	300	350	____
Creamer, 3.25"	30	40	____
Cup	20	50	____
Goblet, 4", 1 oz. cordial	300		____
Goblet, 4.75", 4 oz. oyster cocktail	100		____
Goblet, 4.75", 3 oz. cocktail	200		____
Goblet, 5.5", 7 oz. champagne or sherbet	125		____
Goblet, 7.5", 11 oz. water	200		____
Mayonnaise, 4.75" w/3 feet, under plate & spoon	300	400	____
Pitcher, 8"	800	800	____
Plate, 7" salad	20	35	____
Plate, 8.75" luncheon	20	45	____
Plate, 11" sandwich w/2 handles	50	70	____
Saucer, 2 styles	5	15	____
Sherbet (only 11 petals on this piece), 3.5" diam, 2.75" deep	100		____
Sugar, 3.25"	30	40	____
Tumbler, 5" ftd. juice	120		____
Tumbler, 6" tall, 3.5" diam. ftd. water	40	80	____
Tumbler, 6.25" ftd. iced tea	175		____
Tray, 11" sandwich w/center handle	225	225	____
Tray, 13" salad w/3 feet	250	250	____
Vase, 10" bud		800	____
Vase, 12" tall, 3.75" opening	450	650	____

Note: Crystal items worth ½ yellow prices.

KATY
(1935-? Imperial Glass Company)

	All opalescent colors	Qty
Basket	275	____
Bowls with "flat" rims:		
4.5" diam., 1.5" deep, sauce	45	
8.25" diam., 2" deep	100	____
11" x 8.25" x 1.75" deep, 2-part relish	150	____
11.25" x 8.5" x 1.75" deep, oval vegetable	150	____
Bowls with "stand-up" rims:		
4.5" diam., 1.5" deep, sauce	45	____
5" diam., cereal	60	____
5.25" diam., 1.5" deep	60	____
6.75" diam., 2" deep	60	____
7" diam., 1.75" deep soup	125	____
8.25" diam., 4.5" opening, 4.25" deep w/flower frog	175	____
9" diam., 3.25" deep, console	150	____
9.25" x 6" x 4.25" deep	130	____
11" diam. w/large loops	300	____
Candlestick, ea. 3.5" tall, 4.25" diam. base	120	____
Creamer, 3.25" tall	60	____
Cup	55	____
Mayonnaise, 3.25" tall, 5.5" diam compote w/underplate & spoon	185	____
Plate, 6.25" bread & butter	35	____
Plate, 8" salad	45	____
Plate, 9.75" dinner	130	____
Plate, 12.75" cake	110	____
Platter, 12.75" x 10"	225	____
Saucer	25	____
Sugar, 3.25" tall	60	____
Tidbit, 8" & 9.75" plates	200	____
Tumbler, 4" tall, 3" diam.	80	____

LA FURISTE

(1920s-1930s   Lotus Glass Company)

	Rose, Green, Amber, Crystal	Qty
Bowl, 7.75" x 5.5" rose bowl w/3 feet	90	____
Bowl, 8.5" x 11" oval	115	____
Bowl, 8.75" x 5.5" rose bowl	90	____
Bowl, 9" bell w/ handles (8-sided)	115	____
Bowl, 10" nut w/center handle (8-sided)	125	____
Bowl, 10" w/rolled edge	115	____
Bowl, 10.5" x 4.5" celery (boat shaped)	150	____
Bowl, 10.5" x 5", pinched oval	150	____
Bowl, 11.25" w/rolled edge w/3 feet	125	____
Bowl, 12" crimped w/3 feet	115	____
Bowl, 12" flared rim w/3 feet	115	____
Bowl, 12" x 3.5" w/rolled edge	125	____
Bowl, 12.25" x 4.5" celery w/2 handles	115	____
Bowl, 12.5" x 3" w/flared rim	115	____
Bowl, 13" w/flared rim	125	____
Bowl, 13" diam, 4" deep, rolled edge console	150	____
Candlestick, ea. 3" tall, 4.25" diam. base	115	____
Candlestick, ea. 6"	115	____
Candy dish w/lid, 7" diam, 4.5" tall, 3-parts	125	____
Cheese & Cracker	120	____
Comport, 7"	75	____
Creamer	50	____
Cup	50	____
Decanter w/stopper	250	____
Fruit Salad w/foot (similar to a sherbet in other patterns)	60	____
Goblet, 4.75" wine	65	____
Goblet, 6" tall, 2" diam., 9 oz.	65	____

LA FURISTE *(cont.)*

	Rose, Green Amber, Crystal	Qty
Goblet, 8" tall, 3.5" diam	50	____
Ice tub, 5.75" diam., 4" deep, w/2 handles	90	____
Pitcher, 9.75" tall	200	____
Plate, 6.25" bread & butter	40	____
Plate, 7.5" salad	50	____
Plate, 8"-8.5" salad	50	____
Plate, 9" dinner	50	____
Plate, 10" cake w/center handle	60	____
Plate, 10.5" muffin w/2 handles that turn up	70	____
Plate, 10.5"-11" sandwich w/2 open handles	175	____
Plate, 12" service (8-sided)	75	____
Plate, 12"-12.5" pastry w/2 handles	65	____
Platter, 12.5" x 10" w/2 open handles (8-sided)	75	____
Relish, 6" w/3 sections & lid	65	____
Saucer	20	____
Sherbet, 6.5 oz. high (tall stem)	60	____
Sherbet, 6.5 oz. low (short stem)	60	____
Stem, 1.5 oz. cordial	65	____
Stem, 6", 2.75 oz. wine	65	____
Stem, 3.5 oz. cocktail	65	____
Sugar	60	____
Tumbler, 2.5 oz. whiskey w/foot	60	____
Tumbler, 6 oz. w/foot	60	____
Tumbler, 4.75", 10 oz. w/foot	60	____
Tumbler, 12 oz. iced tea w/foot	65	____
Vase, 7" w/diamond optic	175	____
Vase, 9" w/diamond optic	175	____
Whipped cream, 3 pieces (comport, under plate, & spoon)	175	____

LACE EDGE

(1935-1938 Hocking Glass Company)

	Pink	Qty
Ashtray	trtp*	____
Bowl, 6" cereal, 1.5" deep	30	
Bowl, 6" cereal satin finish, 1.5" deep	20	____
Bowl, 7.75" salad w/ribs, 1.75" deep	40	____
Bowl, 7.75" smooth, 1.75" deep	45	
Bowl, 8.25" (in crystal)	12	____
Bowl, 9.5" smooth	30	____
Bowl, 9.5" w/ribs, 2.5" deep	38	
Bowl, 9.5" satin finish	25	____
Bowl, 10.5" w/3 feet	350	____
Bowl, 10.5" w/3 feet satin finish	55	____
Bowl, ribbed flower w/crystal frog, 3.5" tall, 7" diam.	60	____
Bowl, fish (in crystal; similar to cookie jar base)	40	____
Butter dish base	45	____
Butter dish lid	65	____
Butter complete	110	____
Candle holder, ea.	225	____
Candle holder, ea. satin finish	40	____
Candy jar w/lid, ribbed, 3.25" deep, 4.75" opening	100	____
Comport, 7"	40	____
Comport, 7" satin finish	25	____
Comport w/lid, 7"	80	____
Comport, 9"	trtp*	____
Cookie jar w/lid, base 5" deep, 4" opening	100	____
Cookie jar w/lid, satin finish, base 5" deep, 4" opening	50	____
Creamer	50	____
Cup	40	____
Plate, 7.25" salad	35	____
Plate, 8.25" luncheon	30	____
Plate, 10.5" dinner	40	____
Plate, 10.5" grill	25	____
Plate, 13" solid lace	70	____
Plate, 13" solid lace, 4-part	70	____

LACE EDGE *(cont.)*

	Pink	Qty
Plate, 13" solid lace		
w/satin finish, 4-part	40	____
Platter, 12.75"	60	____
Platter, 12.75", 5-part	50	____
Relish, 7.5", 3-part	100	____
Relish, 10.5", 3-part	35	____
Saucer	25	____
Sherbet, 3" tall, almost		
5" diam.	175	____
Sugar	60	____
Tumbler, 3.5" flat	225	____
Tumbler, 4.25" flat	40	____
Tumbler, 5" w/foot	100	____
Vase, 7"	950	____
Vase, 7" satin finish	85	____

Note: 6.5" green cereal bowl, $100. White sherbet, $8. Fired-on sherbet, $20. Crystal fish bowl, 8.25" tall, 10" diam., trtp*

*trtp = too rare to price

LAKE COMO

(1935-1937   Anchor Hocking Glass Company)

	White w/ decorations	Qty
Bowl, 6" cereal	30	____
Bowl, 9.75" vegetable	70	____
Bowl, flat soup	100	____
Creamer	30	____
Cup	30	____
Cup, St. Denis	30	____
Plate, 7.25" salad	20	____
Plate, 9.25" dinner	35	____
Platter, 11"	75	____
Salt & pepper, 3"	45	____
Saucer	10	____
Saucer, St. Denis	10	____
Sugar	30	____

LAUREL
(1930s McKee Glass Company)

	Jade & Poudre blue	Other colors	Qty
Bowl, 4.75" diam., 1.75" deep berry	30	10	____
Bowl, 5.75" diam., 1.5" deep oatmeal	175		____
Bowl, 6" diam., 1.5" deep cereal	50	15	____
Bowl, 6" diam., almost 2" deep, w/3 feet	60	20	____
Bowl, 7.75" soup	125	40	____
Bowl, 8" diam, 1.5" deep	80		____
Bowl, 8.75" diam., 2.5" deep berry	100	30	____
Bowl, 9.75" oval vegetable	85	30	____
Bowl, 10.5" w/3 feet	95	65	____
Bowl, 11"	95	40	____
Candlestick, ea., 4.25" diam, 1.75" tall	100	20	____
Cheese dish w/lid, base 7.5" plate; lid 5" diam.	375	45	____
Creamer, 3" & 4"	45	15	____
Cup	25	10	____
Plate, 5.75" sherbet	22	8	____
Plate, 7.5" salad/cheese base	25	25	____
Plate, 9" dinner	30	15	____
Plate, 9" grill	30	15	____
Platter, 10.75" x 8"	125	30	____
Salt & pepper	300	75	____
Saucer	12	5	____
Sherbet, 3.75" diam., 3.5" tall	30	12	____
Sugar, 3" & 4"	45	15	____
Tumbler, 3.5" tall, 3" diam	120		____
Tumbler, 4.5" tall, 9 oz.	120	50	____
Tumbler, 5" tall, 12 oz.		90	____
Wine, 3.75" tall, 2.75" diam.	185		____
Wine, 4.5" tall, 3.25" diam.		125	____

Note: Round edges are 75% of scalloped edges as priced above. Add 20% for decorated rims. Crystal candle holder too rare to price.

Laurel Child's Tea Set

	Jade-ite	Ivory	Decorated rim	Scotty on Jade	Scotty on Ivory	Qty
Creamer	35	50	150	120	65	____
Cup	30	40	125	75	50	____
Plate, 6"	20	25	125	75	30	____
Saucer	12	15	100	50	20	____
Sugar	35	50	150	120	65	
Complete 14-piece set	318	370	1700	1040	530	____

LILY PONS & PEBBLE LEAF
(late 1920s-early 1930s Indiana Glass Company)

	Green	Qty
Bowl, 6.5" Bon Bon with three feet	30	____
Bowl, 7" diam., 2.75" deep preserve	20	____
Bowl, 8.5" leaf	40	____
Bowl, 8.5" oval pickle with 2 handles	30	____
Creamer, 2.75" tall	35	____
Plate,* 5.25"	20	____
Plate, 6" sherbet/fruit cocktail	20	____
Plate,* 8.5" salad	20	____
Sherbet, 4" diam., 2.25" deep fruit cocktail	25	____
Sugar, 2.75" tall	35	____

Note: Lily Pons and Pebble Leaf are similar and often used together. Crystal and fired-on colors, $5 each. Red 7" bowl, $40. Crystal satinized 5.25" plate, $5 each.

*Pebble Leaf

LINCOLN INN

(1928-1929   Fenton Art Glass Company)

	All Colors	Qty
Ashtray	30	____
Bonbon, handles square or oval	30	____
Bowl, 4.5" diam, 2.25" deep w/rolled in rim, nut	75	____
Bowl, 4.75" fruit	20	____
Bowl, 5" diam., 1.5" deep, curves inward	40	____
Bowl, finger, 5"	30	____
Bowl, 5" ruffled w/handles	30	____
Bowl, 5" w/foot	40	____
Bowl, 5.5" 1-handled olive	40	____
Bowl, 6" cereal	25	____
Bowl, 6" crimped	25	____
Bowl, 7"	30	____
Bowl, 9"	40	____
Bowl, 9.25" footed	85	____
Bowl, 10"	40	____
Bowl, 10.5" footed	75	____
Bowl, 10.75" crimped	50	____
Cigarette holder, 2.75" tall, 2" diam.	40	____
Comport plate	45	____
Comport, 4" tall, flat surface	55	____
Comport, 4.25" tall, cupped rim	55	____
Comport, 4.25" tall, crimped	55	____
Creamer	40	____
Cup	20	____
Goblet, 3.75" tall, 2.75" diam. juice	45	____
Goblet, 4" wine	45	____
Goblet, 4.5" martini/ cone-shaped sherbet	45	____
Goblet, 5.25" juice or claret	45	____
Goblet, 5.75"water	45	____
Goblet, 6" water	45	____
Goblet, 6" iced tea, shorter stem than water	45	____
Mint, flat, 5" diam., 6" handle-to-handle	30	____
Mint, oval	30	____
Nut, 4" tall, 3.5" diam.	35	____
Pitcher, 7.25"	1000	____
Plate, 6" bread & butter	20	____
Plate, 7" to line finger bowl	20	____

LINCOLN INN *(cont.)*

	All Colors	Qty
Plate, 8" salad	25	____
Plate, 9.25" dinner	50	____
Plate, 11.5"-12"	50	____
Salt & pepper	375	____
Sandwich server w/ center handle	200	____
Saucer	12	____
Sherbet, 4" w/stem	35	____
Sherbet, 4.25" w/stem	35	____
Sherbet, 4.5" cone/martini	30	____
Sherbet, 4.75" w/stem	35	____
Sugar	40	____
Tray, 5-part	50	____
Tumbler, 4" water, no foot or stem	35	____
Tumbler, 4.25", no foot or stem	35	____
Tumbler, 5" water	35	____
Tumbler, 5.5", no foot or stem	35	____
Vase, 9.75"	150	____
Vase, 12"	175	____

Note: Black & Jade-ite salt & pepper, $500 each pair. Other Jade-ite pieces 2x values listed. Add 30% for items with fruit design pressed into center. Crystal items worth half the value of colors.

LORAIN *Reproduced*
(1929-1932   Indiana Glass Company)

	Green	Yellow	Qty
Bowl, 6" cereal	70	75	____
Bowl, 7.5" diam., 2.5" deep salad	55	60	____
Bowl, 8" berry	150	175	____
Bowl, 9.5" x 6.5" x 1.75" deep oval vegetable	55	60	____
Creamer	40	45	____
Cup	15	20	____
Goblet, 5.75"	40		____
Plate, 5.5" sherbet	15	18	____
Plate, 7.75" salad	20	25	____
Plate, 8.75" luncheon	35	40	____
Plate, 10.25" dinner	95	100	____
Platter, 11.5" x 7.25"	48	58	____
Relish, 8.5" x 7.25", 4-part	30	45	____
Saucer	8	10	____
Sherbet, 3" tall, 3.5" diam. *R*	35	35	____
Sugar	40	45	____
Tumbler, 5"	38	38	____

Note: Crystal prices ½ of yellow, except for Snack Tray, 11.5" x 7.25" with tab handles, cup ring, and colored trim, $50.

Reproduction Information: Sherbets made in avocado green and milk white are from the 1960s.

MADRID *Reproduced*
(1932-1938 Federal Glass Company)

	Amber	Green	Pink	Blue	Qty
Ashtray	600	600			____
Bowl, 4.75" cream soup	25				____
Bowl, 5" diam., 1.75" deep dessert	12	12	12	35	____
Bowl, 7" soup *R*	30	40		75	____
Bowl, 8" salad	20	22			____
Bowl, 9.25" berry	30		30		____
Bowl, 9.5" deep salad	40				____
Bowl, 10" oval vegetable	30	30	30	55	____
Bowl, 11" diam., 2.25" deep, flared rim console	25		22		____
Butter dish base *R*	30	40			____
Butter dish lid *R*	55	65			____
Butter complete *R*	85	105			____
Candlestick, ea. *R*	18		15		____
Cookie jar/lid	60		70		____
Creamer *R*	20	20		35	____
Cup *R*	12	14	14	22	____
Gravy boat w/6" x 8.25" tray	3000				____
Hot dish coaster, 5"	175	175			____
Hot dish coaster w/indent, 5"	175	175			____
Jam dish, 7"	30	40		50	____
Jello mold, 2" high	18				____
Lampshade	trtp*				____
Lazy Susan, wooden w/glass cold cut coasters	trtp*				____
Mug, 3.25" tall, 3.75" diam	trtp*				____
Pitcher, 5.5", 36 oz., juice	55				____
Pitcher, 8", 60 oz., square w/applied handle		200		250	____
Pitcher, 8", 60 oz., square w/molded handle	55	150	50	200	____
Pitcher, 8", 80 oz., no ice lip	90	250			____
Pitcher, 8.5", 80 oz., with ice lip	90	250			____
Plate, 6" sherbet	9	12	7	15	____
Plate, 7.5" salad	15	18	12	25	____
Plate, 8.75" luncheon	10	18	12	25	____
Plate, 10.25" relish	25	25	18		____
Plate, 10.5" dinner *R*	70	70		120	____
Plate, 10.5" grill *R*	12	22			____
Plate, 11.25" cake	40		30		____
Platter for under gravy boat	800				____
Platter, 11.5"	34	50	50	60	____
Salt & pepper, footed	140	145		175	____
Salt & pepper, flat *R*	55	75			____
Saucer *R*	5	7	7	12	____
Sherbet, 2.75" cone (Similar to Sylvan sherbet)	5	12	trtp*	18	____
Sherbet, 2.25", squatty	30				____
Sugar base *R*	20	20		35	____
Sugar lid	65	65		200	____
Tidbit, saucer & 7.5" plate, clear glass base	45				____

MADRID *(cont.)*

	Amber	Green	Pink	Blue	Qty
Tumbler, 3.75", just over 2" diam. 5 oz., juice, flat	18	35		45	____
Tumbler, 4" tall, 2.75" diam., 5 oz., footed	30	45			____
Tumbler, 4", 2.75" diam. 9 oz., water, flat	18	25	20	40	____
Tumbler, 5.5", 12 oz., iced tea, 2 styles, flat	25	35		45	____
Tumbler, 5.5", 2.75" diam., 10 oz., footed	35	50			____

*trtp = too rare to price

Reproduction information: New colors: AMBER may be too dark and may have a "76" worked into the design, BLUE may be too dark and appear to be glowing, PINK: may be too pale or too bright and the design may be less distinct, CRYSTAL: difficult to discern. The following items were never originally produced: 9.5" footed bowl, footed (pedestal) cake stand, footed goblet, 2-part grill plate, preserve stand, short salt & pepper shakers, 10.25" snack tray with 2" cup indent, 11 oz. tumbler with design different from vintage tumblers, and vase. 7" soup bowl: old-design on rim is compact, new-design seems to have 4 layers. Butter: new made in amber & pink and is too dark, knob on lid has vertical mold seam rather than old having horizontal mold seam. Candlestick: new made in amber & crystal with glass ridges to grasp a candle, old are smooth inside. Creamer: new made in amber, crystal, pink, and perhaps blue: new- spouts are formed by applying extra glass, old spouts are formed below top rim. The old handles form pointed pear shape where they meet the sides. New handles form a rounder shape. New has a cup-like appearance and the color may be wrong, particularly amber which may be considerably darker. Saucer: new made in amber, crystal, & pink. New amber & pink have colors that just look wrong, crystal is difficult to discern but the saucer will have less quality. 10.5" dinner plate: new made in amber, blue, crystal, and pink. New- diamond in Madrid motif found in center of dinner plate is surrounded by filled in glass resembling a fat blade of grass with a hook, old- diamond is surrounded by glass that resembles a curved sewing needle with an eye, and then there is the same hook. Points in corners of old dinners are more pronounced than those on new ones. Shakers: new shakers made in crystal & blue are shorter & heavier than old and were issued with plastic lids. Sugar: new made in amber, blue, & crystal. The old handles form pointed pear shape where they meet the sides. New handles form a rounder shape and the color may be wrong.

Note: Crystal hot dish coaster, $40, 8" pitcher, $175. Iridescent items same price as Amber. Satinized amber cookie jar: $120.

MANHATTAN *Reproduced*
(1938-1941   Anchor Hocking Glass Company)

	Crystal	Pink	Ruby	Qty
Ashtray, sherbet style	35			____
Ashtray, 4" round	15			____
Ashtray, 4.5" square	18			____
Bowl, 4.5" sauce				
w/handles	10			____
Bowl, 5.25" berry				
w/handles	20	25		____
Bowl, 5.25" cereal	65	125		____
Bowl, 7.25" berry				
w/handles	15			____
Bowl, 8" w/handles	20	25		____
Bowl, 9" salad	25			____
Bowl, 9.5" fruit, w/foot				
& 2 open handles	45	45		____
Candlestick, 4.5"				
square, ea.	10			____
Candy dish, open w/3 feet		18		____
Coaster	20			____
Comport, 5.25" tall	50	70		____
Creamer	18	18		____
Cup	20	200		____
Insert for relish tray, outer	10	10	8	____
Insert for relish tray, center	14			____
Pitcher, 24 oz., tilted *R*	50			____
Pitcher, 80 oz., tilted	60	85	450	____
Plate, 6" sherbet/saucer	12	75		____
Plate, 8.5" salad *R*	20			____
Plate, 10.25" dinner *R*	25	275		____
Plate, 14" sandwich	35			____
Salt & pepper, square	40	75		____
Sherbet, bubble foot	12	25		____
Sugar	15	18		____
Tray, 14" relish, 5 sections	20	35		____
Tray, 14" relish, no sections	20			____
Tumbler, bubble foot *R*	20	24		____
Vase, 8", bubble foot *R*	30			____

Note: Companion pieces by Anchor Hocking: Candy dish w/lid, $45; Cocktail & Wine, 3.5", $12; Decanter w/stopper, $25. Water bottle: clear, $18; Ruby, $250; Forest Green, $150. Go-along cookie jar, crystal $50; pink, $125. Ashtray w/advertisement, $15. Ruby 24 oz. Pitcher, $500. Green: tumblers, $25; dinner plate, $135. Iridized tumblers, $15 each. Jade-ite pitcher, too rare to price. Satinized crystal, 1/2 values of crystal.

Reproduction Information: 8.5" salad plate new measures 8". Tumblers new made without bubble feet. Vase new is

9.75" rather than 8". Many new pieces in light green are being found. Items include: tumblers, large bowls, and various sizes of plates. This listing may not be complete. 10.25" dinner in crystal: Target Stores were selling new crystal Manhattan dinners. Edges on old are smooth, new have *slight* bead. Old dinners have rounded rings and center circle is 3/8". New dinners have crisp, almost pointy rings, and center circle is 1/4". Pedestal cake plates are new. Ruby juice tilt pitchers are new.

Park Avenue pieces:
- Ashtray, 6" round
- Bowl, 5.5" x 2.5" deep
- Bowl, 6"
- Bowl, 10"
- Cake plate with cover
- Goblet
- Plate, 8"
- Plate, 13"
- Salt & pepper, round
- Sherbet, just over 3 oz.

MAYFAIR "FEDERAL"
(1934   Federal Glass Company)

	Green	Amber	Crystal	Qty
Bowl, 5" cream soup	20	18	8	____
Bowl, 5" sauce	12	8	4	____
Bowl, 6" cereal	8	12	4	____
Bowl, 10" oval vegetable	30	25	12	____
Creamer	18	12	4	____
Cup	12	8	4	____
Plate, 6.75" salad	12	10	4	____
Plate, 9.5" dinner	24	15	8	____
Plate, 9.5" grill	18	10	8	____
Platter, 12"	30	25	12	____
Saucer	7	4	3	____
Sugar, no handles	18	12	4	____
Tumbler, 4.5"	40	25	12	____

MAYFAIR "OPEN ROSE"
Reproduced
(1931-1936   Hocking Glass Company)

	Pink	Blue	Green	Yellow	Qty
Bowl, 5" cream soup	65				____
Bowl, 5.5" cereal	30	70	100	125	____
Bowl, 7" vegetable w/tab handles	40	70	150	160	____
Bowl, 9" console w/3 legs	6000		6000		____
Bowl, 9.5" vegetable, oval	50	85	150	160	____
Bowl, 10.25" vegetable w/handles	35	90		165	____
Bowl, 10.25" vegetable w/cover	150	250		1000	____
Bowl, 11.75", shallow	85	110	85	250	____
Bowl, 12" diam., 5" deep, scalloped fruit, "hat"	80	160	95	380	____
Butter dish base	50	110	300	400	____
Butter dish lid	70	260	1200	1300	____
Butter complete	120	360	1500	1600	____
Candy dish w/lid	75	360	700	600	____
Celery dish, 9", 2 sections	250		250	250	____
Celery dish, 10"	60	85	200	200	____
Celery dish, 10", 2 sections	275	90			____
Coaster, 3.5" diam	trtp*				____
Cookie jar/lid *R*	85	355	700	1000	____
Creamer	35	105	250	275	____
Cup, squarish	20	70	200	200	____
Cup, round	400				____
Decanter w/stopper	275				____
Goblet, 3.75" cordial	1300		1100		____
Goblet, 4" cocktail	100		450		____
Goblet, 4.25" cordial	1100		1100		____
Goblet, 4.5" wine	120		500		____
Goblet, 5.25" claret	1300		1100		____
Goblet, 5.75" water	85		525		____
Goblet, 7.25"	300	270			____
Lamp	trtp*				____
Lid for 10" vegetable bowl	100	160	175	200	____
Pitcher, 6" *R*	70	190	600	625	____
Pitcher, 8", 60 oz.	85	220	600	600	____
Pitcher, 8.5" 80 oz.	130	350	800	800	____
Plate, 5.75"	15	30	100	100	____
Plate, 6.5" sherbet, round	20				____
Plate, 6.5" sherbet, round w/off center indent	50	50	150	150	____
Plate, 8.5" luncheon	35	65	150	150	____
Plate, 9.5" dinner	65	100	200	200	____
Plate, 9.5" grill	45	65	100	100	____
Plate, 10" cake w/feet & tab handles	50	85	200		____
Plate, 11.5" grill w/handles				150	____
Plate, 12" cake w/handles	70	110	100		____
Platter, 12" w/open handles, no feet *R*	45	95	200	200	____

MAYFAIR "OPEN ROSE" *(cont.)*

	Pink	Blue	Green	Yellow	Qty
Platter, 12.5" w/closed handles			300	300	____
Relish, 8.5" w/4 sections	50	85	200	200	____
Relish, 8.5", not sectioned	320		390	390	____
Salt & pepper flat *R*	85	365	1300	1000	____
Salt & pepper, footed	trtp*				____
Sandwich server w/center handle	70	130	80	170	____
Saucer	50			150	____
Sherbet, 2.25" w/out stem or foot	375	300			____
Sherbet, 3.25" w/foot	25				____
Sherbet, 4.75" w/foot	100	110	200	200	____
Sugar base	35	105	250	275	____
Sugar lid	2200		2200	2200	____
Tumbler, 2.25" whiskey *R*	85				____
Tumbler, 3.25" juice, footed	100				____
Tumbler, 3.5" juice, flat *R*	60	160			____
Tumbler, 4.25" water, flat	55	160			____
Tumbler, 4.75" water, flat	225	160	250	250	____
Tumbler, 5.25" iced tea, footed	60	160		225	____
Tumbler, 5.25" iced tea, flat	80	320			____
Tumbler, 6.5" iced tea, footed	60	320	250		____
Vase	350	175	485		____

*trtp = too rare to price

Note: Satinized/frosted pink items worth the same as transparent pink pieces if the paint is in excellent condition with exception of 3-footed console bowl, $850. Crystal items 1/3 of pink prices, except 8.25" vase with foot, trtp*, and 12" tray with handles, $85; add $10 for ormolu.

Reproduction information: Whiskeys were only made in pink; new may be wrong shade. New have one stem for blossoms with veins molded in the leaves; old have branching stems and leaves have no veins. New bottoms have more glass than old ones. Cookie jar bottoms: new have indistinct design & bottom is totally smooth; old bottoms have pronounced 1.75" mold circle rim which is missing from the new ones. Cookie jar lids: new have curved edges of design, almost like a scallop, where design approaches outside edge of flat rim edge; old lids end the design in a straight line. Cookie jar: cookie jars were made in pink, blue, yellow and green. All other colors are new, including dark transparent green, jade-ite, and opaque white-ish custard colors. Shakers: new are made in wrong colors and have opening smaller than the .75" opening of the old. New shakers have ridges on 4 corners that extend to the top of the shaker; old ones have ridges that only go about ½ way up. 6" pitchers: new have totally smooth bottoms missing the pronounced 2.25" mold circle rim found on the old. Handles misshapen, should be able to squeeze a dime between handle & shoulder of pitcher. Old spout does not extend beyond shoulder of pitcher, new spout

MAYFAIR "OPEN ROSE" *(cont.)*

is 1/2" beyond side of pitcher. 3.5" juice tumblers: reproduced in pink & blue. New are missing a smooth band near top of tumbler & have raised ridges around the blossoms. Old tumblers have blossoms inside the smooth band. All jade-ite Mayfair is new. Candy dish: crude glass, often cloudy with bubbles. All ruby, amber, and cobalt blue is new. 12" platter with open handles: *old*–glass is transparent; *new*–cloudier glass measures 13.75" x 8.875".

MISS AMERICA *Reproduced*
(1933-1936 Hocking Glass Company)

	Pink	Crystal	Green	Ruby	Qty
Bowl, 4.5" berry			20		___
Bowl, 6.25" cereal	40	12	30		___
Bowl, 8", curves inward	175	75		600	___
Bowl, 8.75", straight sides	100	50			___
Bowl, 10" oval vegetable	70	15			___
Bowl, 12" diam, 2.25" deep	trtp*			1000	___
Butter dish base (same as 6.25" cereal bowl)	50	15			___
Butter dish lid *R*	800	300			___
Butter dish complete	825	315			___
Candy jar w/lid, 11.5"	200	125			___
Coaster, 5.75"	65	20			___
Comport, 5"	50	20			___
Creamer	40	10		500	___
Cup	40	10	20	400	___
Goblet, 3.75" tall wine	125	25		400	___
Goblet, 4.75" tall, 2.75" diam, juice	150	30		400	___
Goblet, 5.25" tall, 3.25" diam, water	100	25		400	___
Pitcher, 8" w/no ice lip *R*	225	75			___
Pitcher 8.5" w/ice lip	300	85			___
Plate, 5.75" sherbet	30	8	15	65	___
Plate, 6.75"			12		___
Plate, 8.5" salad	60	10	18	225	___
Plate, 10.25" dinner	60	20	35		___
Plate, 10.25" grill	50	12			___
Plate, 10.5" oval celery	50	15			___
Plate, 12" footed cake	90	40			___
Platter, 12.25"	100	20			___
Relish, 8.75", 4 sections	35	15			___
Relish, 11.75", 5 sections	trtp*	50			___
Salt & pepper *R*	100	40	500		___
Saucer	15	6		80	___
Sherbet	35	10		225	___
Sugar	40	10		500	___
Tidbit, 8.5" plate over 10.25" plate	180				___
Tumbler, 3.75" tall 2.25"+ diam, juice *R*	100	25		400	___
Tumbler, 4.5" water *R*	80	20	35		___
Tumbler. 5.75" iced tea *R*	175	35			___

Reproduction information: Anything in cobalt is new. Butter lids: pronounced curve near bottom, inside area where knob touches lid is filled with glass (old lid has hollow area where knob and lid meet). Look for a pronounced "star" with distinct points when looking from the underside of the lid through the knob as evident in only the old lids. Shakers: new measure 3.25" and old are actually a bit taller; old allow one to insert a finger inside and reach almost to the bottom with an absence of extra glass at the base that is found in new. New approx. 2" deep; old approx. 2.5" deep. Old shakers have neat ridges with which to screw & unscrew the lids;

MISS AMERICA *(cont.)*

new have rounded off ridges that overlap. Points of the Miss America design are sharper and consistent in quality with other pieces on old; new are more rounded. Pitchers without ice lip: old have a hump of extra glass above where the handle is attached; new are perfectly even around the rim. Tumblers: new have 2 vertical mold marks, old have 4. New have approx. ½" glass on bottom; old have approx. 1/4".

*trtp = too rare to price

Note: Ice blue pieces 10x the price of pink. Jade-ite pieces 4x the price of pink. Iridized crystal bowl, 10.5" diameter, 3.5" deep, $200.

MODERNTONE
(1934-early 1950s   Hazel-Atlas Glass Company)

	Cobalt	Amethyst	Platonite-pastels	Platonite-others	Qty
Ashtray, 5.5"	75				____
Ashtray, 7.75"	175				____
Bowl, 4.75" cream soup	25	25	8	20	____
Bowl, 5" diam., 1.25" deep, berry	35	30	8	15	____
Bowl, 5" deep cereal, w/white			8		____
Bowl, 5" deep cereal, no white			14		____
Bowl, 5" ruffled nut/ cream soup	100	65			____
Bowl, 6.5" cereal	165	165			____
Bowl, 7.75" soup	250	250			____
Bowl, 8", rim			15	35	____
Bowl, 8", no rim			20		____
Bowl, 9" diam., 2.5" deep, berry	65	50		35	____
Butter dish complete w/metal cover	150				____
Cheese dish complete w/metal cover	500				____
Coaster, 3.5" diam			15		____
Creamer	15	18	10	20	____
Cup	15	15	5	15	____
Custard, 3" diam., 2.5" deep	30	25			____
Mug, 4"				15	____
Plate, 5.75" sherbet	10	10	5	8	____
Plate, 6.75" salad	15	15		10	____
Plate, 7.75" luncheon	15	15			____
Plate 8.75" dinner	20	20	10	20	____
Plate, 10.5" sandwich	100	85	20		____
Platter, 11"	70	65		30	____
Platter, 12" x 9.5"	130	90	15	40	____
Salt & pepper	55	65	28	28	____
Saucer	5	5	3	4	____
Sherbet, 3" tall	15	15	6	12	____
Sugar base	15	18	10	20	____
Sugar lid (metal)	60				____
Tumbler, 2.25" whiskey	90				____
Tumbler, 3.75" juice	65	65			____
Tumbler, 4" water	50	45	14		____
Tumbler, 5.25" iced tea	170	170			____

Note: Items in pink and green ½ price of cobalt EXCEPT pink cup, $100, & pink saucer, $35. Crystal 25% of cobalt. Cobalt with gold trim: 11" platter, cup, saucer, berry bowl, dinner plate, 5.75" sherbet plate, and 7.75" luncheon plate, add 10%. Metal lid fits custard, $15.

MODERNTONE *(cont.)*

Little Hostess Party Set

	Gold, Gray, Orange, Turquoise	Aqua, Pink, Tan, Yellow	Blue, Green, Pink, Yellow	Back, Pink, White	Chartreuse, Green, Gray, Maroon	Qty
Creamer	15	15	15	15	15	____
Cup	10	15	10	15	10	____
Plate, 5.25"	8	12	10	12	8	____
Saucer	5	10	5	10	5	____
Sugar	15	15	15	15	15	____
Teapot	45	50		50	40	____
Teapot lid	75	175		175	70	____

Note: Add $20 for boxes in good condition, $35 for boxes in excellent condition.

MOONDROPS

(1932-1940s New Martinsville Glass
Manufacturing Company)

	Red & Cobalt	Ice Blue	Other colors	Qty
Ashtray, 4" diam.	40	35	20	____
Ashtray, 6" diam., 1" deep	40	35	20	____
Bottle, perfume ("rocket"), 6.25" tall	300	250	200	____
Bowl, cream soup, 4.25"	125	100	50	____
Bowl, 4.5" w/tab handle & 3 ft	50			____
Bowl, 5.25" berry	25	20	15	____
Bowl, 5.25" mayonnaise	75	60	40	____
Bowl, 6.75" soup	125	100	50	____
Bowl, 7.5" pickle	35	25	20	____
Bowl, 8" x 6" casserole (base only)	100	75	50	____
Bowl, 8.25" concave top	65	50	35	____
Bowl, 8.25" relish, divided w/3 feet	50	35	20	____
Bowl, 9.25" diam, 4.5" deep			75	____
Bowl, 9.75" ruffled w/3 legs	80	75	45	____
Bowl, 9.75" oval vegetable	60	45	35	____
Bowl, 9.75" oval w/2 handles	75	60	45	____
Bowl, 11.5" x 4.5 celery, boat shape	45	35	25	____
Bowl, 12" casserole w/3 ft	100	85	45	____
Bowl, 13" console w/wings	150	135	85	____
Butter dish base, 6" diam, 1.25" deep	150	125	100	____
Butter dish lid	400	325	250	____
Butter dish complete	550	450	350	____
Candle holder, 2" ruffled, ea.	40	35	30	____
Candle holder, 4.5", ea.	35	30	25	____
Candle holder, 4.75" ruffled, ea.	35	30	25	____
Candle holder, 5", ea. w/wings	75	60	45	____
Candle holder, 5.25", holds 3, ea.	100	75	50	____
Candle holder, 8.5" metal stem, ea.	30	25	20	____
Candy dish, 4.5"	50			____
Candy dish, 8"	50	40	30	____
Cocktail shaker, may or may not have handle	80	70	50	____

MOONDROPS *(cont.)*

	Red & Cobalt	Ice Blue	Other colors	Qty
Compote, 3.75" tall, just over 5.5" diam.			30	____
Compote, 4" tall, 5.75" diam.			45	____
Compote, 5.5" w/3 feet	35	30	25	____
Compote, 11.5"	75	65	45	____
Creamer, 2.75"	25	20	15	____
Creamer, 3.5"	20	18	12	____
Cup	20	18	12	____
Decanter w/stopper, 9.5"	90	80	60	____
Decanter w/stopper, 10.5"	100	85	70	____
Decanter w/stopper, 12" rocket	525	475	425	____
Decanter w/stopper, 13"	160	135	85	____
Goblet, 3" tall, 1.25" diam., liquor/cordial	50	40	30	____
Goblet, 3" tall, 1.25" diam., whiskey	20	20	20	____
Goblet, 3.25" tall, wine	35	30	20	____
Goblet, 3.5" tall, 2" diam, rocket wine	70	60	40	____
Goblet, 4" tall, cordial w/metal stem	35	30	20	____
Goblet, 4" tall, wine	30	25	20	____
Goblet, 4.25" tall, champagne/sherbet	35	30	20	____
Goblet, 4.5" tall. 3.5" diam.	30			____
Goblet, 4.75" tall, wine	35	30	20	____
Goblet, 5" tall, 2.75" diam., w/chromed stem	30			____
Goblet, 5.25" tall, champagne/sherbet w/metal stem	35	30	20	____
Goblet, 5.25" tall, wine w/metal stem	25	20	15	____
Goblet, 5.75" tall, wine w/mtl stem	25	20	15	____
Goblet, 6" tall, water w/mtl stem	35	30	20	____
Goblet, 6.5" tall, water	35	30	20	____
Gravy	150	125	100	____
Jelly, 4.75"	85	80	45	____
Jigger, 4.75"	100	100	80	____
Lid for 8" x 6" casserole	175	125	75	____
Mug, 5" Beer	50	40	30	____
Pitcher, 6.75"	180	160	120	____
Pitcher, 7" (with ice lip)	200	170	135	____
Pitcher, 8" (no ice lip)	200	175	130	____
Pitcher, 8.25" (no				

	Red & Cobalt	Ice Blue	Other colors	Qty
ice lip)	190	175	130	____
Plate, 5.75" bread & butter	15	12	10	____
Plate, 6" sherbet w/off-center indent	18	15	12	____
Plate, 6.5" sherbet	12	10	8	____
Plate, 7.5" salad	18	15	12	____
Plate, 8.5" luncheon	18	15	12	____
Plate, 9.5" dinner	35	30	20	____
Plate, 11.25" w/3 feet			30	____
Plate, 13.5" sandwich	70	40	30	____
Plate, 14" sandwich w/2 handles	80	50	30	____
Platter, 12"	45	40	30	____
Powder jar w/3 feet	400	350	250	____
Relish, 9.5" x 6" 2-part w/handles	trtp*			____
Relish, 12.75" x 7.75" 3-part w/4 feet	225			____
Saucer	10	8	5	____
Sherbet, 2.75" tall, 3.5" diam.	20	18	15	____
Sherbet, 4.5" tall	40	30	25	____
Sugar, 2.75"	20	18	15	____
Sugar, 3.5"	22	18	15	____
Tray, 7.5" for 2.75" creamer & sugar	50	40	30	____
Tumbler, 2.75" tall, 2.25" diam., whiskey, no handle	20	18	15	____
Tumbler, 2.75" tall whiskey w/handle	20	18	15	____
Tumbler, 3.25" tall, 2.25" diam., wine w/foot	20	18	15	____
Tumbler, 3.5" tall, 2" diam., rocket wine	18	15	12	____
Tumbler, 3.5" tall, 3" diam., w/handle	20			____
Tumbler, 3.75" tall w/foot & handle	20	18	15	____
Tumbler, 3.75" tall, 3" diam., no handle	20	18	15	____
Tumbler, 4.25" tall, 3" diam., no handle	25			____
Tumbler, 4.5" tall, 3" diam., no handle	20	18	15	____
Tumbler, 4.75" tall, w/foot & handle	35	30	20	____
Tumbler, 4.75" tall, 3.25" diam.,				

MOONDROPS *(cont.)*

	Red & Cobalt	Ice Blue	Other colors	Qty
w/handle	25			____
Tumbler, 5" tall, 3.5" diam., no handle	25	20	15	____
Tumbler, 5.25" tall water w/foot, no handle	40	35	20	____
Vase, 7.75"	80	75	65	____
Vase, 8.5" ("rocket")	310	285	210	____
Vase, 9.25" ("rocket")	285	260	185	____
Vase, 9.25" ("rocket")	285	260	185	____

Note: Add 25% for heavy silver or platinum overlay

*trtp = too rare to price

MOONSTONE

(1942-1946   Hocking Glass Company)

	Crystal w/bluish white	Qty
Bonbon, heart-shaped w/one handle	18	____
Bowl, 5.5" berry	20	____
Bowl, 5.5" dessert, crimped edge	15	____
Bowl, 6.5" crimped edge w/handles	22	____
Bowl, 7.75", crimped edge	15	____
Bowl, 7.75" relish, divided	15	____
Bowl, 9.5" crimped edge	38	____
Bowl, cloverleaf (3 sections)	15	____
Candleholder, ea.	15	____
Candy jar w/cover	40	____
Cigarette jar w/cover	38	____
Creamer	12	____
Cup	10	____
Goblet	20	____
Plate, 6.25" sherbet	10	____
Plate, 8.25" luncheon	20	____
Plate, 10.75" sandwich	38	____
Puff box w/cover, 4.75" round	35	____
Saucer	6	____
Sherbet	10	____
Sugar	12	____
Vase, 5.5"	24	____

Note: Items in green 4 times prices of crystal.

MOROCCAN AMETHYST

(1960s HAZEL Ware by Continental Can)

Colony design (square or rectangular base)	Amethyst	Qty
Bowl, dessert, 4.5"	20	_____
Bowl, 5.75" square	20	_____
Bowl, 6" round	18	_____
Bowl, 8" oval	30	_____
Bowl, 9.5" x 4.25" rectangle	18	_____
Bowl, 9.5" x 4.25" rectangle w/white overlay	25	_____
Bowl, 11"	40	_____
Chip & dip (11" & 6" bowls w/metal holder)	65	_____
Cup	5	_____
Plate, square dinner	14	_____
Plate, square snack w/cup rest	20	_____
Plate, 12" round	20	_____
Saucer	3	_____
Tray	20	_____
Tumbler, 4 sizes	10	_____

Note: Bowls may be found with metal handles or holders or used in combinations which will increase the price by a few dollars.

Octagonal (8-sided)	Amethyst	Qty
Bowl, 4.75" fruit	20	_____
Cup	5	_____
Plate, 6" dessert	14	_____
Plate, 7.25" salad	12	_____
Plate, 9.5" dinner	14	_____
Saucer, 6"	3	_____
Tidbit, 2-tier (6" & 7.25" plates)	25	_____
Tidbit, 3-tier (6", 7.25", 9.5" plates)	40	_____

Note: Dinner plate may be found with metal handle which will increase the price by a few dollars

Scalloped	Amethyst	Qty
Bowl, 4.75"	20	_____
Bowl, 8" (same as Punch base)	60	_____
Bowl, 14-piece Punch Set	155	_____
Punch bowl, 10.75" (white/Alpine)	35	_____
Base, 8"	60	_____
Cup	5	_____

MOROCCAN AMETHYST *(cont.)*

	Amethyst	Qty
Plate, 10" fan w/cup rest	12	_____
Salt & pepper	125	_____
Snack set (4 fan plates & 4 milk glass swirled cups), 10" x 6.5"	50	_____

Swirled	Amethyst	Qty
Candy w/lid, 4.75"	35	_____
Candy w/lid, 4.75" etched	45	_____
Candy w/lid, 7.25"	35	_____
Coaster for 6.25" iced tea (white/Alpine)	8	_____
Cocktail, 6.5" w/lip	45	_____
Cocktail shaker w/lid, 8.25"	70	_____
Cocktail stirrer	12	_____
Ice bucket, 5"	45	_____
Tumbler, 2.5"	10	_____
Tumbler, 3"	10	_____
Tumbler, 3.25"	10	_____
Tumbler, 3.75"	10	_____
Tumbler, 4.5" water	10	_____
Tumbler, 6.25" iced tea	15	_____
Vase, ruffled 8.5"	45	_____

Miscellaneous	Amethyst	Qty
Ashtray, 3.25" triangle	10	_____
Ashtray, 3.75" round	10	_____
Ashtray, 5" triangle	15	_____
Ashtray, 7" triangle	15	_____
Ashtray, 8" square	15	_____
Bowl, apple, small	65	_____
Bowl, apple, large	trtp*	_____
Bowl, leaf	35	_____
Bowl, 6.75" triangle w/3 feet and pressed design	15	_____
Candle holder, 5-pointed star 4.5" diam., ea.	25	_____
Coaster/ashtray, 3 sizes	15	_____
Goblet, 4" wine	10	_____
Goblet, 4.25" juice	10	_____
Goblet, 4.25" sherbet	10	_____
Goblet, 5.5" water	12	_____
Tumbler, 3.75" juice w/crinkled bottom	15	_____
Tumbler, 4.25" water w/crinkled bottom	18	_____

*trtp = too rare to price

MT. PLEASANT
(Early 1930s L.E. Smith Glass Company)

	Cobalt	Other colors	Qty
Ashtray	30	25	_____
Bonbon w/2 handles & foot	35	25	_____
Bonbon, 7" w/rolled-up edges & handles	30	20	_____
Bowl, 4" opening w/rolled-in edges (rose bowl)	35	25	_____
Bowl, 4.75" square w/foot	30	20	_____
Bowl, 5.5" mayonnaise w/3 feet	35	20	_____
Bowl, 5.75" w/3 feet		25	_____
Bowl, 6" square w/handles	35	20	_____
Bowl, 7" rolled-out edge w/3 feet	30	20	_____
Bowl, 8" scalloped w/2 handles	40	20	_____
Bowl, 8" square w/2 handles	40	20	_____
Bowl, 9" scalloped w/foot	40	20	_____
Bowl, 9.25" square w/foot	45	25	_____
Bowl, 10" scalloped	50	35	_____
Bowl, 10" rolled-up edge w/2 handles	50	35	_____
Candlestick, single ea.	25	15	_____
Candlestick, double ea.	35	20	_____
Creamer	25	15	_____
Cup	15	10	_____
Plate, 6" mint w/center handle	30	20	_____
Plate, 7" scalloped w/2 handles	15	10	_____
Plate, 8" scalloped (no handles)	15	10	_____
Plate, 8" square (no handles)	15	10	_____
Plate, 8" w/2 handles	15	10	_____
Plate, 8" leaf	25		_____
Plate, 8.25" square w/cup indent	18	10	_____
Plate, 9" grill	15	10	_____
Plate, 10.5" cake w/2 handles	30	15	_____
Plate, 10.5" cake, 1.25" high	40	15	_____

MT. PLEASANT *(cont.)*

	Cobalt	Other colors	Qty
Plate, 12" w/2 handles	40	15	____
Plate, sandwich server w/center handle	45	15	____
Salt & pepper, 2 styles	75	50	____
Saucer	10	5	____
Sherbet, 2 styles	20	12	____
Sugar	25	15	____
Tray, 8.75" w/center handle		35	____
Tray, 9" x 7.25" w/4 indents		40	____
Tumbler, 5.75"	28		____
Vase, 7.25"	30	15	____

Note: Sandwich server with Dogwood motif in silver overlay, $300.

NATIONAL (2200 Line)

(1940s-1950s Jeannette Glass Company)

	Crystal	Qty
Ashtray, 3"	3	____
Ashtray, 5" (indents for 4 cigarettes)	5	____
Bowl, 4.5" small berry	5	____
Bowl, 8.75" large berry	12	____
Bowl, 12" low	18	____
Bowl, 12" punch	35	____
Bowl, 15" console	20	____
Box w/lid, cigarette, 5" x 4", 2.25" deep	18	____
Candlestick holder, 2.75" w/3 feet, ea.	10	____
Candy jar w/lid	25	____
Coaster, 4"	5	____
Creamer	10	____
Cup, coffee	5	____
Cup, punch	3	____
Jar w/lid, 4.5" tall (condiment)	20	____
Lazy Susan, complete	65	____
15" tray	15	____
outer inserts, ea.	8	____
center insert	10	____
Pitcher, 4.75" juice/milk	25	____
Pitcher w/ice lip, 7"	22	____
Pitcher w/out ice lip, 7"	20	____
Plate, 8" luncheon	8	____
Relish, 12.5" 6-part (14.75" handle to handle)	12	____
Salt & pepper	15	____
Saucer	3	____
Sherbet, 3"	5	____
Sugar	10	____
Tray, 8" w/handles (13" handle to handle)	8	____
Tumbler, 3.5" w/foot	8	____
Tumbler, 5" w/foot	8	____
Tumbler, 4" flat	5	____
Tumbler, 6" flat	5	____
Vase, 9" tall	12	____

Note: Shell Pink vase, $70. Add $5 for chrome ormolu.

NEW CENTURY

(late 1920s-early 1930s   Hazel-Atlas Glass Company)

	Green	Amethyst & Pink	Cobalt	Qty
Ashtray/coaster, 5.25"	30			____
Bowl, 4.5" diam., 1.75" deep, berry	35			____
Bowl, 4.5" diam., 2.25" deep, berry	45			____
Bowl, 4.75" diam., 2.25" deep, cream soup	25			____
Bowl, 8" diam., 2.5" deep, berry	30			____
Bowl, 9" casserole base	30			____
Bowl, 9" casserole w/lid	75			____
Butter dish base, 6.75" diam.	30			____
Butter dish lid, 5.5" diam.	45			____
Butter dish complete	75			____
Creamer	12			____
Cup	12	15	22	____
Decanter w/stopper, 10.5"	90			____
Goblet, 4.25" tall, wine	50			____
Goblet, 4.5" tall, cocktail	50			____
Lid, 9" diam., fits 9" bowl	45			____
Pitcher, 7.75" w/or w/o ice lip	55	45	60	____
Pitcher, 8" w/or w/out ice lip	65	55	80	____
Plate, 6" sherbet	10			____
Plate, 7" breakfast	15			____
Plate, 8.5" salad	15	15		____
Plate, 9.5" luncheon		10		____
Plate, 10" dinner	35			____
Plate, 10" grill	15			____
Platter, 11" x 8.25"	30			____
Salt & pepper	45			____
Saucer	7	10	15	____
Sherbet, 3.75" diam., 3" tall	10			____
Sugar base	12			____
Sugar lid	28			____
Tumbler, 2.25" tall, 1.75" diam., whiskey	35			____
Tumbler, 3.5", 5 oz. flat	15	20	22	____
Tumbler, 3.5", 8 oz. flat	25			____
Tumbler, 4" tall, 2.75" diam., footed	40			____
Tumbler, 4.25" tall, 3" diam., flat water	15	20	22	____
Tumbler, 4.75", 9 oz. footed	30			____
Tumbler, 5" tall, 3.25" diam., footed	30	25	28	____
Tumbler, 5", 12 oz. flat	30	35	40	____

Note: Items in crystal ½ of green. Crystal with red trim: 6" sherbet plate, $9; sherbet, $10; 8.5" salad plate, $10; 10" dinner plate, $14; 4.25" tall, 3" diam. wine goblet, $12.

NEWPORT
(mid-1930s   Hazel-Atlas Glass Company)

	Cobalt	Amethyst	Fired-on colors & white	Qty
Bowl, 4.25" berry	20	20	8	____
Bowl, 4.75" cream soup	20	20	10	____
Bowl, 5.25" cereal	40	40		____
Bowl, 8.25" berry	45	40	15	____
Creamer	15	15	8	____
Cup	15	10	8	____
Plate, 6" sherbet	12	10	5	____
Plate, 8.5" luncheon	15	12	8	____
Plate, 8.75" & 9" dinner	30	30		____
Plate, 11.5" sandwich	55	55	15	____
Platter, 11.75"	50	50	15	____
Salt & pepper	70	70	30	____
Saucer	8	6	2	____
Sherbet	15	15	8	____
Sugar	15	15	8	____
Tumbler, 4.5"	45	45	15	____

Note: Pink pieces ½ price of Amethyst. Crystal pieces ½ price of fired-on colors.

NORMANDIE *Reproduced*
(1933-1939   Federal Glass Company)

	Amber	Pink	Iridescent	Qty
Bowl, 5" berry	12	18	4	____
Bowl, 6.5" cereal	20	40	8	____
Bowl, 6.75" soup, 1.25" deep		70		____
Bowl, 8.5" berry	30	50	15	____
Bowl, 10" oval vegetable	30	60	15	____
Creamer *R*	12	20	10	____
Cup *R*	10	12	8	____
Pitcher *R*	95	210		____
Plate, 6" sherbet	10	14	4	____
Plate, 7.75" salad	25	20	50	____
Plate, 9.75" luncheon	25	20	10	____
Plate, 11" dinner	60	350	10	____
Plate, 11" grill	18	45	8	____
Platter, 11.75"	45	45	15	____
Salt & pepper *R*	70	120		____
Saucer *R*	8	12	2	____
Sherbet	7	10	5	____
Sugar base *R*	15	20	10	____
Sugar lid, pointed edges *R*	125	500		____
Sugar lid, round edges *R*	trtp*	trtp*		____
Tumbler, 4" tall	50	130		____
Tumbler, 4.5" tall, 2.75" diam	40	100		____
Tumbler, 5" tall, 3" diam	65	165		____

*trtp = too rare to price

Reproduction information: Brand new line of glass similar to pink
Normandie is being imported from China: cup, saucer, 9" plate,
creamer, sugar with lid, pitcher, and shakers with metal lids that
look old.

OLD CAFÉ

(1936-1938 Hocking Glass Company)

	Pink	Ruby	Crystal	Qty
Ashtray, 3.75″ diam			20	____
Bowl, 3.75″ diam., 1.5″ deep, berry w/handles	12	40	5	____
Bowl, 4.5″ diam., 1.5″ deep, w/handles	12		6	____
Bowl, 5″ diam., 2″ deep, w/1 handle	12			
Bowl, 5.5″ cereal	28	22	10	____
Bowl, 6.5″ w/handles	30			____
Bowl, 9″ w/handles	24	34	8	____
Candy jar w/lid (crystal or pink base, ruby lid), 7″	34		20	____
Cup	10	10	5	____
Lamp, 7.5″ tall	145	310	130	____
Lazy Susan pedestal, 2-2.25″ tall			150	
Mint tray, 8″ low & flared	20	20	6	____
Olive dish, 6″ oval	20			____
Pitcher, 6″, 36 oz., juice	350			____
Pitcher, 8″, 80 oz., water	200			____
Plate, 6″ sherbet	15		2	____
Plate, 10″ dinner	70			____
Relish set 15″ crystal base, 5 ruby inserts, 7″ candy jar w/lid		200		
Saucer	8		2	____
Sherbet, 2″ tall, 3.75″ diam	18	20	5	____
Tumbler, 3″ tall, 2.5″ diam, juice	20	25	8	____
Tumbler, 4″ tall, 3.25″ diam, water	24	34	8	____
Vase, 7.25″ tall, 5.75″ diam	40	50	20	____

Note: Mint tray, 8″, add $5 for metal handle. Relish set, 15″ crystal base, 5 green inserts, clear candy jar with lid, $150. Iridized purple, 8″ mint tray, trtp*. White/VitrocK: candy jar, $15; vase, $25.

*trtp = too rare to price

OLD ENGLISH

(1928-1929 Indiana Glass Company)

	All colors	Qty
Bowl, 4"	45	____
Bowl, 9" w/foot	35	____
Bowl, 9.5" flat	50	____
Bowl, 11" diam., 3.5" deep, w/foot, fruit	50	____
Candlestick, 4" tall, 4.25" diam., ea.	30	____
Candy jar w/lid, 4.5"	90	____
Candy jar w/lid, 7.5"	75	____
Cheese & crackers	75	____
10.25" plate w/3.75" indent	40	____
2.75" tall comport, 4.75" diameter	35	____
Comport, 3.5", 2 styles	35	____
Comport, 4.75", ruffled	50	____
Creamer, 4.5"	25	____
Egg cup (only in crystal)	12	____
Goblet, 5.75"	40	____
Pitcher, 9.25"	100	____
Pitcher cover, 6" diam.	140	____
Sandwich server w/ center handle	75	____
Sherbet, 2 styles	25	____
Sugar base	25	____
Sugar lid	40	____
Tumbler, 4.5" tall, 3.25" diam.	30	____
Tumbler, 5.5" tall, 3.75" diam.	40	____
Vase, 5.25" fan	65	____
Vase, 8"	65	____
Vase, 8.25"	65	____
Vase, 12"	80	____

Note: Fired-on colors: 9.25" tall pitcher, $125; cover for pitcher, $175; candy jar w/lid, too rare to price.

ORCHID

(1929-1930s   Paden City Glass
Manufacturing Company)

	Black, Cobalt blue, & Red	Other colors	Qty
Bowl, 4.75"	65	30	＿＿＿
Bowl, 8.5" w/handles	150	100	＿＿＿
Bowl, 8.75"	150	100	＿＿＿
Bowl, 10" w/foot	200	125	＿＿＿
Bowl, 11"	200	100	＿＿＿
Cake stand, 9.5" diam	175	100	＿＿＿
Candlestick, 5.75" ea.	220	120	＿＿＿
Candy box w/cover (square shape)	220	120	＿＿＿
Candy box w/cover (3-leaf clover shape)	250	120	＿＿＿
Candy w/lid, 10.5" tall, 6.25" diam.		120	＿＿＿
Comport, 3.25" tall	65	30	＿＿＿
Comport, 6.75" tall	150	75	＿＿＿
Comport, 10.5" tall, 6.25" diam.		85	＿＿＿
Creamer	100	60	＿＿＿
Decanter, 10.5" tall w/crystal stopper	*trtp		＿＿＿
Ice Bucket, 6"	220	120	＿＿＿
Mayonnaise, 3-piece set	200	120	＿＿＿
Plate, 8.5"	85		＿＿＿
Plate, 10.5" w/2 handles & foot	150		＿＿＿
Sandwich server w/ center handle, 10" diam	125	75	＿＿＿
Sugar	100	60	＿＿＿
Vase, 5"	300		＿＿＿
Vase, 8"	400		＿＿＿
Vase, 8.25" elliptical	280	120	＿＿＿
Vase, 10"	400	150	＿＿＿

*trtp = too rare to price

OVIDE

(1923-1935   Hazel-Atlas Glass Company)

	Decor-ated	Deco	Black	Green	Qty
Bowl, 3.75" diam., 1" deep				15	____
Bowl, 4.75" berry	10				____
Bowl, 5" diam., 1.75" deep				15	____
Bowl, 5.5" cereal	15				____
Bowl, 8" berry	25				____
Candy dish w/lid	40		50	30	____
Cocktail, stemmed			8	4	____
Creamer	15	85	12	4	____
Cup	10	60	8	3	____
Plate, 6" sherbet	8			3	____
Plate, 8" luncheon	10	45		4	____
Plate, 9" dinner	20				____
Platter, 11"	25				____
Salt & pepper	35		35	30	____
Saucer	5	18	5	3	____
Sherbet, 3" tall, 3.5" diam.	12	50	8	3	____
Sugar	15	85	12	4	____
Tumbler, 3.75" tall, 2.5" diam.	35	95			____
Tumbler, 4" tall, 2.5" diam.	35				____

Note: Pink creamer & sugar, $14 ea. Add $5 for silver overlay.

OYSTER AND PEARL

(1938-1940   Anchor Hocking Glass Corporation)

	Ruby	Pink	Crystal, other colors, & fired-on	Qty
Bowl, 5.25" diam, 1.5" deep, jelly, heart-shaped w/1 handle	25	15	10	___
Bowl, 5.5" diam, round w/1 handle	25	15		___
Bowl, 6.5" diam, 2.5" deep, bon bon w/2 handles	40	18		___
Bowl, 10.5" diam, 3.75" deep console	70	40	12	___
Candle holder, 3.5" ea.	35	25	8	___
Plate, 13.5" sandwich	60	35	10	___
Relish, 10.25" oval, 2-part		25		___
Relish, 10.25" oval, 3-part		trtp*		___
Tray, 10.5" x 7.75"			12	___

*trtp=too rare to price

PARK AVENUE

(1941-early 1970s   Federal Glass Company)

	Crystal & Amber	Qty
Ashtray, 3.5"	5	____
Ashtray, 4.5"	5	____
Bowl, 4.75" dessert	5	____
Bowl, 8.5" vegetable	10	____
Candle holder, 5" each	10	____
Tumbler, 2.25" whiskey, 1.25 oz.	4	____
Tumbler, 3.5" juice, 4.5 oz.	4	____
Tumbler, 3.75", water 9 oz.	4	____
Tumbler, 4.75", water 10 oz.	6	____
Tumbler, 5.25" iced tea, 12 oz.	6	____

Note: 4.75" dessert bowls in frosted colors $8 each.

PARROT (SYLVAN)
(1931-1932 Federal Glass Company)

	Green	Amber	Qty
Bowl, 5" berry	55	45	____
Bowl, 7" soup	80	70	____
Bowl, 8" berry	110	95	____
Bowl, 10" vegetable	90	95	____
Butter dish base	90	230	____
Butter dish lid	500	1400	____
Butter complete	590	1630	____
Creamer	75	85	____
Cup	60	65	____
Hot dish/coaster, 5" scalloped	1000	1200	____
Hot dish/coaster, 5" smooth	1200		____
Jam dish, 7"		60	____
Pitcher	trtp*		____
Plate, 5.75" sherbet	65	50	____
Plate, 7.5" salad	60		____
Plate, 9" dinner	95	65	____
Plate, 10.5" round grill	95		____
Plate, 10.5" square grill		75	____
Platter, 11.25"	90	110	____
Salt & pepper	400		____
Saucer	25	25	____
Sherbet, cone-shaped w/foot (Madrid style)	40	40	____
Sherbet, 4.25" tall w/stem	1700		____
Sugar base	60	60	____
Sugar lid	320	675	____
Tumbler, 4.25" flat	200	150	____
Tumbler, 5.5" flat	225	175	____
Tumbler, 5.5" w/foot		200	____
Tumbler, 5.75" w/foot	185	150	____

Note: Blue sherbet, $275. Crystal square grill plate, $200.

*trtp = too rare to price

PATRICIAN *Reproduced*
(1933-1937 Federal Glass Company)

	Green	Pink	Amber	Qty
Bowl, 4.75" cream soup	25	20	17	_____
Bowl, 5" berry	15	14	14	_____
Bowl, 6" cereal	32	28	28	_____
Bowl, 8.5" berry	50	45	50	_____
Bowl, 10" x 7.5" vegetable, 2" deep	45	40	35	_____
Butter dish base, 6.75" x 1.25" deep	100	165	65	_____
Butter dish lid	60	75	35	_____
Butter complete	160	240	100	_____
Cookie jar/lid	600		100	_____
Creamer	18	18	14	_____
Cup	12	14	10	_____
Jam dish, 6.75"	55	45	40	_____
Pitcher, 8" molded handle	150	130	120	_____
Pitcher, 8.25" applied handle	175	160	160	_____
Plate, 6" bread & butter	16	16	10	_____
Plate, 7.5" salad	24	24	18	_____
Plate, 9.25" luncheon	20	22	15	_____
Plate, 11" dinner	50	45	14	_____
Plate, 11" grill	25	20	14	_____
Platter, 11.5" x 8.5"	45	50	40	_____
Salt & pepper	75	120	65	_____
Saucer	12	12	10	_____
Sherbet *R*	18	15	12	_____
Sugar base	18	18	14	_____
Sugar lid	70	70	70	_____
Tumbler, 4" flat	45	45	30	_____
Tumbler, 4.25" tall, 2.75" diam., flat	40	40	30	_____
Tumbler, 5.25" tall, 3" diam., w/foot	95		70	_____
Tumbler, 5.5" tall, just over 3" diam., flat	55	50	45	_____

Note: Crystal 1/2 of Amber EXCEPT: complete butter, $125; 8.25" pitcher w/applied handle, $175; 10.5" dinner plate, $25.

Reproduction information: New sherbets amber only, color too light, pattern crude.

PATRICK

(1930s   Lancaster Glass Company)

	Rose	Topaz	Qty
Bowl, 9" fruit w/handles	200	150	____
Bowl, 11.5" low console	180	140	____
Candlestick, ea.	85	85	____
Candy bowl w/cover, 7" diam., 4.5" tall w/3 feet	200	175	____
Cheese & cracker set, 2-pcs	200	175	____
Creamer	90	50	____
Cup	85	50	____
Goblet, 4" tall, stemmed cocktail	100	100	____
Goblet, 4.75" tall, juice	100	100	____
Goblet, 6" tall, 2.75" diam, water	100	100	____
Mayonnaise, 3-piece set	240	220	____
Plate, 7" sherbet	30	20	____
Plate, 7.5" salad	40	30	____
Plate, 8.75" luncheon	60	40	____
Plate, 9"	60		____
Plate, 11" sandwich w/handles	100	85	____
Saucer	25	15	____
Sherbet, 4.75" tall, 3.5" diam, w/stem	80	65	____
Sugar	90	50	____
Tray, 11" sandwich w/center handle	175	140	____

PEACOCK & ROSE

(1928-1930s   Paden City Glass Manufacturing Company)

	Any color	Qty
Bowl, 8.5" flat	130	____
Bowl, 8.5" oval	200	____
Bowl, 8.75" w/foot	200	____
Bowl, 9" w/handles, 10-sided	150	____
Bowl, 9.5" center handle	175	____
Bowl, 9.5" w/foot	200	____
Bowl, 10" w/foot	200	____
Bowl, 10" w/2 handles	275	____
Bowl, 10.5" w/rolled edge	500	____
Bowl, 10.5" center handle	175	____
Bowl, 10.5" w/foot	200	____
Bowl, 10.5" flat	200	____
Bowl, 11" rolled edge	475	____
Bowl, 14" rolled edge	220	____
Cake plate, 10.5" w/foot	150	____
Candlestick, 5" across, ea.	85	____
Candy box w/lid, 7"	200	____
Cheese and cracker	200	____
Comport, 3.25" tall	130	____
Comport, 5.5" tall, 7.5" diam.	150	____
Comport, 6.25" tall	150	____
Comport, 7.75" diam., flared & scalloped	150	____
Comport, 8" diam., rolled & scalloped	150	____
Creamer, small	60	____
Creamer, 4"	80	____
Creamer, 4.5"	70	____
Ice bucket, 6"	200	____
Ice tub, 6.25"	200	____
Mayonnaise, 3 piece set	130	____
Pitcher, 5"	265	____
Plate, 10" w/ 8 sides	100	____
Plate, 11" x 7.75" w/foot	150	____
Relish, 6.25"	130	____
Sugar, small	60	____
Sugar, 4"	80	____
Sugar, 4.5"	70	____
Tray, 10" sandwich w/center handle	150	____
Tray, 10.75" oval w/foot	200	____
Tray, muffin, 11" x 7", 3.75" tall	150	____
Tumbler, 2.25"	100	____
Tumbler, 3"	80	____

PEACOCK & ROSE *(cont.)*

Tumbler, 4"	80	____
Tumbler, 4.75" ftd.	80	____
Tumbler, 5.25"	100	____
Vase, 5", elliptical	250	____
Vase, 6.5"	400	____
Vase, 8.25", elliptical	400	____
Vase, 10" 2 styles	275	____
Vase, 12" 2 styles	300	____

Note: 12" vase in Ruby, yellow, or cobalt, $850 each. 10.5" rolled edge bowl only known to be in blue.

PEBBLE OPTIC
(1927-1932   Federal Glass Company)

	Green	Qty
Bowl, 4.5" fruit	12	____
Bowl, 6" cereal	16	____
Bowl, 7.5" berry	40	____
Creamer	14	____
Cup	8	____
Plate, 6" sherbet	8	____
Plate, 8" luncheon	12	____
Salt & pepper	trtp*	____
Saucer	4	____
Sherbet	10	____
Sugar base	14	____
Sugar lid	125	____
Tumbler, 1.75" whiskey	10	____
Tumbler, 2.25"	10	____
Tumbler, 3"	10	____
Tumbler, 3.75"	12	____
Tumbler, 4.25"	12	____
Tumbler, 5"	12	____
Tumbler, 5.25"	15	____

*trtp = too rare too price

Note: Crystal items half those in green.

PETALWARE
(1930-1942 Macbeth-Evans Glass Company)

	Pink & Fired-On Colors	Monax & Cremax Plain	Decorated w/colored bands or ivy, & Ivrene	Crystal	Qty
Bowl, cream soup, 4.5"	24	18	22	5	___
Bowl, 5.75" dessert/cereal	18	12	20	5	___
Bowl, 7" soup		60	90		___
Bowl, 8.75" berry	35	45	40	12	___
Creamer, 3.25"	15	10	15	5	___
Cup	10	8	12	5	___
Lampshade (multiple shapes)		25			
Pitcher				30	___
Plate, cream soup liner		20			___
Plate, 6.5" bread & butter	10	10	15	4	___
Plate, 8" salad	15	12	18	4	___
Plate, 9" dinner	25	25	28	6	___
Plate, 9.25" dinner			18		___
Plate, 10.5"		15			___
Plate, 10.75" salver	20				___
Plate, 11" salver	22	15	30	8	___
Plate, 12" salver	24	20			___
Platter, 13"	34	25	40	10	___
Saucer	5	5	7		___
Sherbet, 4"		22			___
Sherbet, 4.25"	18	15	22	5	___
Sugar, 3.5"	15	10	15	5	___
Tidbits, 2-tier, 8.75" berry on top of inverted 7" soup bowl		120		5	___
Tidbits, 2- or 3-tier servers, several sizes of plates	40	25	40	15	___
Tidbits, 4-tier		75			___
Tumbler, 3.5" tall				15	___
Tumbler, 4" tall, 2.75" diam			40		___
Tumbler, 4.5" tall, 2.75" diam	120		40	15	___
Tumbler, 5.25" tall, 2.75" diam			40		___

Note: Cobalt Blue condiment, $10; add $5 for metal lid with wooden knob; add $8 for metal lid with Bakelite knob. Cobalt 9" berry bowl, $50; 4.5" sherbet, $30. **Red trim with flowers** (Mountain Flowers) twice prices of pink. Monax with gold trim 1/2 price of plain. Bluebirds: 7.75" plate, $45; 11" plate, $85. Plates with black floral motif, $25 each.

"PHILBE" FIRE-KING DINNERWARE

(1940   Hocking Glass Company)

	Blue	Pink & Green	Crystal	Qty
Bowl, 7.25" salad	300	120	50	____
Bowl, 10" oval vegetable	500	200	100	____
Candy jar w/lid, 4"	2000	1500	500	____
Cookie jar w/lid	trtp*	trtp*	trtp*	____
Creamer, 3.25"	320	220	75	____
Cup	300	200	100	____
Goblet, 7.25"	600	300	150	____
Pitcher, 6" juice	2200	1200	500	____
Pitcher, 8.5"	4000	2500	600	____
Plate, 6" sherbet	200	100	50	____
Plate, 8" luncheon	180	100	40	____
Plate, 10" heavy sandwich	350	200	50	____
Plate, 10.5" salver	250	125	50	____
Plate, 10.5" grill	250	125	50	____
Plate, 11.5" salver	300	125	50	____
Platter, 12" w/tab handles	500	300	80	____
Saucer/sherbet plate	200	100	50	____
Sherbet, 4.75" stemmed	1500	500		____
Sugar	320	220	75	____
Tumbler, 3.5" juice w/foot	500	350	80	____
Tumbler, 4" water, no foot	400	300	80	____
Tumbler, 5.5" tall, 3.5" diam. w/foot	300	200	80	____
Tumbler, 6.5" iced tea w/foot	300	200	80	____

Note: Royal Ruby too rare to price.

*trtp = too rare to price

PIECRUST

(1946-1954   Pyrex, Macbeth-Evans Division of
Corning Glass Works)

	Blue	Qty
Bowl, 5" small berry	8	____
Bowl, 6" oatmeal	15	____
Bowl, 7.75" soup	25	____
Bowl, 9" large berry	35	____
Bowl, 9.25" rimmed soup	50	____
Creamer	10	____
Cup	7	____
Mug	45	____
Pitcher, 5.25"	45	____
Plate, 6.75" sherbet	6	____
Plate, 7" salad	10	____
Plate, 9.25" dinner	15	____
Plate, 12" salver	28	____
Saucer	3	____
Sherbet	20	____
Sugar	10	____

PILLAR OPTIC

(1930s Hocking Glass Company)

Dinnerware	Green	Pink	Crystal	Qty
Ashtray	20			___
Cup	12	15		___
Mug	60		20	___
Pitcher, 8" tall, 60 oz.	30	30	30	___
Pitcher, 8.5" tall w/ice lip	50	50	25	___
Pitcher, 8.5" tall, no ice lip, fancy handle, beer	45	45	20	___
Pitcher, tilted ball	85	85		___
Plate, 8" luncheon	20			___
Pretzel jar w/lid	150	125	60	___
Saucer	5	5		___
Sherbet, 3.25" w/foot	15			___
Tumbler, 2.25" whiskey, no foot		15		___
Tumbler, 3" cordial w/foot	15	15		___
Tumbler, 4" water, no foot		15		___
Tumbler, 5.5" tall water w/foot	25			___
Tumbler, 5.5" tall iced tea, no foot		25		___

Note: Aquamarine pitcher, too rare to price. Satinized/frosted pretzel jar with lid, $45. Add $5 for striped decorations. Royal Ruby items, $75 each.

Kitchenware	Green & Pink	Qty
Canister, glass lid, 8.5" tall, 4 oz.	100	___
Jar, metal screw lid, 8" tall, 64 oz.	85	___
Jar, metal screw lid, 8" tall, 64 oz. with original label in good condition	135	___
Mixing bowl, 6.75" diam	25	___
Mixing bowl, 7.5" diam	25	___
Mixing bowl, 8.75" diam	25	___
Mixing bowl, 9.75" diam	35	___
Mixing bowl, 10.5" diam	45	___
Mixing bowl, 11.5" diam	100	___
Percolator top	18	___
Reamer, orange	55	___
Refrigerator dish, 6" oval	65	___
Refrigerator dish, 7" oval	65	___
Refrigerator dish, 8" oval	65	___
Shaker, Range size	35	___
Shaker, Range size with original sticker (salt, pepper, flour, sugar) in good condition	45	___
Syrup dispenser, metal lid, 4.5" tall	75	___
Water bottle, 8.5" tall	45	___
Water bottle, 10" tall	45	___

PINEAPPLE AND FLORAL
Reproduced
(1932-1937   Indiana Glass Company)

	Crystal, Fired-on red, & Amber	Qty
Ashtray, 4.5" x 3"	8	____
Bowl, cream soup	12	____
Bowl, 4.75" berry	10	____
Bowl, 6" oatmeal	20	____
Bowl, 7.25" diam., 2.5" deep, berry *R*	5	____
Bowl, 10" oblong vegetable	8	____
Comport, 3" tall	8	____
Comport, 6.5" diamond shaped *R*	4	____
Creamer	5	____
Cup	5	____
Plate, 6" sherbet	3	____
Plate, 8.25" salad	5	____
Plate, 9" dinner	12	____
Plate, 9.5" w/center indent	8	____
Plate, 11" cake	8	____
Plate, 11.5" w/center indent	10	____
Platter	8	
Relish, 11.5" 3-part, 11.5" x 7.25"	8	____
Saucer	2	____
"Servitor" 2-tier 8" & 11" plates	15	____
"Servitor" 2-tier 6" & 9" plate	15	____
Sherbet	8	____
Sugar	5	____
Tumbler, 4"	15	____
Tumbler, 4.5" iced tea	20	____
Vase, 12"	30	____
Vase holder (metal)	30	____

Reproduction information: Other fired on colors and light pink are new. The new 7.25"-7.5" bowl has a 9-pointed star halfway between the two largest blossoms and about 1.5" below them. The rim is smooth.

Note: Green: dinner plate, $15; comport, $15. White: 4" tumbler, $20; comport, $5. 2x value for sterling silver overlay. Advertising ashtray, $20.

PRETZEL

(1930s-1970s   Indiana Glass Company)

	Crystal	Qty
Bowl, 4.5" fruit cup	10	____
Bowl, 7.75" soup, 1.5" deep	12	____
Bowl, 8.5" x 4" oblong pickle w/handles, 1.5" deep	8	____
Bowl, 9.5" berry, 3" deep	20	____
Bowl, 10.25" x 5" oblong celery, 1.5" deep	5	____
Creamer	10	____
Cup	8	____
Leaf, 7" x 5.75" olive	8	____
Pitcher	trtp*	____
Plate, 6"	4	____
Plate, 6.25" w/tab (fruit cup plate or cheese plate)	12	____
Plate, 7.25" square snack plate w/cup indent	12	____
Plate, 7.25" 3-part square	12	____
Plate, 8.25" salad	8	____
Plate, 9.25" dinner	12	____
Plate, 11.5" sandwich/cake	15	____
Saucer	2	____
Sugar	10	____
Tray, 7" x 7" snack w/cup ring	15	____
Tray, 10.25" oblong celery	5	____
Tumbler, 3.5"	75	____
Tumbler, 4.5"	75	____
Tumbler, 5.5"	100	____

*trtp = too rare to price

Note: Teal cup, $125; saucer, $45. Plates with center design twice those with plain center. Fired-on pink 7.5" soup bowl, $12; 6.25" plate with tab, $12; 9.25" dinner plate, $12.

PRIMO

(1932   United States Glass Company)

	Yellow	Green	Qty
Bowl, 4.5"	22	18	____
Bowl, 6.25"	35	30	____
Bowl, 11" footed console bowl	45	35	____
Cake plate, 10"	35	30	____
Coaster or ashtray, 5.25" x 4.75"	15	12	____
Creamer	20	15	____
Cup	15	12	____
Plate, 5.5" sherbet w/indent	12		____
Plate, 6.25"	12	10	____
Plate, 7.5"	12	10	____
Plate, 9.5" grill w/cup ring	50	50	____
Plate, 9.5" grill no cup ring	20	15	____
Plate, 10" dinner	25	22	____
Saucer	5	4	____
Sherbet	18	15	____
Sugar	20	15	____
Tumbler, 5.75"	30	25	____

Note: Black items 3x those in yellow.

PRINCESS *Reproduced*
(1931-1934 Hocking Glass Company)

	Pink & Green	Topaz & Apricot	Qty
Ashtray, 4.5″	85	120	____
Bowl, 4.25″ berry	30	50	____
Bowl, 5.5″ oatmeal	45	40	____
Bowl, 7.25″ diam., almost 1.5″ deep		50	____
Bowl, 8″ diam., 2.5″ deep		50	____
Bowl, 9″ salad, octagonal	65	150	____
Bowl, 9.5″ orange or flower (hat shaped)	80	160	____
Bowl 10″ vegetable	50	65	____
Butter dish base	55	trtp*	____
Butter dish lid	80	trtp*	____
Butter complete	135	trtp*	____
Cake stand, 10″	50		____
Candy jar w/lid *R*	95		____
Coaster	85	120	____
Cookie jar/lid	85		____
Creamer	20	20	____
Cup	15	10	____
Pitcher, 5.75″ no foot	80	700	____
Pitcher, 7.5″ w/foot	800		____
Pitcher, 8″ no foot	70	125	____
Plate, 5.5″ sherbet or saucer	14	6	____
Plate, 8.25″ salad	25	20	____
Plate, 9″ dinner		35	____
Plate, 9.5″ dinner	35	25	____
Plate, 9.5″ grill	16	8	____
Plate, 10.25″ sandwich w/closed handles (add 1″ if measuring handles)	30	175	____
Plate, 10.5″ grill w/closed handles	15	10	____
Platter, 12″	50	65	____
Relish, 7.5″ divided	50	100	____
Relish, 7.5″	200	250	____
Relish, 10″, 3-part w/3feet	trtp*		____
Salt & pepper, 4.5″ *R*	75	90	____
Spice shaker, 5.5″ ea	30		____
Saucer or sherbet plate	14	5	____
Sherbet	25	35	____
Sugar base	20	20	____
Sugar lid	25	20	____
Tidbit, 8.25″ plate above 9.5″ plate	75		____
Tumbler, 3.5″ juice	35	35	____
Tumbler, 4″ water	32	30	____
Tumbler. 4.75″ square foot	65		____

PRINCESS *(cont.)*

	Pink & Green	Topaz & Apricot	Qty
Tumbler, 5.5" iced tea	40	30	____
Tumbler, 5.5" round foot	30	25	____
Tumbler. 6.5" iced tea, round foot	125	175	____
Vase, 8"	65		____

Reproduction information: Candy jar in green: crude & foot missing rays. In pink the new foot is smooth & missing rays. Old knobs have 2 flat sides & two round sides; new knobs are flat on all 4 sides. All blue candy jars or other odd colors or shades of colors are new. Shakers new crude, low quality glass may have bubbles, odd colors and shades of colors. Anything in cobalt blue is new. The candy jar is reproduced in dark amber.

Note: Satinized pieces 1/2 value of transparent items in same color.

Note: Rare Items in	**Pink**	**Qty:**
Celery, 11.5"	500	____
Plate, 10.5" dinner	500	____
Plate, 11.5" grill	250	____
Relish, 8.75" 3-part round	trtp*	____
Relish, 9" w/foot, no sections	trtp*	____

Note: Items in	**Ice Blue**	**Qty:**
Cookie jar w/lid	1000	____
Cup	175	____
Plate, 5.5" sherbet/saucer	175	____
Plate, 9" dinner	225	____
Plate, 9.5" grill	175	____
Relish, 3-part	225	____

*trtp = too rare to price

PYRAMID *Reproduced*

(1928-1932...see note below
Indiana Glass Company)

	Green	Pink	Yellow	Crystal	Qty
Bowl, 4.75" berry *R*	45	45	50	20	____
Bowl, 8.5" berry	60	60	95	30	____
Bowl, 9.5" oval	60	60	85	30	____
Bowl, 9.5" oval pickle w/handles & rounded edges	65	65	95	30	____
Creamer	40	45	55	25	____
Ice tub, 5.25" diam., 6" deep	140	140	275	55	____
Ice tub cover, 5.25" diam			555	trtp*	____
Pitcher, 9.5" tall	375	375	600	555	____
Relish, 4-part, 8" x 8" x 5.75" tall at handle *R*	70	70	85	30	____
Sugar	40	45	55	25	____
Tray w/center handle for creamer & sugar	50	50	80	35	____
Tumbler, 8 oz., 5.5" tall w/2.25" or 2.5" base *R*	75	75	125	100	____
Tumbler, 11 oz.	95	95	140	125	____

Reproduction information: Items marked as reproduced were part of Indiana Glass Company's Tiara line in the 1970s and were issued in the new colors of blue and black.

*trtp = too rare to price

QUEEN MARY

(1936-1939   Hocking Glass Company)

	Pink	Crystal	Qty
Ashtray, 2 styles	10	5	____
Bowl, 4" diam, 2" deep, w/ or w/out single handle	8	5	____
Bowl, 4.5" berry w/2 handles	8	5	____
Bowl, 5" berry	15	8	____
Bowl, 5" diam., 2.75" deep, flared, mayonaise	50	25	____
Bowl, 6" cereal	30	10	____
Bowl, 6.5" diam, 2.25" deep lug soup w/handles	15	8	____
Bowl, 7.5" diam, berry	15	8	____
Bowl, 8" berry w/2 handles	20	10	____
Butter dish base	30	10	____
Butter dish metal lid	35		____
Butter complete w/metal lid	65		____
Butter dish glass lid	120	20	____
Butter complete w/glass lid	150	30	____
Candy Dish, 7" cloverleaf	75	15	____
Candy Jar w/lid	65	25	____
Candlestick, 4.5" ea.		15	____
Celery/pickle, 5" x 10"	40	15	____
Cigarette holder, 3" x 1.75" x 2" deep		14	____
Cigarette Jar, 2" x 3" oval w/metal lid	30	15	____
Coaster, 3.5" round	12	5	____
Coaster/ashtray, 4.25" sq.	12	5	____
Comport, 5.75"	40	15	____
Creamer w/foot, 2.75"	125	25	____
Creamer, flat, 2.5"	18	8	____
Cup, 2 sizes	8	6	____
Custard, 3.75" diam.	30		____
Plate, 6" sherbet	10	4	____
Plate, 6.5"	10	4	____
Plate, 8.5" salad		6	____
Plate, 10" dinner	65	28	____
Plate, 12" sandwich	35	15	____
Plate, 12" 3-part relish	40	20	____
Plate, 12.75" 6-part relish		40	____
Plate, 14" sandwich	40	25	____
Plate, 14" 4-part relish	40	25	____
Punch Bowl Set:Ladle & bowl w/metal ring on which rests 6 cups	trtp*	trtp*	____
Salt & pepper		30	____
Saucer	10	4	____

	Pink	Crystal	Qty
Sherbet	15	8	____
Sugar w/foot, 2.75"	125	25	____
Sugar, flat, 2.5"	18	8	____
Tumbler, 3.5" juice	20	8	____
Tumbler, 4" water	26	8	____
Tumbler, 5" w/foot	85	30	____

Note: Royal Ruby: salt & pepper, $125; candlesticks, trtp*; 3.5" round ashtray, $10. Forest Green: 3.5" round ashtray, $10. Yellow: ashtray & cigarette jar, trtp*. Amethyst salt & pepper shakers, $60. Fired-on candlesticks, $50 each.

*trtp = too rare to price

RADIANCE

(1936-1939 New Martinsville Glass Company)

	Pink, Ice Blue, Red	Amber	Qty
Bon Bon, 6" ftd. open	50	25	____
Bon Bon, 6" flared open	50	25	____
Bon Bon, 6" crimped open	50	25	____
Bon Bon, 6" diam., 2.25" deep, highly crimped open	50	25	____
Bon Bon, 6" covered	130	60	____
Bowl, 5" nut	30	15	____
Bowl, punch, 8"	250	150	____
Bowl, 8"	60		____
Bowl, 9.75" flared, no foot	60	30	____
Bowl, 10" flared w/foot	60	30	____
Bowl, 10" crimped	60	30	____
Bowl, 10" w/short stem crimped	60	30	____
Bowl, 10" w/short stem flared	60	30	____
Bowl, 12" crimped, 2 styles	70	30	____
Bowl, 12" flared (shallow)	60	30	____
Bowl, 12" flared fruit	60	30	____
Butter/Cheese base	200	80	____
Butter/Cheese lid	300	170	____
Butter/Cheese complete	500	250	____
Candelabra, 2 lights w/prisms ea.	250	100	____
Candlestick, 6" ruffled ea.	120	60	____
Candlestick, 8" 1 light w/prisms ea.	200	75	____
Candlestick, 2 lights, no prisms ea.	80	40	____
Candy Box w/ cover	250	150	____
Celery, 10"	40	20	____
Cheese & Cracker	90	60	____
Compote/Mint 5" stemmed	60	30	____
Compote, 6" crimped ftd.	60	30	____
Compote, 6" tall, 9.5" diam.	60	30	____
Condiment set, 5 pieces: tray, 2 cruets, salt & pepper	295	165	____
Creamer	30	20	____
Cruet	100	40	____
Cup, coffee	30	14	____
Cup, punch, 2.75" diam., 2.25" deep	16	10	____

	Pink, Ice Blue, Red	Amber	Qty
Decanter w/stopper	200	120	_____
Goblet, 1 oz. Cordial, 2.75" tall, 1.25" diam.	50	30	_____
Goblet, 4.5" tall, 2.25" diam.	100		_____
Honey jar w/lid	250	150	_____
Ladle (for Punch Bowl)	150	120	_____
Lamp shade, 12"	125	75	_____
Mayonnaise w/under plate and spoon	120	80	_____
Mint, 5" w/handles, 2 styles	30	15	_____
Pickle, 7"	45	30	_____
Pitcher, 10" tall	300	200	_____
Plate, 8" salad	20	12	_____
Plate, 8" ftd salver	60	30	_____
Plate, 9.5"	70		_____
Plate, 11"	60	30	_____
Plate, 14"/Punch bowl liner	90	50	_____
Relish, 7" 2-part crimped	45	25	_____
Relish, 7" 2-part flared	45	25	_____
Relish, 7" 2-part flat rim	45	35	_____
Relish, 8" 3-part	50	30	_____
Relish, 8" 3-part crimped	50	30	_____
Relish, 8" 3-part flared	50	30	_____
Salt & pepper	125	75	_____
Saucer	10	7	_____
Service Set, 5 pieces: tray, creamer, sugar, salt & pepper	195	125	_____
Sugar	30	20	_____
Tray for sugar & creamer, 10.25"	35	20	_____
Tray, 10.25" x 5.75"		50	_____
Tumbler, 4.5"	50	35	_____
Vase, 10" crimped	100	80	_____
Vase, 10" flared	100	80	_____
Vase, 12" crimped	125	100	_____
Vase, 12" flared	125	100	_____

Note: Cobalt Blue is twice the price of Red, Pink, and Ice Blue. Emerald Green: 9" punch bowl, $200; 14" punch bowl liner, $150; 6" tall, 9.5" diam. compote, $200; decanter w/stopper, $300; 18" plate, $175. Crystal: 1/2 amber values. Add 20% for Corn Flower cut. Ruby flash lamp: $100. Add 20% for sterling overlay. Add 10% for gold embellishment.

RENA

(1920s Paden City Glass Glass Manufacturing
Company)

	Green & Pink	Qty
Bowl, 4.75" diam., 2.25" deep	60	_____
Cocktail, 3" oyster, 2.5" diam.	40	_____
Cocktail, 3.75", 2.5" diam., cone-shaped	40	_____
Creamer, 2.75" tall at handle	60	_____
Cruet, 6"	180	_____
Ice tub, 4" deep, 5.5" diam.	90	_____
Parfait, 6" tall, 2.5" diam.	60	_____
Pitcher, 6" tall at handle w/o ice lip (crystal)	50	_____
Pitcher, 7.25" tall at handle w/ice lip	200	_____
Plate, 6.25"	40	_____
Plate, 8"	40	_____
Salt & pepper, 3.5"	100	_____
Sherbet, 3.75" tall, 2.5" diam.	40	_____
Sugar, two handles, 2.75" tall at handle	40	_____
Sugar base, hotel, no handles, 2.5" tall, 3.5" diam.	160	_____
Sugar lid for hotel sugar	160	_____
Sugar shaker/ dispenser, 5"	300	_____
Sugar shaker/ individual, 3.75", 2 oz.	50	_____
Sundae, 5" tall, 4" diam., w/ruffled rim	40	_____
Sundae, 6.25" tall, 3.75" diam.	40	_____
Tumbler, 3.75" tall, no foot,	30	_____
Tumbler, 4" no foot, 2.25" diam.	40	_____
Tumbler, 5" soda, 2.5" diam.	40	_____
Tumbler, no foot, 5.5" Coca Cola	40	_____
Tumbler, 5.5", 2.75" diam.	40	_____
Tumbler, 6" soda, 2.75" diam.	40	_____
Tumbler, 7" soda, 3" diam.	40	_____

Note: Crystal items 1/2 those in pink and green.

RIBBON

(1930-1931   Hazel-Atlas Glass Company)

	Green	Black	Pink	Qty
Bowl, 4" diam., 1.5" deep, berry w/plain base	30			____
Bowl, 4" diam., 1.5" deep, berry w/design in base	30			____
Bowl, 5" diam., 1.75" deep, cereal	30			____
Bowl, 7" diam., 3" deep	50			____
Bowl, 8" diam., 3" deep	50	40		____
Bowl, 9" diam., 2.75" deep w/flared rim	40			____
Candy jar w/cover, base 4.75" diam., 3.5" deep, lid 5" diam.	40			____
Creamer, 3.5"	15			____
Cup	5			____
Plate, 6.25" sherbet, no indent	12			____
Plate, 6.25"sherbet w/indent	12			____
Plate, 8" luncheon	12	12		____
Salt & pepper	40	60	60	____
Saucer	3			____
Sherbet, 3" tall, 3.5" diam.	5			____
Sugar, 3.5"	15			____
Tumbler, 6" tall, 3.25" diam.	30			____

RING
(1927-1933 Hocking Glass Company)

	Crystal w/Colors	Green	Crystal & Satinized	Qty
Bowl, 5" berry	16	6	2	____
Bowl, 5.25" divided	60	35	15	____
Bowl, 5.5" diam, 1.25" deep			30	____
Bowl, 7" soup	40	15	8	____
Bowl, 7" diam., 2" deep, ruffled w/3 feet		45		____
Bowl, 8"	30	15	8	____
Butter tub/ice bucket	60	35	20	____
Candy, curves inward, 5.75" opening, 2" tall w/3 feet		trtp*		____
Candy, 7" diam, fluted w/3 feet		trtp*		____
Candy, 7.25" diam., smooth rim w/3 feet		trtp*		____
Cocktail shaker w/wide opening & straight sides, just over 6" tall	80		80	____
Cocktail shaker w/wide opening, 7" tall	80		60	____
Cocktail shaker, 9" tall	60	30	25	____
Cocktail shaker, 11.5" tall	60	30	25	____
Creamer	30	8	5	____
Cup	20	6	2	____
Decanter w/stopper, sloping sides, 11.5"	100	40	30	____
Decanter w/stopper, cyclindrical base, 11.5"	100	40	30	____
Goblet, 3.75" cocktail plain foot	40	15	8	____
Goblet, 4.5" wine	40	15	8	____
Goblet, 7.25"	40	15	8	____
Ice bucket, 5" diam., 5.5" deep	65	25	15	____
Pitcher, 8"	80	35	25	____
Pitcher, 8.5"	80	45	25	____
Plate, 6.25" sherbet	14	5	2	____
Plate, 6.75" sherbet w/off-center indent	16	6	3	____
Plate, 8.25" salad	16	6	2	____
Plate, 11.25" sandwich	30	14	8	____
Salt & pepper	85	60	20	____
Sandwich server w/open center handle, 11.75"	40	24	18	____
Saucer	10	3	2	____
Sherbet (fits 6.5" sherbet plate)	30	12	5	____
Sherbet, 4.75" stemmed	25	8	4	____

	Crystal w/Colors	Green	Crystal & Satinized	Qty
Sugar	30	8	5	____
Tumbler, 2.5" whiskey, 1.5 oz.	20	12	5	____
Tumbler, 3" tall, flat, 3 oz.	25	7	3	____
Tumbler, 3.75" tall, flat juice	25	7	3	____
Tumbler, 3.75" tall, footed juice (cone-shaped), 3 oz.	25	10	5	____
Tumbler, 4.25" tall, flat, 9 oz.	25	10	3	____
Tumbler, 4.75" tall, flat, 10 oz.			5	____
Tumbler, 5" tall, 2.75" diam, flat water, 10 oz.	25	7	5	____
Tumbler, 5.5" tall, footed water (cone-shaped), 10 oz.	30	10	5	____
Tumbler, 6.5" tall, footed iced tea (cone-shaped), 14 oz.	30	15	7	____
Vase, 8"	50	30	20	____

*trtp = too rare to price

Note: Distinguish this pattern from similar ones by looking for bands of 4 rings.

Note: Pink: pitcher, 8.25" tall, $75; 4.75" flat tumbler, $20. Red & Blue: cup, $65; 8" luncheon, $25. Green salt & pepper, $60 for the pair. Open candy, 7.75", w/3 feet, black amethyst, $50, pink, $35, yellow, $35. Iridescent vase, 8", $15. Ruby: creamer, $30; sugar, $30; dinner plate, $60; 8" luncheon plate, $30; 3" tumbler, $25; 4" tumbler, $25; 5" tumbler, $65; 3.75" flat juice tumbler, $25. Fired-on vase, $50. Vase in multiple fired-on colors, $50.

ROCK CRYSTAL FLOWER
(1925-1949 McKee Glass Company)

Note: s.e. = scalloped edge; p.e. = plain edge

	Red	Cobalt	Other Colors	Crystal	Qty
Bon bon, 7.5" s.e.	60	50	30	20	____
Bowl, 4" s.e., sauce	35	30	20	10	____
Bowl, 4.5" s.e., fruit	35	30	20	10	____
Bowl, 4.75" p.e.	65				____
Bowl, 5" s.e., fruit	45	35	25	15	____
Bowl, 5" p.e., finger	60	50	40	20	____
Bowl, 5.25" diam, 4.5" deep w/3 feet				50	____
Bowl, 7" s.e., salad	65	55	35	25	____
Bowl, 8" s.e., salad	80	60	40	30	____
Bowl, 8.25" s.e.			160		____
Bowl, 8.5" p.e., open center handle	250				____
Bowl, 9" s.e., salad	120	100	50	25	____
Bowl, 10.5" s.e., salad	100	80	50	25	____
Bowl, 11.5" p.e., 5.75" tall w/foot			200		____
Bowl, 12.5" s.e., "Center Bowl", ftd.	300	450	150	75	____
Butter dish base				200	____
Butter dish lid				150	____
Butter complete				350	____
Cake stand, 11"	125	100	60	40	____
Candelabra, 2-lite, 5.25" tall, 6.5" wide, ea.	150	450	60	20	____
Candelabra, 3-lite, ea.	185	85	70	30	____
Candlestick, flat w/stem, ea.	70	60	40	20	____
Candlestick, 5.5", ea.	100	70	40	20	____
Candlestick, 8.5", ea.	225	175	80	40	____
Candy w/lid, 7" diam., 5" tall	250	200	80	60	____
Candy w/lid, 10.25" tall	275	225	100	70	____
Cheese & crackers	150		150		____
10.5" plate w/indent	75		75		
3" tall, 4.25" diam. comport	75		75		____
Comport, 5.5" diam., 7" tall	100	80	50	40	____
Comport, 8.5" diam., 3.75" tall			85		____
Creamer, s.e., flat	70			30	____
Creamer, s.e., ftd., 4.25"	70	50	30	20	____
Cruet w/stopper, 6 oz.				100	____
Cup	70	50	20	15	____
Devilled egg plate				65	____
Goblet, 4 oz., 3.75" tall				15	____
Goblet, 7.5 oz, 5.75" tall, 3.25" diam	60	50	25	15	____
Goblet, 8 oz., 6.5" tall	60	50	25	15	____
Goblet, 8 oz., large footed	60	50	25	15	____

ROCK CRYSTAL FLOWER *(cont.)*

	Red	Cobalt	Other Colors	Crystal	Qty
Goblet, 11 oz. iced tea	70	50	20	15	____
Ice Dish, 3 designs				35	____
Jelly, 5" s.e.	50	40	30	20	____
Lamp	750	600	350	225	____
Parfait, 3.5 oz.	80	60	40	20	____
Pitcher, 1 qt. squat, 5" tall, 3.75" inside diam.			250	175	____
Pitcher, ½ gal. squat, s.e. 6.5" tall, 5" inside diam.			200	130	____
Pitcher, Fancy Tankard, 8.25" tall, 4.5" inside diam.			200		____
Pitcher, Covered Tankard, 9" tall, 4.25+" inside diam.				300	____
Pitcher, Fancy Tankard, 10.25" tall, 4.75" inside diam.	500		300	200	____
Plate, 6" s.e., bread & butter	20	18	12	8	____
Plate, 7" p.e., under plate for finger bowl	20	18	12	8	____
Plate, 7.5" p.e. & s.e., salad	20	18	12	8	____
Plate, 8.5" p.e. & s.e., salad	30	20	18	10	____
Plate, 9" s.e., cake	65	45	25	20	____
Plate, 10.5" s.e., cake (small center design)	65	45	35	25	____
Plate, 10.5" s.e., dinner (large center design)	180	100	80	60	____
Plate, 11.5" s.e., cake	60	40	30	20	____
Punch bowl, 14", 2 styles				400	____
Punch bowl base, 6" tall, 2 styles				225	____
Relish, 11.5" p.e., 5-part			50	50	____
Relish, 11.5" p.e., 2-part		70	60	40	____
Relish, 14" p.e., 6-part			100	80	____
Relish, 14" diam. (handle to handle), 7-part w/closed handles, p.e.				80	____
Salt & pepper			140	85	____
Salt dip				30	____
Sandwich server, center handle	150	100	60	40	____
Saucer	20	18	12	8	____
Sherbet/Egg, 3 oz.	70	50	30	15	____
Spooner				50	____
Stemmed 1 oz. cordial, 3"	70	50	50	25	____
Stemmed 2 oz. wine	60	40	30	20	____
Stemmed 3 oz. wine	60	40	30	20	____
Stemmed 3.5" cocktail	50	30	25	20	____
Stemmed 6 oz. champagne/ tall sundae, 4.5"	40	30	25	20	____
Stemmed 7 oz. goblet, 5.75"	60	40	30	20	____

ROCK CRYSTAL FLOWER *(cont.)*

	Red	Cobalt	Other Colors	Crystal	Qty
Stemmed 8 oz. goblet, 6.5"	60	40	30	20	____
Sugar base, s.e., flat	70			30	____
Sugar base, s.e., footed, 4.25" tall	70	40	30	20	____
Sugar lid	150	120	50	40	____
Sundae, 3.25", 6 oz., low foot	40	30	20	15	____
Syrup w/metal lid	800			200	____
Tray, 7" s.e., pickle or spoon				70	____
Tray, 12" x 8" s.e., celery	90	60	50	30	____
Tray, 13" x 6.5" p.e., roll	125	100	75	35	____
Tumbler, 2.5" whiskey	70	50	30	20	____
Tumbler, 5 oz. tomato juice, 3.5"	60	50	30	20	____
Tumbler, 4"	60	50	30	20	____
Tumbler, 5"	60				____
Tumbler, 5.25", 2 styles	60	50	30	20	____
Tumbler, 12 oz., 2 styles, iced tea	70	60	40	30	____
Vase, cornucopia			100	80	____
Vase, 7" tall, 5.5" diam.				65	____
Vase, 11" cupped	200	175	125	65	____
Vase, 12" w/square top	200	175	125	75	____

Note: Red slag 12.5" footed bowl, $450.

ROMANESQUE

(Late 1920s   L.E. Smith Glass Company)

	All colors*	Qty
Base, 4.5" diam., 2" tall, fits 10.5" bowl	85	___
Bowl, 10" w/foot, 4.25" tall	100	___
Bowl, 10.5" flat	100	___
Bowl, 10.5" w/foot	100	___
Bowl, 10.5" flat w/3 parts	100	___
Bowl, 12" console	80	___
Cake plate w/2 open handles	60	___
Cake plate, 11.5" diam., 3" tall, w/3" pedestal	85	___
Candlestick, ea., 2.5" tall	35	___
Candlestick, ea., 3.5" tall	60	___
Cup	40	___
Plate, 5.5", octagonal	15	___
Plate, 6", round	20	___
Plate, 7", octagonal	14	___
Plate, 7", round	20	___
Plate, 8", octagonal	14	___
Plate, 8", round	20	___
Plate, 9", octagonal, 10.75" handle-to-handle w/ship motif	75	___
Plate, 10", octagonal	28	___
Powder dish w/lid, 4" diam., 1.25" deep	250	___
Relish, 11" 3-part, octagonal	100	___
Sherbet, round rim, 3" tall, 3.5" diam.	18	___
Sherbet, crimped rim	24	___
Tidbit, 2 8" oct. plates	35	___
Tray, snack, 10" x 8"	35	___
Vase, 7" fan	70	___
Vase, 7.5" fan	70	___
Vase, 8" fan	70	___
Vase, 8.5" fan w/Romanesque foot	70	___
Vase, 8.5" w/swirled foot	70	___

*Made In Amber, Black Amethyst, Crystal, Green, Yellow, & Pink.

ROSE CAMEO
(1931   Belmont Tumbler Company)

	Green	Qty
Bowl, 4.5" berry, 1.5" deep	20	____
Bowl, 5" cereal, 2" deep	24	____
Bowl, 5.5", straight sided	80	____
Plate, 7" luncheon	18	____
Sherbet	15	____
Tumbler, 5"	20	____
Tumbler, 5.25"	20	____

ROSEMARY
(1935-1936   Federal Glass Company)

	Amber	Green	Pink	Qty
Bowl, 4.75" diam. cream soup	12	25	30	____
Bowl, 5" diam., 1.25" deep, berry	8	10	15	____
Bowl, 6" diam., 1.25" deep, cereal	30	30	35	____
Bowl, 10" oval	15	30	40	____
Creamer	8	15	20	____
Cup	6	8	10	____
Plate, 6.75" salad	8	8	12	____
Plate, 9.5" dinner	12	15	25	____
Plate, 9.5" grill	8	15	20	____
Platter, 12" x 8.75"	20	30	40	____
Saucer	4	5	5	____
Sugar, 4", no handles	8	15	20	____
Tumbler, 4.25"	25	35	50	____

ROULETTE
(1936-1937 Hocking Glass Company)

	Green	Pink	Crystal	Qty
Bowl, 9.5" fruit, 2.5" deep	35		7	____
Cup	12		5	____
Pitcher, 7.5" tall	70	75	30	____
Plate, just over 5" sherbet	14		3	____
Plate, 8.5" luncheon	18		4	____
Plate, 11.5" sandwich	35		8	____
Saucer	8		2	____
Sherbet	10		3	____
Tumbler, 2.5" whiskey, 1.5 oz.	28	30	10	____
Tumbler, 3.25" old-fashioned, 7.5 oz.	55	50	20	____
Tumbler, 3.5" juice, 5 oz.	45	40	12	____
Tumbler, 4" water, 9 oz.	45	40	10	____
Tumbler, 5" iced tea, 12 oz.	45	40	10	____
Tumbler 5.5" footed, 3.5" diam., 10 oz.	50		10	____

ROUND ROBIN
(1928 Economy Glass Company)

	Green	Iridescent	Qty
Bowl, 4" berry	15	3	____
Bowl, 7" diam., 2.5" deep	20		____
Creamer	10	4	____
Cup	5		____
Domino tray (Sugar cube tray), 7.5" w/3" indent	55		____
Plate, 6" sherbet	5	2	____
Plate, 8" luncheon	10	3	____
Plate, 12" sandwich	40	5	____
Saucer	2		____
Sherbet	10	4	____
Sugar	10	4	____

Note: Crystal candleholders, $15 each.

ROXANA

(1932   Hazel-Atlas Glass Company)

	Yellow	White	Qty
Bowl, 4.5" diam, 2.25" deep	20	15	____
Bowl, 5" diam, 1.25" deep. berry	12		____
Bowl, 6" diam, 1.25" deep cereal	15		____
Plate, 5.5"	10		____
Plate, 6" sherbet	10		____
Sherbet, 3" diam, 2.5" deep	10		____
Tumbler, 4.25" tall, 3" diam	20		____

Note: 4.5" bowl, crystal with green rim, $20.

ROYAL LACE *Reproduced*
(1934-1941 Hazel-Atlas Glass Company)

	Blue	Green	Pink	Crystal	Qty
Bowl, 4.5" diam., 2.25" deep, cream soup	50	40	30	15	____
Bowl, 5" diam., 2.25" deep, nut	trtp*	trtp*	trtp*	trtp*	____
Bowl, 5.25" diam., 1.5" deep, berry	145	120	90	65	____
Bowl, 10" diam., 2.75" deep, round	85	75	65	30	____
Bowl, 10" diam., 4.5" deep, straight edge	100	80	65	45	____
Bowl, 10" diam., 3.5" deep, rolled edge	1200	400	200	400	____
Bowl, 10.5" diam., 4.25" deep, ruffled edge	1400	300	200	100	____
Bowl, 11" rolled & ruffled, 3" deep			trtp*		____
Bowl, 11" diam., 2" deep, oval	95	85	75	45	____
Butter dish base, 6.25" diam., 1.5" deep,	450	250	150	75	____
Butter dish lid, 4.75" diam.	350	200	100	50	____
Butter complete	800	450	250	125	____
Candle holder, ea., straight edge	110	80	70	40	____
Candle holder, ea., rolled edge, 5" diam., 2.25" tall	250	150	140	85	____
Candle holder, ea., ruffled edge, 5.25" diam., 2.25" tall	300	150	165	75	____
Cookie jar/lid *R*	450	150	90	45	____
Creamer	65	45	25	15	____
Cup	40	30	20	10	____
Pitcher, straight	180	150	120	375	____
Pitcher, 64 oz., 8" no ice lip	350	225	125	75	____
Pitcher, 68 oz., 8" w/ ice lip	500	trtp*	125	100	____
Pitcher, 86 oz., 8" no ice lip	500	300	200	125	____
Pitcher, 96 oz., 8.5" w/ ice lip	600	275	225	150	____
Plate, 6" sherbet	18	15	12	8	____
Plate, 6.5" chrome w/indent	65				____
Plate, 8.5" luncheon	65	45	40	20	____
Plate, 10" dinner	55	50	45	25	____
Plate, 10" grill	35	30	25	15	____
Platter, 12.75" x 9.75"	75	65	50	30	____
Salt & pepper	350	200	150	75	____
Saucer	18	15	12	8	____
Sherbet, all glass	60	60	35	20	____
Sherbet w/chrome base	40			8	____

ROYAL LACE *(cont.)*

Sugar base	65	45	25	15	____
Sugar lid	200	150	100	75	____
Toddy set, cookie jar w/metal lid & tray, 8 plain cobalt roly-polies, ladle	400				____
Tumbler, 3.5" tall, 2.75" diam. *R*	65	60	60	25	____
Tumbler, 4.25" tall, 3.25" diam. *R*	50	45	35	20	____
Tumbler, 4.75"	225	135	135	75	____
Tumbler, 5" tall, 3.5" diam.	165	125	125	80	____

Reproduction information: Tumblers: new may have smooth bottoms; some have no design; color too dark. Cookie jar lid: cobalt only, new missing mold seam across knob & down 2 sides. Cookie jar base: new missing circular mold mark on bottom. Cookie jars in any other color are new. Cobalt too dark, green too light, pink difficult to discern. All red is new.

Note: Amethyst: 11" rolled edge console bowl, $2000; rolled edge candlesticks, $1000 ea.; sherbet w/chrome base, $65; Toddy set, $500. Fired-on, rolled edge candleholder, trtp*. Satinized green 10" lampshade, trtp*. Crystal with ruby trim straight-sided candle holders, trtp*. Iridized pink platter, trtp*.

*trtp = too rare to price

ROYAL RUBY *Reproduced*
(1938-1960s, 1977   Anchor Hocking Glass Company)

		Qty
Ashtrays *R*		
3.25″ square	10	____
4.25″ square	10	____
4.5″ square	10	____
5.75″ square	10	____
Leaf	15	____
Bottles		
Beer, 9.75″, 32 oz	100	____
Ketchup, 8.25″	125	____
Water, ribbed	250	____
Water, smooth	250	____
Bowls		
Baltic (rounded foot/base), 4.75″	10	____
Bubble		
4.5″ dessert	12	____
8.25″ vegetable	30	____
Burple (vertical rows of balls & lines)		
Dessert, 4.5″	8	____
Berry, 8″	25	____
Charm (square)		
Dessert, 4.75″	8	____
Salad, 7.25″	30	____
Classic		
11″x 5″ deep	45	____
12″ x 8″, 3.25″ deep	45	____
Fairfield		
5.25″ diam, w/2 handles	25	____
Oyster & Pearl		
5.25″ heart-shaped w/1 handle	25	____
5.5″ round w/1 handle	25	____
6.5″ bon bon, deep	40	____
10.5″ console	70	____
Sandwich		
4.75″	20	____
5.25″ w/smooth rim	25	____
5.25″ w/scalloped rim	25	____
6.5″	30	____
8.25″	80	____
Whirly Twirly (series of horizontal bulges), 3.75″	14	____
Other bowls		
4.25″ dessert	6	____
5.25″ popcorn	18	____
6.5″ soup	18	____
6.75″ cereal	18	____
7.5″ soup	15	____
8.25″ vegetable	20	____
10″ diam., 5.25″ deep, punch	35	____
Boxes		
Cigarette, 4.25″ x 3.5″ x 2.5″ deep		

ROYAL RUBY *(cont.)*

		Qty
(crystal base, ruby lid)	30	____
Cigarette 6" x 4" x 1.5" deep		
(crystal 2-part base, ruby lid)	40	____
Puff (round 4.5" diam., 1.75" deep		
crystal base, ruby lid)	40	____
Candlesticks		
Bubble, ea.	45	____
Oyster & Pearl, 3.5", ea.	35	____
Queen Mary, 4.5", ea.	trtp*	____
Cocktail Glasses (metal stems)	15	____
Cocktail Shaker, 5.5"	35	____
Cocktail Shaker, 9.5"	85	____
Creamers		
Flat (no foot)	10	____
Footed, 2 styles	12	____
Cups		
Bubble	10	____
Charm (square)	8	____
Coffee, 2 styles	8	____
Punch *R*	5	____
Ice Bucket	70	____
Lamp, Old Cafe, 7.5" tall	310	____
Maple Leaf (spoon rest)	10	____
Mint tray w/center handle, 7.5"	14	____
Moskeeto-lites, ea.	25	____
Pitchers		
Bubble/Provincial (large bubbles that just touch each other)	60	____
Georgian (honeycomb-like bottoms)	50	____
High Point (vertical ribs w/series of 3 circular shapes in between, tapered in at base)	85	____
Hobnail (small bumps that do not touch one another)	40	____
Roly Poly (flat bottom, smooth sides curve inward at base)	40	____
Swirl, 2 styles	60	____
Tilted, 2 styles	50	____
Upright water, 8" tall	50	____
Whirly Twirly (series of horizontal bulges)	85	____
Windsor (small cube-like design at bottom)	45	____
Plates		
Classic, 14.5"	65	____
Sherbet, 6.5"	8	____
Salad, 2 styles, 7.75"	12	____
Snack w/cup indent, 8.25"	40	____
Luncheon, Charm (square) 8.25"	12	____
Dinner, 2 styles, 9.25"	14	____
Dinner, 9.25" Bubble	35	____
Sandwich, 13.5" Oyster & Pearl	60	____
Platter, 10" x 6" oval w/tab handles	200	____

		Qty
Punch bowl, 10"	35	___
Punch bowl base	50	___
Salt & Pepper (Georgian)	60	___
Saucers		
Bubble	5	___
Charm (square)	3	___
Round, 2 styles	3	___
Sherbets		
Baltic (rounded foot/base), 2.25" tall, 2.5" diam.,	8	___
Balled Stem	10	___
Smooth Stem	8	___
Spoon rest (Maple Leaf)	10	___
Sugar bases		
Flat (no foot)	10	___
Footed, 2 styles	12	___
Sugar Lid	20	___
Tidbit		
Bubble, 2-tier	50	___
Tumblers		
Baltic (rounded foot/base)		
Juice, 2.5"	7	___
Cocktail, 3.5"	5	___
Water, 4.5"	5	___
Bubble/Provincial (large bubbles that just touch each other)		
Old Fashioned, 3.25"	16	___
Juice, 3.75"	12	___
Water, 4.5"	12	___
Iced Tea, 5.75"	18	___
Clear "bubble" foot		
Berwick (single row of "balls")		
Sherbet, 3.5"	14	___
Cocktail, 3.75"	16	___
Juice/wine, 4.5"	16	___
Goblet, 5.5"	16	___
Early American (rows of "balls" w/largest ones at outer edge)		
Cocktail, 3.25"	16	___
Sherbet, 4"	16	___
Juice, 4.25"	16	___
Goblet, 5.25"	16	___
Georglan (honeycomb-like bottoms)		
3.25"	10	___
3.5"	8	___
4.5"	8	___
5"	8	___
5.5" (flat)	8	___
5.5" (pedestal)	15	___
High Point (vertical ribs w/series of 3 circular shapes in between, tapered in at base)		

ROYAL RUBY *(cont.)*

		Qty
Fruit, 3.25"	15	____
Table, 4.25"	15	____
Iced Tea, 5.5"	40	____
Hobnail (small bumps that do not touch one another)	8	____
Newport (straight sides, sharp inward taper near base)		
Old fashioned, 3"	6	____
Juice, 4"	6	____
Water, 5"	6	____
Iced Tea, 6"	8	____
Roly Poly (flat bottom, smooth sides curve inward at base)		
Juice, 3.25"	5	____
Table, 4.25"	6	____
Water, 4.75"	6	____
Iced Tea, 5"	8	____
Swirl, 4"	20	____
Whirly Twirly (series of horizontal bulges)		
3.25"	10	____
4"	10	____
5"	10	____
Windsor (small cube-like design at bottom)		
3.25"	7	____
4"	7	____
Other Tumblers		
Brandy snifter, 5.5" tall	30	____
Whiskey, just under 3" tall, 1.75" diam.	10	____
Grape decorations, 5.25" tall	8	____
Hoe Down, 2 sizes	5	____
3.25" footed wine	15	____
4.75" footed iced tea	10	____
4.75" flat w/gold trim	5	____
Vases		
Bud, 3.75" *R*	5	____
Bud, 5.75"	10	____
Classic, 10"	50	____
Coolidge, 6.75"	6	____
Harding, 6.75"	6	____
Hoover, 9" (plain)	15	____
Hoover, 9" (decorated)	20	____
Ivy ball, two styles, 4"	5	____
Ivy ball, 6"	7	____
Pineapple, 9"	35	____
Square textured bottom, flared top w/or w/out crimped top, 9"	20	____
Squatty, 3.75"	18	____

Reproduction information: Ashtrays, punch cups, 3.75" vases: most reproductions have "Anchor" symbols. Covered pedestal plates are new.

Note: Ashtrays, add $5 for collectible advertisements.

*trtp = too rare to price

(1930-1932 & Fired-on red 1934-1935 Macbeth-Evans Glass Company)

	Topaz	Crystal w/ variations	Crystal	Red (Fired-on)	Qty
Bowl, 5.5" diam, 1.25" deep, cereal	8	4	2	16	____
Bowl, 8.5" diam, berry	18	9	5		____
Creamer, 2.75" thin & 3" thick	8	4	3	16	____
Cup, 2 styles	8	3	2	12	____
Pitcher, round sides, 8"		60	50		____
Pitcher, straight sides	125	50	40		____
Plate, 6" bread & butter	6	2	1		____
Plate, 8" luncheon	8	3	2	40	____
Plate, 9.25" dinner	10	6			____
Plate, 10.5" grill	10	4	3		____
Plate, 11.75" cake	40	20	15		____
Plate, 13" cake	60	30	20		____
Saucer	4	2	1		____
Sherbet	8	3	2		____
Sugar, 2.5" thin & 3" thick	8	4	3	16	____
Tumbler, 3.5" tall, juice	15	5	5		____
Tumbler, 4" tall, water	10	4	4		____
Tumbler, 4.75" tall, 2.5" diam	10	4	4		____
Tumbler, 5" tall	15	6	6		____

Note: Monax: 6" sherbet plate, $8; 8" luncheon, $10. Amber 11.75" cake plate, $80. Green: Pitcher, $600; 4" tumbler, $65; saucer, $3. Pink: Pitcher, $600; 4" tumbler, $65; 4.75" tumbler, $65.

SAGUENAY
(1941-1950 Dominion Glass Company)

	Fired-on colors	Crystal	Qty
Bowl, 4.25" berry w/handles	10	5	____
Butter dish base	30	20	____
Butter dish lid	30	20	____
Butter dish complete	60	40	____
Creamer	12	6	____
Cup	7	3	____
Egg cup, 2.5"		7	____
Plate, 6" sherbet	6	4	____
Plate, 8" luncheon	10	7	____
Salt & pepper	25	12	____
Saucer	4	2	____
Sherbet	10	5	____
Sugar	10	6	____
Tumbler, 3.5", 5 oz. juice	12	7	____
Tumbler, 4.25", 9 0z. water	18	10	____

Note: Orange, turquoise, white, too rare to price.

SANDWICH *Reproduced*
(1939-1964 Anchor Hocking Glass Corporation)

	Crystal	Forest Green	Amber	Qty
Bowl, 4.25" w/smooth rim	6	5		____
Bowl, 4.75" dessert w/ crimped rim	25		5	____
Bowl, 4.75" w/smooth rim	6		6	____
Bowl, 5" w/scalloped rim	8			____
Bowl, 5.25" w/scalloped rim	8			____
Bowl, 6.5" w/smooth rim	8		6	____
Bowl, 6.5" scalloped	8		30	____
Bowl, 6.75" w/scalloped rim	100	50		____
Bowl, 6.75" cereal	35		14	____
Bowl, 7" salad	8			____
Bowl, 7.5" salad w/scalloped rim	8	80		____
Bowl, 8.25" w/scalloped rim	10	85		____
Bowl, 8.25" oval w/scalloped rim	12			____
Bowl, 9" salad	25		30	____
Bowl, 9.75" punch/salad	30			____
Butter dish base	20			____
Butter dish lid	25			____
Butter complete	45			____
Cookie jar open, never had lid		20		____
Cookie jar w/lid *R*	40		45	____
Creamer	8	45		____
Cup, coffee	4	20	5	____
Cup, punch	4			____
Custard w/crimped rim	15	25		____
Custard w/smooth rim	4	4		____
Custard liner/under plate	20	4		____
Hot plate, 5.5"	150			____
Pitcher, 7" juice	70	200		____
Pitcher, ½ gallon, 8.5"	90	500		____
Plate, 7" dessert	14			____
Plate, 8"	7			____
Plate, 9" dinner	30	140	12	____
Plate, 9" w/indent tor cup	8			____
Plate, 12" sandwich	25		15	____
Punch bowl (salad bowl), 9.75"	30			____
Punch bowl stand	40			____
Saucer	3	18	4	____
Sherbet	8			____
Sugar base	8	45		____

SANDWICH *(cont.)*

	Crystal	Forest Green	Amber	Qty
Sugar lid	18			___
Tumbler, 3" juice, 5 oz., flat	8	8		___
Tumbler, 3.25" juice, 3 oz., flat	20			___
Tumbler, water, 9 oz., flat, 4"	8	12		___
Tumbler, water w/foot, 9 oz., 4.75"	45		275	___

Reproduction information: New cookie jar is taller & wider than old. New measures 10.25" tall; old measures 9.75" tall. New measures 5.5" across at opening; old measures 4.75".

Note: Ruby items: 4.75" bowl, $20; 5.25" bowl, $25 (smooth or scalloped); 6.5" bowl, $30; 8.25" bowl, $80. Pink items: 4.75" bowl, $8; 5.25" bowl, $10; 8.25" bowl, $20; 6" juice pitcher, $300. Ivory & white: punch bowl, $20; punch bowl base, $25; punch cup, $3.

SANDWICH *Reproduced*
(1920s-1990s Indiana Glass Company)

	Crystal	Teal	Red	Pink & Green	Qty
Ashtrays shaped in 4 suits for bridge parties	5				____
Basket, 10"	35				____
Bowl, 4.25" berry	4				____
Bowl, mayonnaise w/foot	15			30	____
Bowl, 6" round	4				____
Bowl, 6", hexagonal	5	20			____
Bowl, 8.5"	10				____
Bowl, 9" console	22			40	____
Bowl, 10" diam., 5" deep, ruffled	100				____
Bowl, 11.5" console	18			50	____
Butter dish base *R*	10	75			____
Butter dish lid *R*	20	100			____
Butter complete *R*	30	175			____
Candlestick, 3.5" ea.	10			25	____
Candlestick, 7" ea.	15				____
Celery, 10.5" oval w/scallops	18				____
Creamer	10		50		____
Creamer, diamond-shaped	10	12			____
Cruet w/stopper	30	150		175	____
Cup	4	10	30		____
Decanter w/stopper *(R in green)*	75		85	125	____
Goblet, 4 oz. wine, 3" *R*	8		15	28	____
Goblet, 9 oz., 5.75"	14		50		____
Pitcher	30		130		____
Plate, 6" sherbet	4	10			____
Plate, 7" bread & butter	4				____
Plate, 8" oval w/cup indent	5	12			____
Plate, 8.25" luncheon	5		20		____
Plate, 10.5" dinner	12			30	____
Plate, 13" sandwich	14	30	38	28	____
Puff box w/lid	18				____
Salt & pepper	30				____
Sandwich server w/center handle	24		50	35	____
Saucer	3	5	8		____
Sherbet	7	18			____
Sugar base	10		50		____
Sugar, diamond-shaped	10	12			____
Sugar lid	20				____
Tray w/tab handles for diamond-shaped creamer & sugar	10				____
Tumbler, 3 oz. cocktail w/foot, 3"	10				____
Tumbler, 8 oz. water w/foot	10				____
Tumbler, 12 oz. iced tea w/foot, 6.5"	10				____

SANDWICH *Reproduced (cont.)*

Note: Amber items twice those in crystal. Tidbit found in amber only, 8.25" luncheon plate over 10.5" dinner plate, $45.

Reproduction information: Green & pink items that are too light in color are new. Items not shown in this list are new. Wine goblet: old measures 2" across top; new is larger, about 2.75" across top. Butter dish, as well as other items, made new using old molds. Beware! Old green will glow under black light. Cookie jars in cobalt and pink are new. Tiara Exclusives includes dozens of items made from Indiana Glass Co. molds. If you find an item not listed, it probably is a piece of Tiara.

SHARON *Reproduced*
(1935-1939 Federal Glass Company)

	Green	Pink	Amber	Qty
Bowl, 5" diam, 2.25" deep, cream soup	70	50	30	____
Bowl, 5" diam, 1.25" deep, berry	18	15	10	____
Bowl, 6" diam, 1.5" deep, cereal	30	30	25	____
Bowl, 7.75" diam, 1.75" deep, flat soup,		55	55	____
Bowl, 8.5" diam, 2.5" deep, berry	40	38	5	____
Bowl, 9.5" diam, 2.5" deep, oval	40	38	22	____
Bowl, 10.25" diam, 3" deep, fruit	60	60	30	____
Butter dish base *R* 7.5" x 1.25"	45	25	15	____
Butter dish lid *R*	75	40	30	____
Butter complete *R*	120	65	45	____
Cake plate, 11.5" diam	75	50	20	____
Candy jar w/ lid *R*	180	65	50	____
Cheese dish base *R* 7.25" x .75" w/rim		1500	200	____
Cheese dish lid *R* (Butter dish lid)		40	30	____
Cheese dish complete		1540	230	____
Creamer *R*	25	20	16	____
Cup	20	15	7	____
Jam dish, 7.75", 1.25" deep	75	250	50	____
Pitcher, 9" ice lip	450	200	150	____
Pitcher, 9" no ice lip	500	180	150	____
Plate, 6" bread & butter	14	12	7	____
Plate, 7.25" salad	35	35	20	____
Plate, 9" dinner	30	25	12	____
Platter, 12.5"	40	35	25	____
Salt & pepper *R*	90	75	35	____
Saucer	12	12	5	____
Sherbet	38	18	14	____
Sugar base *R*	25	20	16	____
Sugar lid *R*	45	35	25	____
Tumbler, 4" tall, thick, flat	75	50	35	____
Tumbler, 4" tall, 2.75" diam, thin (blown), flat	80	50	35	____
Tumbler, 5.25" tall, thick, flat	100	100	65	____
Tumbler, 5.25" tall, 2.75" diam, thin (blown), flat	120	50	55	____
Tumbler, 6.75" tall, footed		65	150	____

SHARON *(cont.)*

Note: Items in Crystal: 11.5" cake plate, $10; 7.5" salad plate, $10; 6.5" footed tumbler, $15. Satinized Sharon, trtp*.

Reproduction information: All jade-ite & chalaine (opaque blue) is new. Butter: new lid has easy-to-grasp knob as it is about 1"; new base has true rim with a hard edge in which lid fits.

Old lid's knob is about .75" high and the base has rounded, smooth rim for lid. No blue butters are old. Cheese dish: new base too thick, not flat enough but rather bowl shaped. Creamer: new pink is too pale, mold seam is not centered on spout. Sugar: new handles meet bowl in a circle; new lid missing extra glass from mold seam around the middle. Shakers: crude flowers with 4 petals rather than a bud with 3 leaves. Candy dish: thick glass, poor quality. Old foot is 3.25" in diameter; new foot is just under 3". If you find a piece of Sharon in an odd color, beware! 7.5" biscuit jar in blue or pink is new.

*trtp = too rare to price

SHELL PINK

(1958-1959 Jeannette Glass Company)

	Opaque pink	Qty
Ashtray, Butterfly, 4.25" x 2.25" w/4 toes	25	____
Base or pedestal for punch bowl, 4.5"	40	____
Bell	350	____
Bottle, bulbous ribbed bottom, thin tapered neck	75	____
Bowls		
Floragold (motif inside, "woven" exterior), 6.25" tall, 9" diameter, footed (more like a pedestal)	50	____
Gondola fruit bowl w/2 handles, 17.5" x 5" x 4.25"	300	____
Holiday, 10.75" diameter, 3.75" deep	320	____
Pheasant bowl, 8" diameter, almost 3" deep	120	____
Punch, 13.5" diameter, 6" deep	40	____
Lombardi bowl, 10.5" x 6.5", 5.25" deep, w/4 toes	65	____
Box, Cigarette, 4.25" x 6.25" divided base with butterfly finial on lid that has chrysanthemum motif inside	120	____
Cake plate, Diamond Cut (Anniversary) pattern	75	____
Cake stand with pedestal, Harp pattern	100	____
Candle holders		
Eagles, 3" tall, ea.	50	____
Double, Chrysanthemum and oak leaf design, 5.25" tall, ea.	65	____
Votive with metal stand	125	____
Candy dish, Floragold pattern, 5.25" oval scalloped w/4 ft	50	____
Compote, Windsor style, 5.5" tall, 6" diameter	20	____
Covered containers		
Bee hive jar (honey pot), shaped like hive, 4.25"	125	____
Candy with acorns & leaves, base 3.25" tall, 5.25"	40	____
Candy with grapes, 6" tall overall; base 3.5" deep, 4.25" diameter, 7" tall overall	20	____
Cookie jar; base 6.5" tall, 5.75" diameter, 10" tall overall	200	____
Powder jar, round with rose buds	50	____
Wedding bowl, 3412/P, square, 6.5" tall	25	____
Wedding bowl, square, 8.25" tall	35	____
Creamer, Baltimore pear, 5" tall	18	____
Dishes		
Florentine, 10" x 7.75" w/4 feet (resembles a bowl)	125	____

	Opaque pink	Qty
Octagonal Vineyard with Partitions (4-part) 12" x 12" x 1.5" deep	200	____
Goblets		
Sherbet/champagne, Thumbprint design, 4" tall, 3.5" diameter	25	____
Water, Thumbprint design, 6.25" tall, 3.25" diameter	25	____
Lazy Susan, 5-part round relish, 13" ball bearing base, 6.5" diam on bottom, 4.75" diam. On top	60	____
Pitcher, Thumbprint design, 6"	35	____
Planters		
Diamond texture, 5"	50	____
Grape motif, footed, 5" tall, 4.25" diameter	18	____
Square with foot, smooth sides, flared, 4.75" tall, 5.25" diameter	40	____
"Stars" & "Wheat", 6" tall, 4.5" diameter	18	____
Punch Bowl Set, Feather design		
Bowl, 13.5" diameter, 6" deep	40	____
Cup, 3" diameter, 2.5" deep	5	____
Ladle, 12" long, plastic	15	____
Base or pedestal, 3.5" tall, 5.25" diameter at top, 6.5" diameter at bottom	50	____
Relish platters		
3-part rectangle w/sunburst motif in each section, beaded rim	65	____
5-part, Feather design	40	____
5-part, Crosshatch design, round with scalloped rim, 13.5"	40	____
6-part, Feather design	40	____
Tray, Harp pattern, 2 open handles, 10" x 15.5" (handle to handle)	100	____
Tumbler, juice, footed with Thumbprint design, 4.25" tall, 2.5" diameter	20	____
Snack set, Feather design		
Cup,	5	____
Plate, 7.75"	12	____
Sugar base, Baltimore pear, 5" tall	18	____
Sugar lid, Baltimore pear, 2.25"	35	____
Vases		
5" Cornucopia	70	____
7" Crosshatch	50	____
9" National pattern, heavy bottom	70	____

Note: Crystal Butterfly cigarette box, $100.

(1931-1933 Jeannette Glass Company)

	Pink	Green	Qty
Bowl, 5.25" cereal, 1.75" deep	30	35	____
Bowl, 8.5" berry, 3.5" deep	45	45	____
Bowl, 9.25" oval vegetable	90	185	____
Butter dish base, 6" diam, 1.25" deep	40	50	____
Butter dish lid	40	50	____
Butter complete	80	100	____
Butter w/Sierra bottom & Adam/Sierra lid	trtp*		____
Creamer, 3.25" tall	28	28	____
Cup	18	18	____
Pitcher, 6.5"	145	175	____
Plate, 9" dinner	25	35	____
Platter, 11" x 7.75" oval	60	70	____
Salt & pepper	60	60	____
Saucer	10	12	____
Smoking set	trtp*		____
ashtray, 2.75" diam, 3.5" diam including holder; cigarette jar, 3.5" tall base, 2.75" tall, 2.75 diam lid, 3" diam metal holder, 6" tall, 9" x 4.75"			
Sugar base, 3" tall	28	28	____
Sugar lid, 3.25" diam	30	30	____
Tray, 10" sandwich w/2 open handles	25	25	____
Tumbler, 4.5" tall, 3.75" diam	90	200	____

Note: Ultra-marine: cup, $175; 5.5" cereal bowl, $225.

*trtp= too rare to price

SPIRAL

(1920s   Federal Glass Company)

	Green & Pink	Qty
Bowl, 6" diam., 2.5" deep (marked)	12	____
Bowl, 7.75" diam., 1.75" deep (marked)	12	____
Creamer	12	____
Cup	8	____
Goblet, 5.75" (marked)	18	____
Pitcher, 7.75" at handle	40	____
Pitcher, 8" at handle	50	____
Plate, 6"	10	____
Plate, 8" w/1.25" wide band of spiral design	10	____
Plate, 8" w/2" wide band of spiral design	10	____
Saucer, 5.75" (marked)	6	____
Sherbet, 2.75" tall, 4" diam. (marked)	10	____
Sugar	10	____
Tumbler, 1.75" tall	14	____
Tumbler, 2" tall	10	____
Tumbler, 3" tall	10	____
Tumbler, 3.75" tall, 2.5" diam.	10	____
Tumbler, 4" tall juice	10	____
Tumbler, 4" tall water	10	____
Tumbler, 4.75" tall	10	____
Tumbler, 5" tall	10	____

Note: Crystal items half the value of colored pieces.

SPIRAL (HAZEL-ATLAS)
(1929-early 1930s   Hazel-Atlas Glass Company)

	Green	Qty
Goblet, 5.5"	12	____
Plate, 8.25"	8	____
Tumbler, 3.75"	10	____
Tumbler, 5.25"	10	____

SPIRAL *Reproduced*
(1928-1930   Hocking Glass Company)

	Green & Iridized Crystal	Qty
Bowl, 4.75" berry	60	_____
Bowl, 5.5", 1" deep berry	10	_____
Bowl, finger (iridescent w/ green base	45	_____
Bowl, 7" salad, 1.5" deep	20	_____
Bowl, batter w/spout & 1 handle, 7" diam., 3.5" deep	55	_____
Bowl, 8.5" berry, 2" deep (swirls in opposite direction)	18	_____
Butter tub or Ice tub, 3" deep, 5.5" diam.	45	_____
Cake plate, 10" w/3 feet *R*	40	_____
Cake plate, 10" w/3 feet & adv. on rim	125	_____
Candy w/lid, 4.5" tall	45	_____
Creamer, 2.5" flat	12	_____
Creamer, 3" w/foot	14	_____
Cup, 3 styles	10	_____
Ice tub	35	_____
Lid for 10" pitcher	100	_____
Mug, 2.75" tall	45	_____
Percolator top, 2" tall	12	_____
Pitcher, 7.5" tall, 3.5" diam, w/smooth rim bulbous	65	_____
Pitcher, 8" tall, 4" diam, w/rope at tim	65	_____
Pitcher, 8.25" tall, 4" diam, w/rope at rim, straight sided	65	_____
Pitcher, 8.25" tall, 5" diam, w/rope at rim, Jumbo, 80 oz	65	_____
Pitcher, 10" tall, 5" diam, w/foot	75	_____
Plate, 6" sherbet	10	_____
Plate, 8" luncheon	14	_____
Plate, 8.25" luncheon	14	_____
Plate, 10" sandwich (swirls in opposite direction)	15	_____
Plate, 10" cake w/3 feet	40	_____
Platter, 12" x 8"	35	_____
Preserve w/notched lid (for spoon)	70	_____
Salt & pepper	80	_____

	Green & Iridized Crystal	Qty
Sandwich server w/center handle (swirls in opposite direction)	18	____
Saucer, 6"	3	____
Saucer, 6.25"	3	____
Sherbet, 2.5" tall cone	12	____
Sherbet, stemmed	12	____
Sherbet, 3" tall, 4" diam	12	____
Sugar, 2.5" flat	12	____
Sugar, 3" w/foot	14	____
Syrup pitcher, 4.5" tall	70	____
Syrup pitcher, w/metal lid	85	____
Tumbler, 3.75" flat	14	____
Tumbler, 3.25" tall, 2.5" diam, w/foot	14	____
Tumbler, 4" tall	14	____
Tumbler, 4.75" tall, 3.5" diam, w/foot	14	____
Tumbler, 5" tall, flat water	16	____
Tumbler, 5.25" tall, flat iced tea	20	____
Tumbler, 6" tall, footed (found with 2 foot designs)	25	____
Vase, 5.75" tall	50	____
Vase, 6" tall	50	____
Vase, 6.75" tall	50	____

Reproduction information. 10" diameter cake plate difficult to discern; perhaps the new color is a bit too dark.

Note: Pink pieces worth twice green, crystal pieces worth 1/4. Satinized green 1/3 value of transparent green.

SPIRAL OPTIC
(Late 1920s-1930s Fostoria Glass Company)

	All colors	Qty
Bowl, 4095 ind. salt	25	____
Bowl, 4095 ind. almond	25	____
Bowl, 1769 finger	15	____
Bowl, 4095 4.5" diam. nappy	15	____
Bowl, 4295 4.5" diam.	15	____
Bowl, 4095 5" diam. nappy	15	____
Bowl, 4095 6" diam. nappy	20	____
Bowl, 4095 7" diam. nappy	20	____
Bowl, 2297 cupped, 7.25", 5" deep	50	____
Bowl, 8" with foot, 4.75" deep	65	____
Bowl, 2315 8.5" diam. w/foot	55	____
Bowl, 2297 11" diam. w/rolled edge	60	____
Bowl, 2350 rolled edge, 10"	65	____
Bowl, 2350 flared salad with flat foot, 10.5"	65	____
Bowl, 2297 cupped w/3 toes, 10.5"	70	____
Bowl, 2315 flared w/ foot, 10.5"	65	____
Bowl, 2329 rolled edge, 11"	60	____
Bowl, 2297 rolled, 11"	60	____
Bowl, 2297 flared w/3 toes, 12"	75	____
Bowl, 2371 rolled edge, 13"	65	____
Bowl, 2297 13" diam. cupped	60	____
Bowl, 2329 rolled edge, 14"	65	____
Candle holder, 2372, 1.5" x 4.25" ea.	45	____
Candle holder, 2393, 2" rolled low ruffle	50	____
Candy jar w/lid, 4095.5	45	____
Candy jar w/lid, 5084	60	____
Carafe, 1697	60	____
Centerpiece, 2393, 12" diam., rolled low ruffle	65	____
Centerpiece, 2293, 12" diam.	60	____
Centerpiece, 2371, 13" diam.	40	____
Centerpiece, 2293, 15" diam.	80	____
Confection and cover, 2380	175	____
Creamer, 2255	25	____
Cup, 2350	20	____
Flower block, 2309, 3.75"	25	____
Ice pail, 2378, 6"	75	____
Jug No. 7, 2082, 9" tall, straight sides, no foot	120	____
Jug No. 7, 4095	120	____
Jug No. 7, 5200, straight sides w/foot 10" tall	120	____
Jug No. 7, 4295, curved sides w/foot, 10.5" tall	120	____
Pail ice, 2378, 6"	75	____
Pail sugar, 2378, 3.5"	60	____
Pail, whipped cream, 2378, 2.5"	80	____
Pitcher, (jug no. 7), 2082, 9" tall, straight sides, no foot	120	____
Pitcher, (jug no. 7), 4095	120	____
Pitcher, (jug no. 7), 5200, straight sides w/foot, 10" tall	120	____

SPIRAL OPTIC *(cont.)*

	All colors	Qty
Pitcher, (jug no. 7), 4295, curved sides w/foot, 10.5" tall	120	___
Plate, 2283, 6.5" bread & butter	22	___
Plate, 2283, 7.25"	22	___
Plate, 2283, 8.5"	22	___
Plate, 2287 sandwich server w/ctr handle, 11.5"	55	___
Plate, 2283, 13.5"	60	___
Salt, individual	35	___
Saucer, 2350, 5.75"	18	___
Stem, 5082, 3.75" tall, 3.75" diameter	45	___
Stem, 5297, 4" tall	45	___
Stem, 5083, 5" tall, 2.25" diameter	50	___
Stem, 5282, just over 5" tall	45	___
Stem, 5082, just over 5" tall, 2.25" diameter	50	___
Stem, 5082, 5.5" tall, 2.75" diameter	45	___
Stem, 5282, 5.75" tall	45	___
Stem, 5083, 6" tall, 2.75" diameter	45	___
Stem, 5283, 7.25" tall	45	___
Stem, 5282, 7.5" tall, 3.5" diameter	55	___
Sugar, 2255	25	___
Sugar pail, 2378, 3.5"	60	___
Tray, 2297, w/3 toes 13"	55	___
Tumbler, 4295, 2.5" w/foot	35	___
Tumbler, 858, 3.75"	30	___
Tumbler, 4095, 3.25" tall, just under 3.25" diam., w/foot	30	___
Tumbler, 4095, 4.75" w/foot	25	___
Tumbler, 4295, 4.75" w/foot, 3.25" diameter	25	___
Tumbler, 5200, 5.25"	35	___
Tumbler, 4095, 5.5" w/foot, 3.5" diameter	35	___
Vase, 4095, 7" tall, 8.5" diameter	45	___
Vase, 2360, 8" tall	65	___
Vase, 4087, 8" tall	65	___
Vase, 5087, 8" tall	65	___
Vase, 2292, 8" tall, 8.5" diameter	65	___
Vase, 5085, 8" tall, narrow	65	___
Vase, 4095, 9" tall,	65	___
Vase, 4095.5, 9" tall	65	___
Vase, 5086, 9" tall	65	___
Vase, 2360, 10" urn w/2 handles, 4.25" diam.	65	___
Whipped cream pail, 2378, 2.5"	80	___

SPIRAL OPTIC
(late 1920s Hazel-Atlas Glass Company)

	Green	Qty
Decanter, 11.5"	125	____
Jar with cover, 3" deep, 2.5" diameter	45	____
Pitcher, 7" tall at handle, ice lip	50	____
Pitcher, 7.25" at handle, no ice lip	60	____
Pitcher, 8.25" at handle, no ice lip	50	____
Tumbler, whiskey	25	____
Tumbler, 3" tall, 2.5" diameter	12	____
Tumbler, 4" tall, 2.75" diameter, thin	15	____
Tumbler, 4" tall with flared rim, 3" diameter	12	____
Tumbler, 4" tall, 3" diameter	12	____
Tumbler, 4.25" tall, 2.75" diameter	12	____
Tumbler, 5" tall, 2.75" diameter	12	____
Tumbler, 5.25" tall, 3" diameter	12	____

Note: Items in pink 50% more than green. Items in cobalt blue 2x value of green.

SPIRAL OPTIC
(Late 1920s Hocking Glass Company)

	Green	Qty
Goblet, 7", 3.25" diam.	18	____
Pitcher, bulbous, 7.5" tall, 3.5" diameter	35	____
Pitcher, 8.5" tall, 4.25" diameter	35	____
Plate, 6.25", sherbet	8	____
Plate, 8.25"	6	____
Sherbet, 3.25", 3.5" diam., 2.5" foot	5	____
Sherbet, 3.25", 3.5" diam., 2.75" foot	5	____
Tumbler, 400, 1.75" whiskey	8	____
Tumbler, 404, juice	5	____
Tumbler, 405, 3"	5	____
Tumbler, 401, 3.75", wider than 403 tumbler	5	____
Tumbler, 403, 3.75" tall, 2.25" diameter	5	____
Tumbler, 414, 3.75" tall, curves outward	5	____
Tumbler, 406, water	5	____
Tumbler, 409, iced tea	7	____

SPIRAL OPTIC
(1920s Indiana Glass Company)

	Amber & Green	Qty
Bowl, 9", 5.25" deep with 2 handles, w/foot	65	____
Bowl, 10.5", 4" deep with 2 handles, w/foot	65	____
Candlestick, 3.5" tall, 5" base, ea.	18	____
Candlestick, 8.5" tall, 4.25" base, ea.	30	____

Note: Fired-on 8.5" tall candlestick, $25 each.

SPIRAL OPTIC
(Late 1920s Jeannette Glass Company)

	Green	Qty
Base for 10.5" bowl, .75" tall, 5.5" diam.	35	____
Bowl, 10.5" diameter rolled edge	40	____
Candle holder, 2.25" tall, 4.25" diam., ea.	18	____
Candy jar, 9"	40	____
Cup	5	____
Plate, 6"	6	____
Plate, 8"	8	____
Saucer	2	____

Note: Iridescent sherbet, $4. Pink 8" plate with Liberty Flour Advertisement, $25.

SPIRAL OPTIC
(1920s Tiffin - United States Glass Company)

	All Colors	Qty
Basket, 10.75" tall	65	____
Bowl, 6.75" with foot	20	____
Bowl, 8.25" diameter, `5" deep with foot	35	____
Bowl, 8.75", cupped	35	____
Bowl, 9.25" berry, highly flared rim	35	____
Bowl, 9.5", console	40	____
Bowl, 10.25"	40	____
Bowl, 10.75", 3.5" deep, epergne, ruffled edge	65	____
Bowl, 10.75", greatly rolled edge	35	____
Bowl, 10.75", rolled edge	35	____
Bowl, 11" orange	40	____
Bowl, 11.75" low, scalloped edge	35	____
Bowl, 11.75" fruit, 3.5" deep, rolled edge	40	____
Bowl, 11.75", 2.5" deep epergne, shallow, ruffled edge	65	____
Candlestick, 2.25", octagonal base, ea.	18	____
Candlestick, 3.5" x 5", round base, ea.	18	____
Candlestick, 5.25", round, humped base, ea.	20	____
Candlestick, 9.25", ea.	24	____
Candy jar, 7.5", 6.25" diameter coned-shaped	60	____
Cheese and cracker set	35	____
Plate with center indent, 10"	20	____
Center comport, 4.75"	15	____
Compote 7" tall	30	____
Plate, 7.5" salad	10	____
Plate, 7.75"	10	____
Plate, 10"	20	____
Plate, 10" sandwich server with center handle	30	____
Plate, 13.25"	35	____
Sherbet, 3.75" tall	20	____
Vase, 8.25" Dehlia, cupped	50	____
Vase, 8.5" Lily, flared top	50	____
Vase, ruffled top, fits two "epergne bowls"	40	____

STARLIGHT
(1938-1940   Hazel-Atlas Glass Company)

	Pink	Cobalt	White, Crystal	Qty
Bowl, 4.75" diam, 1.75" deep, w/closed handles			10	____
Bowl, 5.5" diam, cereal w/closed handles	14		7	____
Bowl, 8.5" diam, 3" deep, w/closed handles	20	40	10	____
Bowl, punch, 8.5" diam bowl, w/ 3" diam chrome rim			35	____
Bowl, 11" diam, salad			20	____
Bowl, 12" diam			20	____
Creamer			7	____
Cup			7	____
Plate, 6" bread & butter			4	____
Plate, 8.5" luncheon			4	____
Plate, 9" dinner			10	____
Plate, 13" sandwich	25		18	____
Relish dish, 8" x 4.25"			10	____
Salt & pepper			30	____
Saucer			2	____
Sherbet			10	____
Sugar			7	____

STARS AND STRIPES
(1942   Anchor Hocking Glass Company)

	Crystal	Qty
Plate, 8"	30	____
Sherbet	15	____
Tumbler, 5"	35	____

STRAWBERRY

(Early 1930s   U.S. Glass Company)

	Pink, Green	Crystal, Iridescent	Qty
Bowl, 4" diam	15	8	____
Bowl, 6.25" diam, 2" deep	130	15	____
Bowl, 6.5" diam, salad	28	12	____
Bowl, 7.5" diam, 3" deep berry	45	15	____
Butter dish base	75	30	____
Butter dish lid	150	80	____
Butter complete	225	110	____
Comport, 5.5" diam., 3.5" tall	45	12	____
Creamer, small, 3.75"	40	8	____
Creamer, large, 4.5"	40	12	____
Olive dish, 5" w/1 handle	30	8	____
Pickle dish, 8.25" oval	30	8	____
Pitcher	250	150	____
Plate, 6" sherbet	20	4	____
Plate, 7.5" salad	26	4	____
Sherbet, 3.25" tall, 3.75" diam.	10	4	____
Sugar, small	40	12	____
Sugar, large (5.5")	38	12	____
Sugar lid for 5.5" piece	70	12	____
Tumbler, 3.5" tall	50	8	____

SUNBURST
(Late 1930s   Jeannette Glass Company)

	Crystal	Qty
Bowl, 4.75" diam, 1.5" deep, berry	8	___
Bowl, 8.5" diam, berry	18	___
Bowl, 11" diam, 4" deep	20	___
Candlestick, ea.	12	___
Creamer	10	___
Cup	6	___
Plate, 5.5"	8	___
Plate, 9.25" dinner	20	___
Plate, 11.75" sandwich	15	___
Relish, 2-part, 8" x 5.5"	12	___
Relish, 2-part, 8" x 5.5", w/silver overlay	20	___
Saucer	3	___
Sherbet	12	___
Sugar	10	___
Tray, 5.25" x 8.75" oval	12	___
Tumbler, 4" tall, 3" diam	20	___

Note: Iridized pieces, $8 each.

SUNFLOWER
(1930s   Jeannette Glass Company)

	Green	Pink	Qty
Ashtray	20	20	___
Cake plate, 10"	25	30	___
Creamer	40	35	___
Cup	28	24	___
Hot plate (Trivet), 7"	1000	1000	___
Plate, 8"	*trtp	*trtp	___
Plate, 9" dinner	32	27	___
Saucer	22	20	___
Sugar	40	35	___
Tray, 2 handles, 11.5" diam	*trtp		___
Tumbler, 4.75"	50	45	___

Note: Opaque creamer, cup, & sugar, $85 each. Ultramarine Ashtray, $30, Delphite creamer, $100. Yellow creamer & sugar, $500 each. Caramel creamer & sugar, $500 each.

*trtp = too rare to price

SWIRL

(1937-1938   Jeannette Glass Company)

	Ultra-marine	Pink	Delphite	Qty
Bowl, 4.75" berry	18	14		____
Bowl, lug soup w/2 tab handles, 5" diam., 2" deep	55	45		____
Bowl, 5.5" diam., 1.75" deep, cereal	18	14	15	____
Bowl, 9" diam., 3" deep, salad	28	22	28	____
Bowl, 10" footed w/handles	35	35		____
Bowl, 10.5" diam., 5" deep, console w/foot	40	45		____
Butter dish base	45	45		____
Butter dish lid	280	180		____
Butter complete	325	225		____
Candlestick, ea. (double)	30	35		____
Candlestick, ea. (single)			90	____
Candy dish, open w/3 feet	20	15		____
Candy dish w/lid	175	225		____
Coaster, 3.5"	45	30		____
Creamer	16	12	12	____
Cup	16	12	10	____
Pitcher	trtp*	trtp*		____
Plate, 6.5" sherbet	10	10	8	____
Plate, 7.25"	18	12		____
Plate, 8" salad	20	20	15	____
Plate, 9.25" dinner	25	28	15	____
Plate, 10.5"			25	____
Plate, 12.5" sandwich	35	25		____
Platter, 12"			45	____
Salt & pepper	65			____
Saucer	7	5	5	____
Sherbet, 3.75" diam., 2.5" deep	25	18		____
Sugar	16	12	12	____
Tray, 10.5", 2 handles			35	____
Tumbler, 4", flat	35	25		____
Tumbler, just over 4" tall, 3.25" diam., footed	50	25		____
Tumbler, 4.5", flat		25		____
Tumbler, 5.25", flat	130	65		____
Vase, 6.5"		30		____
Vase, 8.5", 2 styles	30			____

*trtp = too rare to price

TEAROOM

(1926-1931 Indiana Glass Company)

	Green	Pink	Crystal	Amber	Qty
Banana Split, 7.5" flat	125	105	70		____
Banana Split, 7.5" footed	85	75	55		____
Bowl, finger, 4" diam.	75	55	45		____
Bowl, 8" w/2 handles	105	85	45		____
Bowl, 8.75" salad	105	85	45		____
Bowl, 9.5" x 7.5" oval	75	75	40		____
Candlestick, 2.75" tall, ea.	35	30	25		____
Creamer, 3.25" oval & flat	45	45	25		____
Creamer, 3.25" tall, 8-sided w/foot	35				____
Creamer, 4" w/foot, round	45	45	25	85	____
Creamer, 4.25" ftd, 8-sides	30	30	15		____
Creamer, 4.5" w/foot rect.	30	30	15	85	____
Cup	65	65	45		____
Glace, 7 oz. & 6.5" ruffled	90	85	55		____
Goblet, 6.25"	90	85	55		____
Ice Bucket, 6.5" tall	95	95	50		____
Lamp, 11.75" tall	180	180	85		____
Marmalade, 4" tall to top of lid	230	205	105		____
Mustard, 5" tall to top of lid	205	180	95		____
Napkin holder,	trtp*				____
Parfait, 5.25" tall, 2.5" d.	125	105	55		____
Pickle, 8.5"	35	30	20		____
Pitcher, 10"	270	205	trtp*	480	____
Plate, 6.5" sherbet	50	45	25		____
Plate, 7.75" salad	100	55			____
Plate, 8.25" luncheon	50	45	25		____
Plate, 10.5" w/2 handles	60	55	30		____
Plate, 10.5" sandwich w/center handle	60	55	30		____
Relish, 2-part, 8.25" x 4.25"	40	35	25		____
Salt & pepper	120	120	55		____
Saucer, 6.25' diam	45	40	25		____
Sherbet, w/foot, 3" tall	40	35	25		____
Sherbet, tall, sundae, 5"	105	105	55		____
Sherbet, ruffled, 6"	50	45	30		____
Sugar, 3", 8-sided w/foot	35				____
Sugar lid (for 3")	55				____
Sugar base, 3.25", oval/flat	45	45	25		____
Sugar lid (for flat)	35	205	90		____
Sugar base 4.5" w/foot	30	30	15	85	____
Sugar lid (for 4.5")	205	205	55		____
Sugar, rectangular	35	40	15		____
Tray, center handle	205	180	55		____
Tray for ftd. cream & sugar (center handle)	55	45	25		____
Tray for oval, flat cream & sugar (1 side handle), 6.5" x 5.75"	70	60	40		____
Tumbler, 4.25" flat	150	135	55		____
Tumbler, 6 oz. footed, 5"	60	55	25		____
Tumbler, 5.25" footed	55	50	20	105	____
Tumbler, 6.25" footed	75	65	30		____

	Green	Pink	Crystal	Amber	Qty
Tumbler, 12 oz. footed	90	80	40		____
Vase, 4.75" tall, ruffled	130	120			____
Vase, 6.5" tall,	105	95	55		____
Vase, 9.5" tall, ruffled	130	120	20	205	____
Vase, 9.5" tall, straight	85	80	50		____
Vase, 10.25" tall, 7" diam, ruffled	280	330	155		____
Vase, 11" tall, straight	155	130	80		____

Note: 10.25" tall vase, crystal and yellow coloration in checkerboard design, trtp*. 9.25" tall vase in crystal checkerboard, trtp*.

*trtp = too rare to price

TENDRIL
(1930s U.S. Glass Company)

	Green	Qty
Ashtray, 3.75" diam	30	____
Bowl, 5.5" x 4" x 1.75" deep, hat shaped	30	____
Creamer, 2.75" tall	20	____
Cup	12	____
Pitcher, 8" tall	50	____
Plate, 6"	12	____
Plate, 8.25"	20	____
Plate, 9.75", 10.75" handle to handle	30	____
Saucer	8	____
Sugar, 2.75" tall	20	____
Tumbler, 5" tall, 2.75" diam.	20	____

Note: Pink, 9.75" handled plate, $35

THISTLE *Reproduced*
(1929-1930 Macbeth-Evans)

	Pink	Green	Qty
Bowl, 5.5" cereal	38	38	____
Bowl, 10.25" fruit	400	250	____
Cake plate, 13"	160	180	____
Cup	30	30	____
Plate, 8" luncheon	28	28	____
Plate, 10.25" grill w/pattern only on rim	40	45	____
Saucer	15	15	____

Note: Yellow 5.5" cereal bowl, $200.

Reproduction information: These items are new & were never originally produced: butter dish, pitcher, & tumbler.

THUMBPRINT

(1927-1930   Federal Glass Company)

	Green	Qty
Bowl, 4.75" berry	15	____
Bowl, 5" cereal	15	____
Bowl, 8" berry	25	____
Creamer	18	____
Cup	10	____
Pitcher, 6"	80	____
Pitcher, 7.25"	80	____
Plate, 6" sherbet	10	____
Plate, 8" luncheon	15	____
Plate, 9.25" dinner	25	____
Salt & pepper	80	____
Saucer	4	____
Sherbet	10	____
Sugar	18	____
Tumbler, 4" tall, 2.75 diam	20	____
Tumbler, 5" tall	25	____
Tumbler, 5.5" tall	30	____
Vase, 9" tall	60	____

Note: Crystal, 8" plate, $5.

TULIP *Reproduced*
(1930s Dell Glass Company)

	Amethyst & Blue	Green & Amber	Crystal	Qty
Bottle, violin, 7.75" tall	35			____
Bottle, violin, 9.75" tall	45			____
Bowl, 6"	25	20	15	____
Bowl, 13.25" x 6.25" console	115	100	40	____
Candle holder, ea., 3.75" diam., 2" tall, resembles a blossom bowl	40	30	25	____
Candle holder, ea., 5.25" diam. 3" tall, regular candlestick design	48	30	15	____
Candy jar, 8.25" tall, 6.5" diam.	115	85	40	____
Cigarette holder (same as juice)	40	25	15	____
Coaster/ashtray, 4.75" x 4.75"	30			____
Creamer, 2"	30	18	15	____
Cup	20	18	12	____
Decanter w/stopper, 10.75"	trtp*	trtp*	trtp*	____
Decanter, violin shaped w/musical note stopper	trtp*	trtp*	trtp*	____
Goblet, 7" water	trtp*	trtp*	trtp*	____
Ice tub, 4.75" diam, 3" deep	95	75	35	____
Leaf plate, 6.75" wide, go-along	45			____
Leaf plate, 7.25" wide, go-along	45			____
Plate, 6" sherbet	18	12	5	____
Plate, 7.5"	20	15	7	____
Plate, 9"	25	20	12	____
Plate 10.25"	45	35	20	____
Relish, 3-part leaf, 8" x 7.5"	45			____
Saucer	10	8	5	____
Sherbet, 3.75" diam.	25	20	10	____
Stopper, 2.75"	30	35	20	____
Sugar, 2"	30	18	15	____
Toothpick holder, 2.25" tall, 2.25" diam	40			____
Tumbler, 1.75" tall, 1.75" diam, whiskey	35	25	15	____
Tumbler, 2.75" tall, 2.25" diam, juice (Same as cig. holder)	40	25	15	____
Tumbler, 4.75" water	44			____

Reproduction information: New pieces from Taiwan are slightly smaller than the pieces listed above.

*trtp = too rare to price

TWISTED OPTIC

(1927-1930 Imperial Glass Company)

	Pink	Green	Amber, Carn- ival, & Ruby Gold	Blue, Yel- low, & Vase- line	Qty
Basket, 10"	45	40	40	90	____
Bottle, perfume	85	85	85	100	____
Bowl, mayonnaise (resembles a custard cup)	45	40	40	60	____
Bowl, 4.75" fruit	30	25	20	45	____
Bowl, 4.75" with 2 handles, bon bon (resembles a cream soup bowl)	15	12	10	25	____
Bowl, 5.5" jelly w/1 handle	15	12	10	25	____
Bowl, 7" ruffled nappy	40	30	30	60	____
Bowl, 7" straight- sided nappy	40	30	30	60	____
Bowl, 7.5" nut	40	30	30	60	____
Bowl, 8.25" candle (center holds a taper)	100	100	100	125	____
Bowl, 8.5" nut w/bulging rim	40	30	30	60	____
Bowl, 8.75" diam., 2" deep	40	30	30	60	____
Bowl, 9" with 2 handles, 10-sided	20	18	12	30	____
Bowl, 9" nut, curved inward	20	18	12	30	____
Bowl, 9.25" rimmed salad	30	28	22	40	____
Bowl, 9.5" fruit with open center handle	40	30	30	60	____
Bowl, 10" flower with bulging rim	40	30	30	60	____
Bowl, 10" salad, flared rim	40	30	30	60	____
Bowl, 10.5" console with low rolled edge	60	60	25	65	____
Bowl, 10.5" console with high rolled edge	60	60	25	65	____
Bowl, 10.5" octagonal w/foot	60	60	25	65	____
Bowl, 10.5" oval with foot	60	60	25	65	____
Bowl, 11" console with low rolled edge, "center"	60	60	25	65	____
Bowl, 11" console with high rolled edge	60	60	25	65	____
Bowl, 11" flower w/"toes"	80	80	45	85	____
Bowl, 11.5" console with high rolled edge	60	60	25	65	____
Bowl, 11.5" flared console	60	60	25	65	____
Bowl, covered comport	60	60	60	85	____
Bowl, footed mayonnaise comport	25	25	25	45	____
Box, powder	50	50	50	75	____
Candle holder, 2.5" tall, ea.	20	18	15	25	____
Candle holder, 3.5" tall w/flanged top rim, ea.	20	18	15	25	____
Candle holder, 3.5" tall with thick rim, ea.	20	18	15	25	____
Candle holder, 3.5" tall with decorations, ea.	22	20	18	28	____

TWISTED OPTIC *(cont.)*

	Pink	Green	Amber, Carnival, & Ruby Gold	Blue, Yellow, & Vaseline	Qty
Candle holder, 8.25" tall, ea.	25	22	20	35	____
Candle holder, 8.25" tall with decorations, ea.	28	25	24	38	____
Candy box, flat (no foot) w/ lid	50	50	50	75	____
Candy jar, footed, short, w/ lid	50	50	50	75	____
Candy jar, base flanged at rim, w/ lid	60	60	60	85	____
Candy jar, 9" tall overall base 4.5" diam., 5" tall lid, 4.5" diam.	50	50	50	75	____
Cake plate, 10.5" diam.,10-sided w/2 open handles	25	25	25	35	____
Cheese & cracker set	35	30	25	50	____
Comport 9.5" plate with indent	15	12	10	25	____
Cheese dish, footed comport	20	18	15	25	____
Comport, cheese	20	18	15	25	____
Comport, open mayo w/rolled edge & foot	25	22	20	35	____
Comport, covered	50	50	50	75	____
Creamer	15	12	10	25	____
Cup	10	10	10	15	____
Dresser Set (My Lady)	175	165	165	235	____
Perfume bottle	85	85	85	100	____
Powder box	50	50	50	75	____
Tray, 7.5" x 9"	40	30	30	60	____
Goblet, 8 oz.	25	25	25	65	____
Mayonnaise set	60	54	55	95	____
Comport	25	22	20	35	____
Plate with indent	15	12	10	25	____
Spoon	20	20	25	35	____
Night Set	80	80	80	115	____
Decanter	60	60	60	80	____
Tumbler	20	20	20	35	____
Perfume bottle	85	85	85	100	____
Pitcher, 8" tall, 4.5" diam. at rim	85	85	85	100	____
Pitcher, 9" tall, 4" diam. at rim	50	50	50	75	____
Pitcher, 9.75" tall, 4.75" diam. at rim	60	60	60	75	____
Plate, under plate for mayonnaise comport	15	12	10	25	____
Plate, 6" bread & butter	8	8	5	10	____
Plate 6" sherbet with indent	8	8	5	10	____
Plate, 8" salad	10	8	8	14	____
Plate, 9.5" cracker w/center indent for cheese comport	15	12	10	25	____
Plate, 10" sandwich w/open center handled	30	30	30	50	____
Plate, 10.5" cake, 10-sided with 2 open handles	25	25	25	35	____
Plate, 12"	30	30	30	50	____

TWISTED OPTIC *(cont.)*

	Pink	Green	Amber, Carnival, & Ruby Gold	Blue, Yellow, & Vaseline	Qty
Plate, 12" diam., muffin dish w/4 toes, 5" tall	100	100	100	145	____
Plate 14" w/center indent for mayo comport	15	12	10	25	____
Powder box	50	50	50	75	____
Sandwich plate, 10" with open center handle	30	30	30	50	____
Sandwich set	60	54	55	95	____
14" plate with indent	15	12	10	25	____
mayonnaise comport	25	22	20	35	____
spoon	20	20	25	35	____
Saucer	8	8	5	10	____
Sherbet, no stem	15	12	10	25	____
Sherbet, fancy stem	18	15	12	30	____
Sherbet, smooth stem	15	12	10	25	____
Sugar	15	12	10	25	____
Tray, 7.5" x 9" for Dresser Set	40	30	30	60	____
Tray, 7.5" x 9" oval w/indent	40	30	30	60	____
Tumbler, juice, 5 oz.	12	10	10		____
Tumbler, table, 8 oz.	12	10	10		____
Tumbler, water, 10 oz.	14	12	12		____
Tumbler, iced tea, 14 oz.	14	12	12		____
Vase, 6" rose bowl (bulbous)	35	30	25	50	____
Vase, 7.25" rolled rim with 2 handles	35	30	30	65	____
Vase, 7.5" tall, no handles	35	30	30	75	____
Vase, 7.5" tall, narrow bottom, wide opening, w/2 handles	35	30	30	75	____
Vase, 8" tall, slender base, flared rim, w/2 handles	35	30	30	75	____
Vase, 8" rose bowl (bulbous)	35	30	25	50	____
Vase, 8" tall cone shape with 2 handles	35	30	30	75	____
Vase, 8" tall fan w/ 2 handles	35	30	30	75	____
Vase, 8" tall pinched at top with 2 handles	35	30	30	75	____
Vase, 9.5" tall,	35	30	30	75	____

Note: Crystal worth ½ of lowest price shown in any color for that item. Add 20% for silver overlay and other embellishments. Add $75 to the value of any item with a black base or foot. Black bases: 5" diam., 1.75" tall and 6.5" diam., 1.75" tall, $100 ea. Smoked console bowl, $85.

U.S. SWIRL
(Late 1920s   U.S. Glass Company)

	Green	Pink	Qty
Bowl, 4.5" berry	10	12	_____
Bowl, 5.5" w/1 handle	14	16	_____
Bowl, 7.25" pickle, oval w/2 handles	18	22	_____
Bowl, 7.75" round	18	22	_____
Bowl, 8.25" oval 2.75" deep	50	50	_____
Bowl, 8.25" oval, 1.75" deep	75	75	_____
Bowl, footed candy	25	25	_____
Butter dish base	75	75	_____
Butter dish lid	100	110	_____
Butter complete	175	185	_____
Candy w/lid, base has 2 handles	60	65	_____
Comport, 5" diam., 2.75" tall	40	40	_____
Creamer	15	18	_____
Pitcher, 8"	70	75	_____
Plate, 6.25" sherbet	7	7	_____
Plate, 7.75" salad	10	10	_____
Salt & pepper	60	65	_____
Sherbet, 3.25"	5	8	_____
Sugar base	12	14	_____
Sugar lid	28	31	_____
Tumbler, 4.75"	15	18	_____
Vase, 6.5"	25	25	_____

Note: Iridescent & Crystal items ½ the value of green.

VERNON
(1930-1932   Indiana Glass Company)

	Green & Yellow	Crystal	Qty
Creamer	30	10	_____
Cup	20	8	_____
Plate, 8" luncheon	12	5	_____
Plate, 11" sandwich	30	12	_____
Saucer	8	5	_____
Sugar	30	10	_____
Tumbler, 5"	40	12	_____

VICTORY

(1929-1931 Diamond Glass-Ware Company)

	Blue	Black	Other Colors	Qty
Bon bon, 7" hi-footed	30	20	15	_____
Bowl, 5.5" , 2" deep				
w/2 handles			40	_____
Bowl, 6.5" cereal	40	35	15	_____
Bowl, 7.25" w/handles			40	_____
Bowl, 8.5" flat soup	60	50	25	_____
Bowl, 9" oval vegetable	120	100	35	_____
Bowl, 11" rolled edge	65	50	30	_____
Bowl, 12" console	75	65	38	_____
Bowl, 12.5" flat rim	75	65	38	_____
Candlestick, ea., 3.25" tall	65	55	20	_____
Cheese & cracker set				
(12" indented plate &				
6" tall comport)			55	_____
Comport, 6" tall	75		20	_____
Creamer	55	50	18	_____
Cup	40	35	10	_____
Goblet, 5"	100	85	25	_____
Gravy boat, 8.25", 1.5" deep	275	250	125	_____
Gravy under plate,				
7.75" x 5.25"	125	100	100	_____
Mayonnaise 3-piece set	115	90	60	_____
Mayo. comport,				
3.75" tall	50	40	30	_____
Mayo. ladle	25	25	15	_____
Mayo 7.5" under plate,				
w/indent	40	25	15	_____
Plate, 6" bread & butter	20	18	8	_____
Plate, 7" salad	20	18	8	_____
Plate, 7" w/indent for				
5.5" bowl			40	_____
Plate, 7.5"			15	_____
Plate, 8" luncheon	40	35	10	_____
Plate, 9" dinner	55	45	25	_____
Platter, 12"	90	75	35	_____
Sandwich server, 11"				
w/center handle	90	80	35	_____
Saucer	18	15	5	_____
Sherbet	35	30	15	_____
Sugar	55	50	18	_____
Whipped cream set	120			_____
Bowl, 5.5"	75			_____
Plate, 8.5" w/indent	20			_____
Ladle	25			_____

Note: Amethyst: cup, $20; saucer, $10; creamer, $35; sugar, $35.

VITROCK

(1934-1937   Hocking Glass Company)

	White	Fired-on colors & striped trim	Qty
Bowl, 4" diam, dessert	5	8	____
Bowl, 4.75" diam, 2" deep, cream soup	15	20	____
Bowl, 6" diam, 1.5' deep, fruit	7	10	____
Bowl, 7.5" diam, cereal	8	10	____
Bowl, 9" diam, flat soup (soup plate)	30	40	____
Bowl, 9.5" diam, 2.5" deep, vegetable	15	20	____
Creamer	7	10	____
Cup	4	7	____
Plate, 7.5" bread	4	7	____
Plate, 8.5" luncheon	4	7	____
Plate, 10" dinner	10	12	____
Platter, 11.5"	30	40	____
Salt & pepper, 3"		60	____
Saucer	4	7	____
Sugar	7	10	____

WATERFORD

(1939-1944 Hocking Glass Company)

	Pink	Crystal	Qty
Ashtray		8	____
Bowl, 4.75" diam., just over 1.5" deep, berry	22	8	____
Bowl, 5.5" diam, 1.5" deep, cereal	42	20	____
Bowl, 8.25" diam, 3.25" deep, berry	36	10	____
Butter dish base, 6.5" diam	65	8	____
Butter dish lid	300	25	____
Butter complete	365	33	____
Coaster, 4" diam., .5" rim w/rays		5	____
Coaster, 4" diam., .5" rim w/rays & sm. circle at center		5	____
Creamer, oval	18	5	____
Creamer, ftd.		45	____
Cup	20	8	____
Goblet, 5.25" tall, 3.25 diam		18	____
Goblet, 5.5" tall		18	____
Lamp, 4" round base		45	____
Lazy Susan, 14"		35	____
Pitcher, juice (tilted), 42 oz.		34	____
Pitcher, water (tilted), 80 oz.	200	50	____
Plate, 6" sherbet	12	5	____
Plate, 7" salad	22	8	____
Plate, 9.5" dinner	35	10	____
Plate, 10.25" cake w/2 closed handles	35	15	____
Plate, 13.75" sandwich	50	15	____
Plate, 14" lazy Susan		35	____
Relish, 13.75" round w/5 parts		20	____
Relish, 14" round w/6 parts		35	____
Salt & pepper, 4" tall, narrow w/plastic lid		12	____
Salt & pepper, 4.25" tall, wide (flared bottom)w/metal lids		8	____
Saucer	10	5	____
Sherbet, smooth foot & rim, 3.5" tall	20	5	____
Sherbet, scalloped		25	____
Sugar base	18	7	____
Sugar lid	100	20	____
Tumbler, 3.5" juice	120		____
Tumbler, 5.25" tall, 2.75" diam., ftd	30	12	____
Tumbler, 5.75" tall, 3" diam., sm. stm	30	12	____

Note: Ashtray w/advertisement in center, $20. Amber goblet: $20. Yellow goblet and 13.75" sandwich plate: too rare to price. Forest Green, 14" round relish plate, $35; smooth inserts for relish, $12; center insert, $20. Iridescent pieces 4x pink. Satinized yellow, 12" round tray, $40. Crystal with silver inlaid same value as pink. White 6-part relish, $35. Ice blue coaster, $20. Silver inlaid pieces, $20 ea. Royal Ruby: 9.5" dinner plate & 13.75" sandwich plate, $200 each.

WHITE SHIP

(Late 1930s   Hazel Atlas Glass Company)

	Blue glass w/white details	Qty
Ashtray, 2 styles	65	____
Ashtray, 4" square, crystal w/decorations	18	____
Ashtray w/metal sailboat, 4.75" diam.	150	____
Box, 3 sections	250	____
Cocktail mixer, 4.5" diam., 4.25" deep	50	____
Cocktail shaker (see note)	85	____
Cup (no details)	15	____
Ice bowl (7" mixing bowl in metal holder w/tongs), complete	45	____
Ice tub, 5.5" diam., 4" deep	55	____
Pitcher, no ice lip or ribs at neck	70	____
Pitcher with ice lip and ribs at neck, 8"	90	____
Pitcher with ice lip, 80 oz.	85	____
Plate, 6" sherbet	45	____
Plate, 8" salad	45	____
Plate, 9" dinner	60	____
Saucer	35	____
Tray, 2 sizes	165	____
Tray, go-along, 12" x 18" w/chrome & Bakelite handles	80	____
Tray, go-along, 13.75" x 8" w/wooden handles	80	____
Tumbler, 2.25" shot glass	300	____
Tumbler, 2.25" roly poly	10	____
Tumbler, heavy rounded bottom, 3.25"	30	____
Tumbler, 3.25" old fashion	22	____
Tumbler, 3.5" whiskey	70	____
Tumbler, 3.75" juice	15	____
Tumbler, 3.75" straight water	18	____
Tumbler, 4.75" straight water	16	____
Tumbler, 4.75", 10 oz. iced tea	18	____
Tumbler, 5" no clouds	28	____
Tumbler, 12 oz. 5" iced tea	25	____
Tumbler, 5.25"	25	____

Note: Chrome tray to hold cocktail shaker and six tumblers, 11.25" diam., $50. Cocktail shakers and other pieces with other motifs (fish, dancers, etc.) worth 110% to 150% more. Chrome holder for ice tub, $20.

WINDSOR

(1932-1946 Jeannette Glass Company)

	Pink	Green	Crystal	Qty
Ashtray, 5.75"	42	45	15	____
Bowl, 4.75" diam, 1.5" deep, berry w/flat rim	14	14	5	____
Bowl, 4.75" diam zz*, 1.5" deep, finger	40		8	____
Bowl, 5" diam zz*, 1.5" deep	45		5	____
Bowl, 5" diam, 1.25" deep, w/one rd. handle			15	____
Bowl, 5" diam, 1.75" deep			65	____
Bowl, 5" diam, 2.25" deep cream soup	25	34	7	____
Bowl, 5.5" diam, 2.75" deep, cereal	35	38	9	____
Bowl, 7" x 11.75", 2.75" deep, "boat"	45	55	25	____
Bowl, 7.25" w/3 feet, 1.75" deep	45		10	____
Bowl, 8" diam zz*, 2.25" deep	125		15	____
Bowl, 8.5" diam, berry	28	28	7	____
Bowl, 9" diam, w/handles, 2.75" deep	30	30	7	____
Bowl, 9" diam, 2" deep oval vegetable	25	30	8	____
Bowl, 10.5" diam, salad	25			____
Bowl, 10.5" diam zz*, 3.75" deep	225		30	____
Bowl, 12.5" diam, 3" deep, fruit	140		30	____
Butter dish base	30	50	10	____
Butter dish lid	60	70	20	____
Butter complete	90	120	30	____
Cake plate, 10.5"	35	40	10	____
Candlestick, ea.	55		12	____
Candy jar w/lid			30	____
Coaster, 3.25"	20	24	5	____
Compote, 5.5" tall, 6" diam.			20	____
Creamer (2 styles in Crystal)	15	15	7	____
Cup	12	12	4	____
Finger light, 5"			45	____
Pitcher, 4.5", milk	150		25	____
Pitcher, 6.5"	45	75	15	____
Plate, 6" sherbet	10	12	3	____
Plate, 7" salad	22	30	4	____
Plate, 9" dinner	25	40	8	____
Plate, 10" sandwich w/closed handles	25		10	____
Plate, 10.5" w/open handles	25	25	8	____

WINDSOR *(cont.)*

	Pink	Green	Crystal	Qty
Plate, 10.5" zz*			10	____
Plate, 13.5" chop	40	40	15	____
Platter, 11.25" x 8.25"	35	35	8	____
Platter, 3-part	400		30	____
Powder jar complete, 3.5" diam.	350		20	____
Relish, 3-part, 8.25" sq.	400			____
Relish, 2-part, 11.25" x 8.25"			15	____
Salt & pepper, 3"	45	70	20	____
Saucer	10	10	3	____
Sherbet, 2.75" tall	18	20	4	____
Sugar base, 3" w/smooth rim	30	40	15	____
Sugar base, 3.25" w/scalloped rim	15	20	7	____
Sugar lid w/pointy knob	20	30	8	____
Sugar lid w/small knob	120		10	____
Tray, 4" sq. w/handles	12	18	5	____
Tray, 4" sq. no handles	50		10	____
Tray, 4" x 9" w/handles	12	18	5	____
Tray, 4" x 9" no handles	60		12	____
Tray, 8.5" x 9.75" w/handles	25	35	10	____
Tray, 8.5" x 9.75" no handles	95		15	____
Tumbler, 3.25" tall, 3" diam, flat	30	35	10	____
Tumbler, 3.75" tall, flat	18	35	10	____
Tumbler, 4.25" tall, w/foot, cocktail			10	____
Tumbler, 4.5" tall, flat	35	60	10	____
Tumbler, 5" tall, w/foot	35	60	10	____
Tumbler, 5" tall, 3" diam, flat			10	____
Tumbler, 7.25" tall, w/foot			10	____
Vase, 10" tall		150		____

*zz = zigzag or pointed edges

Note: Delphite ashtray, $65. Blue creamer, cup, 9" dinner, 3.25" flat tumbler, & 4" flat tumbler: $75 each; powder jar, $375; 4.75" berry bowl $50. Red pitcher, $500. Yellow powder jar, $375; dinner plate, $250. Crystal one-handled candleholder, $20. Ruby flash, bowl, 8.75" diam zz*, 3" deep, $75; other Ruby flash items twice items in pink. Compote, 5.5" tall, 6" diam., Shell Pink, $80; satinized, $20; amberina, $8; blue, $10; bright green, $25. Iridescent: 3.75" tumbler, $20; 5" diam., 1.25" deep bowl with one handle, $15, milk pitcher, $25. Amberina, 8.25" diam., 2.5" deep bowl, $30.

BIBLIOGRAPHY

Antique & Collectors Reproduction News, *Depression Glass Reproductions*. Des Moines, IA: 1994.

Antiques & Collectors Reproduction News, vol. 11, #8. *Cherry Blossom individual berry bowls*. Des Moines, IA. August 2002.

Coe, Debbie & Randy. *Elegant Glass Early, Depression & Beyond*. Atglen, PA: Schiffer Publishing, 2001.

Florence, Gene. *Anchor Hocking's Fire-King & More*. Paducah, KY: Collector Books, 1998.

Florence, Gene. *Collectible Glassware from the 40s 50s 60s...* Paducah, KY: Collector Books, 1998.

Florence, Gene. *Collector's Encyclopedia of Depression Glass*. Paducah, KY: Collector Books, 1998.

Florence, Gene. *Pocket Guide to Depression Glass and More*. Paducah, KY: Collector Books, 1999.

Glass Review, vol. 17, #2. "Amercian Table Glass Factories." Marietta, OH: 1987.

Goshe, Ed, Ruth Hemminger, and Leslie Piña. *Depression Era Stems & Tableware: Tiffin*. Atglen, PA: Schiffer Publishing Ltd., 1998.

Hopper, Philip. *Forest Green Glass*. Atglen, PA: Schiffer Publishing, 2002.

Hopper, Philip. *More Royal Ruby*. Atglen, PA: Schiffer Publishing, 1999.

Hopper, Philip. *Royal Ruby*. Atglen, PA: Schiffer Publishing, 1998.

Keller, Joe & David Ross. *Jadite: An Identification and Price Guide*. Atglen, PA: Schiffer Publishing, 1999.

Kilgo, Garry & Dale, and Wilkins, Jerry & Gail. *Anchor Hocking's Fire -King Glassware*. Addison, Alabama: K & W Collectibles Publisher, 1997.

Piña, Leslie, and Paula Ockner. *Depression Era Art Deco Glass*. Atglen, PA: Schiffer Publishing Ltd., 1999.

Pina, Leslie. *Fostoria American Line 2056*. Atglen, PA: Schiffer Publishing Ltd., 2006.

Snyder, Jeffery B. *Morgantown Glass: From Depression Glass through the 1960s*. Atglen, PA: Schiffer Publishing Ltd., 1998.

Townsend, Wayne. *Corn Flower*, Winnipeg, Manitoba Canada: Hignell Printing Limited, 2001.

Weatherman, Hazel Marie. *Colored Glassware of the Depression Era*. Ozark, MO: Weatherman Glassbooks, 1970.

Weatherman, Hazel Marie. *Colored Glassware of the Depression Era 2*. Ozark, MO: Weatherman Glassbooks, 1974.

Weatherman, Hazel Marie. *The Decorated Tumbler*. Springfield, MO: Glassbooks, 1978.

Yeske, Doris. *Depression Glass, 3rd Edition*. Atglen, PA: Schiffer Publishing Ltd., 1999.

www.auctionbytes.com

www.epa.gov

www.geocities.com

www.henonnest.com

www.indianaglass.carnivalheaven.com

www.inflationstamps.com

Website:http://www.justglass.com

www.ndga.net

www.shop4antiques.com

www.topix.net

www.victorianweb.org

www.westmorelandglassclubs.org

INDEX...NAMES & NICKNAMES

The numbers C-1 to C-32 refer to the color identification photos found between pages 96 & 97

234

Notes

Notes

Notes